T0270738

The Quantified Self in Precarity

Humans are accustomed to being tool bearers, but what happens when machines become tool bearers, calculating human labour via the use of big data and people analytics by metrics?

The Quantified Self in Precarity highlights how, whether it be in insecure 'gig' work or office work, such digitalisation is not an inevitable process—nor is it one that necessarily improves working conditions. Indeed, through unique research and empirical data, Moore demonstrates how workplace quantification leads to high turnover rates, workplace rationalisation and worker stress and anxiety, with these issues linked to increased rates of subjective and objective precarity.

Scientific management asked us to be efficient. Now, we are asked to be agile. But what does this mean for the everyday lives we lead?

With a fresh perspective on how technology and the use of technology for management and self-management changes the 'quantified', precarious workplace today, *The Quantified Self in Precarity* will appeal to undergraduate and postgraduate students interested in fields such as Science and Technology, Organisation Management, Sociology and Politics.

Phoebe V. Moore is an active researcher and a Senior Lecturer in International Relations at Middlesex University, UK.

Routledge Advances in Sociology

For a full list of titles in this series, please visit www.routledge.com/series/SE0511

The Quantified Self
in Precarity

Work, Technology and What Counts

Phoebe V. Moore

Routledge
Taylor & Francis Group

LONDON AND NEW YORK

First published 2018
by Routledge

2 Park Square, Milton Park, Abingdon, Oxfordshire OX14 4RN
52 Vanderbilt Avenue, New York, NY 10017

Routledge is an imprint of the Taylor & Francis Group, an informa business

First issued in paperback 2019

British Library Cataloguing-in-Publication Data
A catalogue record for this book is available from the British Library

Library of Congress Cataloging-in-Publication Data
A catalog record for this book has been requested.

ISBN: 978-1-138-67406-6 (hbk)
ISBN: 978-0-367-87290-8 (pbk)

Typeset in Sabon
by codeMantra

The Quantified Self in Precarity: Work, Technology and What Counts is dedicated to my families the Carters, Moores, and van Somerens; my dearest Aureol; my partner Dan whose support has been immeasurable; my wonderful friends Christine and Joan who have inspired me since childhood; my more recent friends Ben, Felicity and Michael whose solidarity is unequalled; and Tokyo Rose, my cat whose animal affective labour is an ongoing lifesaver.

Contents

1 Getting to Know the Autonomic Self

Diarising, quantification of activities and self-experimentation are not unprecedented obsessions. King Charles II had a penchant for weighing himself at specific times in the day. A report from the Royal Society's archives from 9 March 1664 written by Sir Robert Moray indicates that Charles II, aged 34 at the time of this report,

> had the Curiosity of weighing himself, very frequently, to observe the severall Emanations of his Body, before and after sleep, Tennis, Riding abroad, Dinners and Suppers: and that he had found he weighed lesse after Tennis, by two pounds three ounces (but the King drinking two draughts of Liquor after play, made up his weight;) after Dinner, by four pounds and an halfe.
>
> (Corden, 2013)

Sanctorious of Padua, noted for introducing quantitative approaches to medicine in the 16th and early 17th century, weighed himself before and after meals, weighed his meals and then weighed his excrement (Neuringer, 1981: 79). Dali is also said to have meticulously measured his excrement.

While the King, the physician and the artist tracked physical expressions, other historical figures measured the less tangible. Benjamin Franklin kept his moral compass in track quite explicitly through daily self-examination and keeping track of his actions in a little book which contained a 'page for each of the virtues', one of which was temperance, where the subheading stated 'eat not to dullness: drink not to elevation'. A grid beneath listed the various types of violations one might commit in relation to the virtue along a timeline of days. Franklin would make a 'little black spot' for 'every fault I found upon examination to have been committed respecting that virtue upon that day'. Buckminster Fuller was an avid self-tracker and gave himself the nickname 'guinea pig b'; he kept a scrapbook diary about his day-to-day life and his ideas.

Humans have, in the 21st century, moved into a new series of fascinations of body tracking. We are interested in knowing about our autonomic systems or an autonomic 'self' that was seen to be largely out-of-bounds for the layman and woman's knowledge and understanding. *Autonomic* refers to the nervous system of a physiological self where the mind, sentiment and body are less separable than mainstream Cartesian modernism dictates. Autonomic means self-governing and comes from the Greek, 'auto' or 'self' + 'nomos', or 'law'. Through intensive and long-term data collection advocated by the Quantified Self movement discussed below, individuals have begun to pursue autonomic self-knowledge to improve ourselves. To gain this knowledge and set out self-improvement plans, we track movement, activity, emotions and attitudes in a quest to gain more intimate knowledge about the self. We wish to control, modify, regulate and understand our 'selves' more precisely in order to control, improve and develop this 'self', as though this 'self' is an identity proxy or a data double such as is discussed by Ruckenstein (2014); a self that requires constant, uncritical self-improvement. We track patterns in exercise, sleeping, running and walking as provided by FitBit; eating habits with dashboards provided by most fitness trackers; body temperatures provided by Microsoft Band 2; exposure to the elements like sunshine, provided by a wearable device called Netatmo's June; and pollution detected by the Tzao; and a range of other personalised pursuits. So, knowledge about the autonomic self is attainable through a mixture of physical, psychological, biometric, quantifiable, and sometimes topographical attributes in ways Franklin and Dali could only have imagined.

'Think about all the times you need to use your identity' says Andrew D'Souza, President of Bionym, a company that has invented a wristband that tracks users' movements and offers biometric authentication (Hennigan, 2014). Start-ups began to look at unprecedented methods to profile consumers. The Bionym is designed to capture a customer's gaze upon entering a shop or restaurant, so wait staff can immediately serve the customer based on previous orders or requests, 'from booking tickets to check in, security, room access, boarding passes and purchases… knowing your name and dietary preferences' (Hennigan, 2014). Consumer tracking has allowed other-tracking and consumer profiling for years, with such things as Tesco Club Cards. Technologies now allow personalised pilgrimages for self-knowledge, allowing people to define the 'self' in ways even more aligned around consumerism.

However, this book examines how self-knowledge involves knowledge of the *working* self, rather than the *consuming* self, examining how technological developments affect the employment relationship in unprecedented ways. The digitally quantified worker is precarious, and the insecurity of quantified workplaces are symptoms of the routes of productivity capture in unstable times. As the machine becomes increasingly central for human resource decisions and appears in more ways in the employment relationship, it is the use of the data made available from technologies that seals an emerging metaphorical social pact that has not yet been agreed by all parties, those parties being workers as self-experimenters and precarious subjects; an ever-invisible management[1] that is sometimes entirely machinic; and the specialists and inventors who develop and implement new technologies to measure our labour. While these new relationships do not arise simply because new technologies have emerged, data allows the seeming neutralisation of the employment relationship in ways that this book reveals. In fact, new technology often accelerates already existing hierarchies whether seen in mental (knowledge economy, professional, cultural, educational work) or manual (warehouse, factory, construction, transport) labour relations.

Digitalised workplaces are located along a continuum from a virtual platform where algorithms determine what work you have and what work will be removed from you in virtual factory and office floors, in competition with other workers and dictated by what journalist Sarah O'Connor (2016) called an algorithmic boss as seen in 'crowd' or 'gig' work made available by such platforms as Uber and Mechanical Turks; to the individual worker in an office whose activities are tracked, monitored, surveilled, and whose work is intensified by the automation dimensions of such technologies, or automated altogether. Humans are accustomed to being tool bearers, but what happens when *machines* become tool bearers, where the tool is seemingly ever more precise calculations about human labour, through the use of big data and people analytics? Data is treated as a neutral arbiter and judge, and is being prioritised over qualitative judgements in key performance indicator management systems and digitalised client-based relationships.

People pursue self-improvement and regulation when they set out to self-track for physical and mental health and other methods of self-improvement, as are celebrated in the Quantified Self movement and community. The flip side of this is when management asks workers to self-track for performance, whether it is reaching the right level of health or working more efficiently and productively; or when the client or employer 'other tracks' workers through electronic performance monitoring and other workplace surveillance methods; and views data either openly or surreptitiously. In digitally quantified workplaces such as those outlined in this book, the employment relationship is ambivalent and often, our work is intensified. Indeed, 'computers, which are meant to help [workers to] do the work more efficiently are also extremely merciless monitoring tools' leading to conditions where 'work rates are close to the maximum that workers can manage' (Peaucelle, 2000: 461). Digitalisation, I claim, is not an inevitable process nor one that necessarily improves working conditions. Indeed, it has already been demonstrated to lead to high turnover rates, workplace rationalisation and worker stress and anxiety, which I link to increased rates of both objective and subjective *precarity* in Chapter 3.

The five years of research informing this book contributes to the literature on the political economy of self-tracking where exercise and casual games become labour (Greenhill and Fletcher, 2013; Till, 2014); to the wealth of research on the growing power of machines and tools over labour via deterritorialisation (Hardt and Negri, 2000); symbolic impacts on society and sociality (Leon, 2015), automation (Frey and Osborne, 2013); the algorithmic boss in crowdwork platforms (Berg, 2016; Bergvall-Kåreborn and Howcroft, 2014; Cheney-Lippold, 2011; Gandini, Pais and Beraldo, 2016) and electronic performance management (Bhave, 2014; Jeske and Santuzzi, 2015); digital reproductive labour (Jarrett, 2016); digitalised precarity (Dyer-Witheford, 2015; Gill and Pratt, 2008; Huws, 2014); virtual work (Holts, 2013; Huws, 2014); digital labour (Fuchs, 2014) and work in the social factory (Terranova, 2000); questions of the intensifying relationship between bodies and the machine (Guéry and Deleule, 2014; Haraway, 1991) and machinic and socio-technical assemblages (DeLanda 2006; Deleuze and Guattari, 1983; Lupton, 2012). By highlighting the political and ideological moments of production, where politics emerge from data captured from hidden labour in the employment relationship and where idealised health and wellbeing become an ideology, I address Burawoy's call to politicise production (1985: 122). New forms of work quantification that involve electronic tracking of what I call 'unseen' labour (involving affective and emotional labour) are capital's latest method to capture surplus value in unstable conditions of agility. So, through emphasising power relations where machines intervene at unprecedented levels of intensity and intimacy, I speak to Massumi's critique of affect theories that begin with stasis rather than process (2002), by identifying systems where workers' reproductive labour symbolically serves machines.

The following sections introduce this book by first looking at evidence of the rise of self-and other-tracking in workplaces and ways it has been conducted, in 'Ways and Means to Quantify the Self at Work'; dealing conceptually with the idea of the 'self' as a way of introducing the theoretical contributions of the text in 'The Self and Science of Quantification' and then, the 'Legal landscape for quantification of workers' just before the 'Introducing possible conclusions' where I present key arguments and outline the subsequent chapters.

Ways to Quantify the Self at Work

With the use of radio frequency identification (RFID), Bluetooth, triangulation algorithms and infrared sensors, a variety of wearable devices entered the market in the early 2000s including Nike Fuelband, Fitbit One, and Bodymedia Armband, which would help people to find their autonomic selves. Noticing the uptake in use of these devices, Kevin Kelly, Executive and Founding Editor of Wired Magazine; Gary Wolf, writer for Wired; and others in the Silicon Valley area, began to meet to discuss their own experiences in quantifying themselves for self-optimisation. It became clear that a new social movement and community was on the horizon where 'self-knowledge through numbers' would become the driving mantra.

The steering group launched the first Quantified Self Conference in San Francisco in 2007, and Kelly's event publicity linked quantifying the self to 'real change [that] will happen in individuals as they work through self-knowledge… of one's body, mind and spirit… a rational [path]: unless something can be measured, it cannot be improved'. For the first Quantified Self conference, Kelly called for projects that, for example, might discuss personal genome sequencing, life logging, measuring chemical body load counts, self-experimentation, location tracking, digitising body info, sharing health records, psychological self-assessments and medical self-diagnostics. The 2014 Quantified Self Conference in San Francisco included 'Quantifying motivation with a smartwatch', 'Photo lifelogging', 'Grief and Mood Tracking', 'My Weight and Sleep' and 'Deciphering my brain fog'. The San Francisco Quantified Self Meetup Group describes itself on its website as 'a regular show and tell for people taking advantage of various kinds of personal tracking – geo-tracking, life-logging, DNA sequencing, etc., to gain more knowledge about themselves' and 'invites topics around but not limited to'

- Chemical Body Load Counts
- Personal Genome Sequencing
- Lifelogging
- Self Experimentation
- Risks/Legal Rights/Duties
- Behavior monitoring
- Location tracking
- Non-invasive Probes
- Digitizing Body Info
- Sharing Health Records
- Psychological Self-Assesments
- Medical Self-Diagnostics (Quantified Self Bay Area Meetup Group, 2017)

The 2015 conference programme included talks such as:

- Know Thy Cycle, Know Thyself
- Three Years of Logging my Inbox Count
- Breaking the TV Habit
- How I Measured my Talk
- Thinking Through Data Access and Privacy
- Mindful Devices – Living Non-Judgementally in a Connected World
- Lifelogging – Quantitating Aspects for Health
- The Digital Health Coach
- Is Your Nervous System Hungry?
- Extreme Productivity: Maniac Week and Other Productivity Hacks

I attended the 2015 Expo and led a breakaway session I called 'The Quantified Self at Work' along with Joost Plattel, who was the data analyst for the Quantified Workplace experiment run by the company in the Netherlands I outline in Chapter 4. We had a very good turnout for our breakaway session and several people asked questions afterwards about what we had identified as patterns in employee usage of wearables and other tracking technologies in the experiment. One notable experience during this session was that while I was giving my talk, Joost looked down at his watch several times. I kept thinking that he was keeping track of how long I had spoken for and so sped up my talk as I was not keeping track of the time myself. Only later did Joost tell me he had just bought the new Apple Watch that had been launched that day and was looking at notifications! Physical movements may represent new significance as technology takes on new functions!

Quantified Self international events and the proliferating use of many new popular tracking devices mark a movement where people in this emerging community seek self-improvement and self-empowerment through capturing data from sensory and logging devices. Lupton notes that interest in more modern types of self-quantification probably started in the 1970s, but the term 'quantified self' advanced in our cultural lexicon in 2008 (Lupton, 2013: 26). Use of the term became increasingly widespread throughout the media in 2012 and 2013 and Quantified Self events have allowed the concept to flourish. Quantified self-improvement started in the extra-curricular realms but has become accepted into workplaces, which is the focus of the current book.

Workplace quantified self projects are often part of corporate wellness offerings, and self-tracking initiatives are focused on other purposes such as productivity, movement, stress and wellbeing. Accelerometers, Bluetooth, triangulation algorithms and infrared sensors allow managers to monitor workers far beyond traditional hours logged by swipecards. Increasingly, 'many wellness programs now address things like emotional well-being, mental health and financial wellness' (Kohll, 2016) and the benefits of improved productivity and employee wellness are continuously trumpeted (Campbell, 2015; Rackspace, 2014; Verma, 2014). Wearables and other tracking devices are manifest in the form of a range of body-worn devices including pins, rings, badges and smartwatches. The technologies used in workplaces measure and track mental and physical performance, via accelerometers, Bluetooth, triangulation algorithms and infrared sensors, allowing self-monitoring beyond the enclosure of a specific workplace and beyond the standard hours logged allowed by human resources software tools such as Patriot Pay and Kronos.

There is a glut of products on the market to track wellness at work, and leaders include Global Corporate Challenge and JawBone Up, both which offer self-tracking packages with dashboards that reveal compared data. FitBit's market share was secured in 2015 largely because of its new corporate wellness packages (Whitney, 2016; also see Gibbs, 2015). Daily activity tracking software allows workers to work as normal in front of a computer terminal, but the software monitors any interruptions to work and measures any inactivity at the terminal. The results are claimed to be automated and accurate. Tracking activity will help workers, the software designers promised, with personal productivity levels. It promises to help you take control of your daily work time. Software companies sell activity logs, timesheets, timekeeping, daily activity tracking, daily time tracking, organisation, personal productivity, productivity management, time reporting, and overtime calculation tools. Going into the domain of emotion, the company John Deere has been experimenting with a 'happiness metric', measuring employee's morale every two weeks, checking workers' motivation, team health and 'regular pulse checks of the morale of their employees' (Power, 2016). They are building on the happiness measure by explicitly looking at human behaviour, communication methods and attitudes. New technologies capture physical and spoken movements and face-to face interactions in the office, capturing excitement and intonation of voices with a very high level of accuracy. With Sociometric Solutions, movement around workspaces can also be documented, and in areas with higher density, productivity levels are also looked at to identify how specific movements and interactions are linked to productivity and outputs. Data shows where and what kinds of communication happens. It is not yet possible to discern identity or words spoken, but data can help with decisions about ideal office furniture location, desk allocations and the like.

As part of my British Academy/Leverhulme funded project 'Agility, Work and the Quantified Self' (2015–2017), my co-investigators and I researched one company in the Netherlands who carried out an experiment with a group of employees who volunteered to be involved in a study that gathered data about the steps they have taken, their heartrates and sleep data taken from FitBits; productivity based on RescueTime; and daily lifelog data where each participant rated their feelings of subjective stress and personally perceived productivity. As I outline in Chapter 4, employees at the company in the Netherlands were set up with personalised dashboards and were asked to consent to data being shared with all colleagues, including management. They could then personally and intra-personally interpret the data accumulated based on the dashboards. A job category has emerged alongside the introduction of new tracking technologies, where 'data analysts' set up related projects with companies, provide consultancy and finally, triangulate data to identify patterns. In the case of my project, the company's data analyst and the behavioural psychologist co-investigator from my project, Lukasz Piwek, and I, could potentially identify specific periods of stress, joy or other emotions as they linked to, for example, productivity and movement.

At a physical level, devices can discern how many calories have been burned based on activity and heartrate. There are discussions for methods to track precise numbers of calories and proteins accumulated from bodily fluids. A lens being developed by Google measures blood glucose levels in tears, using tiny LED lights surrounding the lens which are visible when glucose levels reach a certain threshold. These smart lenses have the ability to take a reading per second. This gives users detailed access to changing blood glucose levels. A rapidly growing research and development area is in measuring emotions, such as an app available from Plasticity Labs – as of 2016 the indicators were not universalisable but this is a rapidly growing area of research. A lot of work is focusing on which emotions can be read by specific physical reactions. Some people may sweat when they are stressed, others may experience increased heart rates whilst others experience reduced heart rates, introducing the question of how fair it will be to use data like this in workplace comparison or judgement-based activities such as appraisals. The homogenising aspect to these studies reflects the dangers in reading data in the workplace where each worker has different life circumstances and desires. Before too long it will be possible for employers to literally track our blood, sweat and tears.

In 2014, Goldsmiths University conducted an experimental project with Rackspace providing wearable devices to office workers to identify whether they improve productivity or not, stating that:

> Wearable technologies are arguably the biggest trend since tablet computing, so it's natural that employees and businesses will look to use these devices in the workplace. Using data generated from the devices, organisations can learn how human behaviours impact productivity, performance, well-being, and job satisfaction. Employees can demand work environments and hours be optimised to maximise their productivity and health and well-being.
>
> (Goldsmiths/Rackspace 2014)

The results of this project indicated that a single employee can create more than thirty gigabytes of data per week when using three devices. Scaled across organisations, this is a significant amount of data that could be stored and analysed.

In 2013, 90 percent of companies made wellbeing programmes available to employees, and increasingly incorporated or encouraged the use of motivational tools to track progress and sustain engagement (Wilson, 2013). A 2014 report indicated that the 'market for enterprise wearable devices, which includes industrial and healthcare wearables, [is] growing from US$21 million in 2013 to US$9.2 billion by 2020' (Nield, 2014), a compound annual growth rate of 138 per cent (Tractica, 2016). 2014 was said to be the 'year of wearable technology' (Spence, 2013) with the launch of Google Glass and the flood of products offering a range of personal enhancement and self-experimentation devices. From 2014 to 2019 more than thirteen million wearable fitness tracking devices are predicted to be incorporated into workplaces (Nield, 2014) and the forecast for wearables shipped worldwide in 2020 is expected to reach 237.1 million (IDC, 2016).

In 2015, nearly a fifth (18 percent) of employees in Europe had access to wearable technology at work (ADP UK, 2015). In 2016, one in five Americans owned a wearable fitness device and 56 percent believed it would lengthen their lives (Pennic, 2016). In 2016, one in three companies provided wearable devices, to track activity (Jiff, 2016), save money (Daws, 2016) and improve employees' health and happiness.

BP America was an early adopter of self- and other-tracking at work in 2013 and offered step-tracking armbands as part of a voluntary company-wide initiative in health and well-being. BP's health and welfare benefits consultant Chris Phalen indicated that more than 90 per cent of employees participated in the initiative and noted that 'the program has improved morale, contributed to the corporate culture, improved the health of employees, and lowered insurance rates for both the company as well as individuals' (Lindzon, 2014). Call centre data reporting has long been used to view workers' emotional responses to customers (Bain and Taylor, 2000; Poster, 2011) but this takes things a step further. 'The battle for space on your body' (Spence, 2013) is fully underway.

Wearable devices at work can be used to record productivity however it is defined, as has been seen in warehouse and factory work for decades in various work design models covered in the next chapter; however new methods track levels and types of physical activity, heart rate variability as well as emotional and mood variances and stress levels at frequent intervals. The 'quantified work environment' (Bersin et al., 2016) can resemble a world of athletes where technology aids people in identifying peak performance times and gaining rapid feedback which resembles the 'agile' methods discussed in the next chapter. Indeed, the measure of physiolytics is a way to extract information from wearables data 'to improve performance' (Wilson, 2013). While physiolytics is predominantly used in sport it is 'spreading to workers in factory and office settings as well' (Ibid.: 1). In this context, the emergence of workplace wearable devices and self-tracking (and what I call other-tracking) technologies are seen in wellness initiatives in advanced countries to be cutting edge methods which improve employees' health and well-being and improve aggregate firm productivity (Nield, 2014; Wilson, 2013). In other cases, devices are provided and used for reduced health insurance premiums and even product discounts, such as at Whole Foods, where employees can save money on food if they prove they have lost weight. These are the markers of the world of work where far more information is shared and known by employers, but it is not always known what is shared, leading to some of the legal concerns discussed below.

Philosophically, by prioritising measure and the quantifiable, there is a risk that we begin to reject or ignore the qualitative aspects of life, despite the intimate areas of investigation that quantified self technologies allow. In Chapter 2, I begin to think through the bigger frame for this trend because capitalism, as the current global political economic model within which we live, is becoming a system of increasingly empty selves, subject to unending capitalist social reproduction, where data simply confirms the order it has already prefabricated. Is there really more that can be known about ourselves? Does quantifying ourselves actually start to shut down possibilities for spontaneity and for undefined vitalities? Or, indeed, are we at risk of creating new possibilities for discrimination when we see the ideal fitness or productivity level in a quantified way? Are we setting a standard that is unattainable for most people but could become seen as a 'norm'? Is the interest in optimal workplace wellness part of a 'wellness syndrome' (Cederström and Spicer, 2015) where, if you are not pursuing optimal wellness, you are abnormal and subject to exclusion? While the Quantified Self ideal starts with a sentiment and an ethos of self-empowerment, there is emerging evidence of an explicit set of corporate led gestures toward controlling the mind/body with management's recognition of their inseparability, potentially subsuming any capability to act except in a corporate programme of efficiency and rational (masculine) affinities around production (Moore, 2015). The worker has only her labour power to sell. The measure and value of our work is continuously judged by the employer in the capitalist framework. As a result, workers suffer from perpetual alienation from both a say in the worth of our work and from that which is produced. We are separated from social forces as our work is individualised. While quantified workplaces now are not identical to scientific management, 'in time and motion studies—the ultimate and most perfected form of this control—the boss even tries to control every second, literally every second, of the time which you spend in his employ' (Mandel and Novak, 1970/2014: 24).

The system of quantifying the self, as it begins to produce new 'knowns', could be seen as circular and beset by a contradiction; functional, but lacking qualities that make life enjoyable, because it does not recognise the qualitative, use-value, or unconscious, symbolic exchange. Capitalism could be reproduced as a functional system whereby everything functions to reproduce a system which absences difference. Meaning and value, as subjective phenomena, are irretrievably lost, and distinct institutions become functionally equivalent. Precarity, which I discuss in Chapter 3, is disguised in this process to look like smooth spaces of time, but as numbering becomes subject, and as we quantify our 'selves', we enter striated experiences. Workers using self-tracking technologies enter into a collective assemblage of enunciation, where incorporeal transformation is attributed to bodies. These devices and related practices quantify experience and perpetuate neoliberal capitalist inequalities and are symptomatic of burgeoning, gendered, globalising precarity.

Tracking for the most efficient methods in industrial work is still a pursuit in production and workplace organisation, and work design gurus have embraced self- and other-tracking with enthusiasm for both professional and industrial workplaces. What is new about self- and other-tracking technologies in workplaces is the technological functions available and the availability of the 'big data' that is derived from tracking activities. Management can know more than ever before about workers as technology constantly tracks second by second information of their movements and internal functioning. While the focus of the book is on tracking, other features of the newest technology in workplaces are addressed in Chapter 3, since automation and platform work are other trends that must be considered. The implications of work intensification, data protection and privacy and possibilities for exclusion from the new kinds of labour markets emerging are already being realised. Furthermore, accelerated physiological tracking may only be the beginning. What happens when management attempts to track workers' thoughts and emotions? Measuring knowledge work has always been difficult. New methods of tracking could be the answer to the problem of measuring qualitative work, but could also put the last nail in the coffin of workers' alienation. Or perhaps the quantified self is the liberated self in this new world of work. In any case, the types of data made available by new technologies provide very real possible changes to previously asymmetrical relationships: the relationship between a doctor and a patient, an athlete and a coach, an employee and a boss (at least for workers whose boss is still a person)!

The Self and Science of Quantification

I use the word 'self' as a signifier for a singular subjectivity. This is a self that is not yet obtained (and perhaps may never be obtained): an idealised, desired self. The ideal quantified self is (a) one who cognitively recognises that the mind and the machine must join forces to control physical movement and the affective experience or emotional responses to work, (b) someone who knows that their non-cognitive self is in constant need of self-improvement, and so, (c) is perpetually imperfect. In this emerging employment relationship, machines are allocated significant authority to measure activity and provide reports on work and responses to work. Machines aid management (or the invisible boss) to identify who the ideal quantified worker might be, along the lines of what Taylor called a 'first class' worker when writing of his 'first class shoveller' (1911/1998: 31) that he referred to in the *Principles of Scientific Management*, an idealised shoveller who Taylor praised for meeting the appropriate standards in the 'science of shovelling' (1911/1998: 31). As we will see in the current book, wearable and other technological tracking devices provide a new science of measure.

Quantifying the self, as I detail in the next chapter, requires intentional abstraction and self-divisibility. I argue that the authentic self, in the structural conditions of capitalism, is the person in the coal face of day-to-day work. This person is a precarious individual who is now under extreme pressure to both work with and against machines in an environment where data produced by machine captures all-of-life to serve capital. Conditions in a digitalised, precarious world of work place the responsibility to capture the affective and emotional labour discussed in Chapters 2 and 4 onto workers, in a form of attempted externalised control over social reproduction. The use-value of labour-power and its reproduction and transformation as exchange-value is, in the case study in Chapter 3, captured within the rubric of agility where the agile self is ever-responsive to machines and market demands and is required to internalise all components of the labour process. Digitalised approaches to workplace management allow capital to attempt to absolutely define value, where the qualitative is subsumed and where nothing can exist outside capitalist relations.

White-collar professional workplaces have readily identified self-tracking with wellbeing initiatives, where such items as FitBits are introduced for workers to use to improve fitness and health. Surely healthier workers are automatically happier and more productive. Insurance premiums can also be reduced. But workers in warehouses and factories are not necessarily given the option to 'enjoy' the use of technologies. In factories, tracking data is more readily used in making human resource related decisions for hiring and firing. However, both warehouse and office contexts imagine an ideal self that collapses the possibilities for difference.

The Homogeneous, Hireable Self, in Precarity

In the following chapters I discuss interviews I have carried out with people who experience urban precarity as self-employed and freelancers, entrepreneurs and office workers in a period of merger. The precarious workers whose working conditions are discussed later in the present book and the people who I have interviewed for the book's empirical sections, share one experience in work. Today, workers must be ready to change. Technology transforms at an extraordinary rate, and markets are never stable. Thus, we must be personally prepared to change. The concept of lifetime employment, once a norm in Japan for example, is a thing of the past, across the world.

The quantified self at work phenomenon is linked to the rise in precarity and in this book I ask, how does the incorporation of self- and other-tracking devices into workplaces and labour processes and the rise of platform management interface systems challenge the meaning of self and 'employability'? This is an important question because the promises of the knowledge-based economy seen in the early part of the 2000s have been largely unmet. Policymakers and management theorists recognised and invested in this new world of work with recommendations for education and work design (Moore, 2006, 2009, 2010; Warhurst and Thompson, 2006). The production-based economy had increasingly become an 'informational' based economy (Castells, 2000) and entrepreneurs and other types of knowledge workers were predicted to become champions of the working world. The much-cited 'creative class' was seen to hold the golden key to change workplace relationships. We were all going to become our own bosses and teamwork was going to overcome the dominant model of production, effectively eliminating controlling employment relationships and ultimately democratising workplaces. However, this renaissance has not happened. Rather than successes from the overhaul of control based workplaces or reduced workloads afforded in the knowledge based economy, we now hear about the 'seven-day weekend' which amounts to hyper-employment, or working too much; the supposed luxuries of working 'anywhere' in the same breath as the 'gig economy'; accelerated expectations of how much work can be done and where, as time and space become apparently nebulous (Wajcman, 2015); glamorisation of being always on and always connected as synonymous with digital macho 'dev' cultures where sleep and food are not seen as essentials; and distributed work, which introduces hyper-flexibilised working conditions within complementary zero-hour contracts. Quantifying and datafying the working self is part of this trend.

In 2017, the Office for National Statistics (ONS) reported that the main rise in employment figures was in self-employment in the UK. Comparing estimates to the same quarter for the previous year, the ONS reported in early 2017 that the number of self-employed people increased by 125,000 to 4.80 million for the period October to December 2016 (ONS, 2017). The reasons Parliament offers for this rise are interesting, stating that 'most people who are self-employed have chosen to be so voluntarily and many value the freedom it provides' (Parliamentary business, 2015). There are no data offered to support this claim, but in following paragraphs reasons are listed as being due to 'the economic cycle', reflecting on the downturn in 2008 where job opportunities fell until 2013. 'Technological change' is the next reason identified, where going 'freelance' is cheaper and easier with apps such as Uber, eBay and AirBnB which 'matches self-employed workers with consumers demanding their services' (Ibid.). The report goes on to state that the Family Resources Survey shows that in 2012/13, the average income from self-employment had fallen by 22 percent from 2008/9, and in 2012/13 was around £11,000 (Ibid.). About 80 percent earn less than £15,000 a year which is 2/3 of the median wage. The Institute of Public Policy Research (IPPR) indicates that the UK is an 'outlier', because self-employment is the main driver for total employment (Hatfield, 2015). In southern and eastern European countries, high rates of self-employment have not fed into job recovery, and where employment is growing in northern and western European economies, self-employment is not also rising. Entrepreneurship and self-employment are considered key economic growth drivers, but the downside is that 'living standards of self-employed have fallen further than for employees' (Ibid.: 33).

'Bogus self-employment' refers to cases where people who meet all legal criteria for employment, are registered as self-employed. There are significant down sides to being self-employed as listed above. It is a stretch to say an Uber taxi driver has no boss when they can be fired, or 'deactivated', for low customer ratings, promoting a competitor, cancelling rides too often or for speaking out against Uber publicly. Most Uber workers across the world have no right to sick pay or holidays given their 'self-employed' status. However, in October 2016, Uber drivers in England and Wales won a landmark employment tribunal backed by GMB that gave them the right to be classified as workers, meaning they should be entitled to paid rest breaks, a national minimum wage and holiday pay. (Uber is in the process of appeal at the time of writing.) The judge stated that the 'notion that Uber in London is a mosaic of 30,000 small businesses linked by a common "platform" is to our mind faintly ridiculous'. This victory reveals the drudgery of the day-to-day experiences of the supposed entrepreneurial 'heroes' driving economic growth and contributing to employment statistics that have been much celebrated by British politicians. The first budget published by Philip Hammond in March 2017 proposed increased taxes for self-employed workers, ignoring the realities of precarity for nearly one million of those who work in the gig economy, their struggle with debt, pay falling an average by £100 a week between 2006/7 and 2013/4 and the impact on women and pensioners. What these people 'are not is a new wave of entrepreneurs about the relaunch the British economy' (Hutton, 2017). Hutton states that the supposed entrepreneurial 'heroism is restricted to a minority and most self-employed are more victims of the system than its exemplars' (Ibid.).

While UK productivity was a bit better in the first half of 2016 than in years preceding, it was worse than all G7 countries except Japan in 2014. So, UK companies with regular employees could argue that the intensification of workplace quantification is happening to improve the country's productivity scores. From a labour process perspective (Knights and Willmott, 1998), the corporate use of technology to intensify and control work is not itself new. Just as implementation of Taylor's scientific management strategies in the late 1800s led to interwar experiments with the Bedaux system and Gilbreth's time-motion study, and similar to swipe cards and the intricate divisions of labour in the factory, technologies have, for a long time, been used to identify the ideal ways of working and define the 'one best way' as named by the Gilbreths, to carry out work (outlined in Chapter 2). To be 'employable' in these conditions would mean that physically, a person can demonstrate efficient bodily movements in the construction or manufacturing context. Now, tracking devices that measure personal as well as work related activities are leading to a new type of relationship to a market where being self-employed has little to do with being employable. The new version of employability individualises and places increased responsibility and accountability onto workers and potentially will be replaced by the term 'hireability' with the rise of precarious, unstable, temporary work and self-employment. Automation of both work and management is underway and intensification of such technologies further puts responsibility on workers for their ability to compete in a world with less and less work for humans.

Workers have experienced the effects of austerity policies as governments seek to make savings in public services to attempt to increase growth whilst removing its accountability to citizens and intense competition for incomes. While some may see self-employment as allowing more autonomy and self-management, as we will see in Chapters 3 and 4, the machine it-self is rapidly becoming a manager. This phenomenon feeds into anxieties about the replacement of labour-power with robots and other machines, as well as our individual selves being replaceable by other humans in a digitalised race to the bottom. We have begun to internalise the imperative to perform in new ways to become 'hire-able'. We go through a subjecti-fication process, effectively becoming observing, entrepreneurial subjects, simultaneous to being constantly observed, whilst remaining objectified, working bodies. Indeed, the rise in attempts to quantify work is a symptom of rising precarity.

To think about wearables and the hardware of external tracking devices used to improve and understand the (precarious) self as well as corporate tracking of selves is to think about mind/body relation as much as it is to think about a technology/society relation. This understanding of the utility of workplace self-archiving devices potentially allows a re-interpretation of radical elements of monism endorsed by the affective and corporeal turns found in feminist research, critical geography and religious studies. So, the-oretically, the book intends to contribute to these literatures by exploring a set of ontological and epistemological questions around the significance of the body/mind relation in the use of wearable and other relevant tracking technologies. I ultimately ask whether the increased role for machines in the employment relationship reduces possibilities for resistance. The liter-ature in feminist critical political economy looks at the ontological in the political, exploring the material in a way that is not disconnected from the immaterial and with the cognitive and corporeal, recognising their insepa-rability and searching for spaces for dissent.

In legal terminology precarity refers to dependency whereby tenancy of one's own land belongs to someone else. This term has been reinterpreted in the neoliberal era to involve shrinkages in welfare states, privatisation and supposed 'reciprocity' between flexible workers and management (Berlant, 2011: 192) resulting in the rise in limited and time sensitive contracts. Precarious life conditions have not led to happiness and fulfilment, but to underemployment, anxiety and sickness. Self-archiving and self- and other-tracking devices in platform work inspire me to interrogate assumptions of the ontology for the mind/body experience of new worlds of work. In this book, I build on a growing literature in precarious labour, bringing a much-needed empirical dimension to how working conditions in many spheres are being affected by monitoring technologies. My arguments intersect with the corporeal and the affective 'turns', research that aims to identify the corporeal dimensions of social life, discussed in the following chapter. And, personally speaking, the book builds on work that I have done on the concept of employability and subjectivity (Moore 2009, 2010, 2011), querying how these technologies change the very basis for how the self can be understood as well as my interest in the quantification of work and the impact on workers (Akhtar and Moore, 2017; Moore, 2015; Moore and Piwek, 2015, 2017; Moore and Robinson, 2016). My 2010 book, *The International Political Economy of Work and Employability* outlined the way that the employability agenda of the 1980s and onward reveals a process of intensified personalisation of subjectivity and individualisation of responsibility for being employable, leaving out social capital and class. I looked at higher education's embrace of the employability drive as course curricula were positioned to aid students toward specific modes of being and behaving. The private sector was given a new role in education and several initiatives were formed to internationalise specific modes of being. In the book, I theorised that education initiatives were a form of *trasformismo* because they capture the 'ability' dimension of new ways of working emerging in, for example, peer to peer production and new collaborative ways of working made possible through new technologies. Building on these arguments, the current book looks at the impact that new technologies of measure which are now being introduced into workplaces have and to what extent these could be considered radical pathways to autonomy, as peer to peer production arenas were seen (Moore, 2011), or will these impacts act as surveillance mechanisms that speed up and intensify work irreversibly?

From the warehouse to the boardroom, tensions between autonomy and control reflect the increased quantification and reduced qualification of the mind/body. Are we engaging with machines, adapting to machines, or being subordinated through a phase of automation both of work and of management, where the role of technology is so significant that we are looking at an imminent scenario where the relationship is inverse, and machines manage humans? Chapter 3 positions the book's arguments in the new materialist literature where the ontological questions that these provocations pose are primary, where the terrain of workers' struggle begins with the fervency of corporeality in the face of quantification and digital labour.

While the focus of this book is not on resistance, it sets the stage for my next phase in research. Previously I mentioned the recent Uber tribunal triumph and the hope that taxi drivers will soon start to see the introduction of basic employee rights. Chapter 4 looks at responses to workplace quantification and to some extent, forms of resistance. Digitally quantified workers carry out everyday forms of resistance like appropriating apps, sousveillance (watching the watcher), carrying out information and sharing jamming, using personal devices rather than company provided ones at work, situational leveraging and feet dragging. I am asking, what is stopping workers from using data generated from self-tracking devices to justify our outputs and activities in the appraisal scenario or however our employability or hireability is determined? Could cross-tabulated data help us to prove that we are more stressed when we have too much work and provide a defense against work intensification or force work programmes to be reduced? The attraction of self-tracking may be that wearable tracking technologies will help to determine what is 'normal' for an individual through a process of 'biopedagogy' (Fotopoulou and O'Riordan, 2016). If we can see what is 'normal' for ourselves, then we can avoid blanket comparison with others, leading to better judgements about our own labour that we could ask management to take into account. The risk, of course, is that rather than allowing for a defensive tool in the workplace, quantifying technologies homogenise what is thought of as 'normal' rather than allow for tailored profiles, and produce an ideal-type, high performing, probably male and probably white, human, against whose image we must all compete.

Monitoring and Tracking Precarity

Before the early 20th century, human 'behaviour' was not a category for scientific study. Animals and plants were seen to demonstrate behaviours, but humans were spiritual beings and our experience of life was understood largely as separate from our biology. John B. Watson is credited with introducing the ascription of behaviour to humans to the research community. In a talk at Columbia University in 1913, this animal psychologist said that 'if psychology would follow the plan I suggest [behaviourism], the educator, physician, the jurist and the businessman could utilize our data in a practical way, as soon as we are able, experimentally, to obtain them' (Watson, 1913, quoted in Davies, 2016: 87). Just a few months later, despite never having worked with humans, Watson was promoted to the presidency of the American Psychological Association. Behaviour soon became a recurring theme for policymaking in finance and health. Behavioural economics and behavioural finance were used to identify best practices in home buying and optimal decision-making. Lifestyles became linked to health practices. Tweaks to everyday practices across populations could, it was decided, reduce social issues like obesity and deal with health care spending. However, behaviourism tended to put the emphasis on individuals' decision making as responsible for personal problems and tends to overlook difference across decision makers. The specifics of each body do not appear relevant in the context of the large statistics generated and physical limitations as influencing behaviour, not always considered. Not all actors have identical opportunity and access to education helping to make decisions about behaviour. Nevertheless, there has been little sign of abatement in attempts to understand, manage and change it.

During the period of industrial betterment discussed in Chapter 2, US factory owners encouraged workers to abstain from drinking and to generally behave in upright ways by maintaining traditionally configured families and regularly going to church. Workers' actions were assessed for precision in scientific management in factories. Far from the US but with a similar ethos in behaviour incentivizing, China introduced radio calisthenics as part of a drive for a healthy population, where good behaviour involved regular physical activity, which was picked up by Mao during the cultural revolution. Outward behaviours were seen as manageable and science, sport and religion were used to experiment with different methods. But workers' internal goings-on and emotions remained somewhat mysterious and there were no attempts to explicitly measure these to analyse their role in work and productivity. Research began to show that happy, as well as healthy, workers were inherently more productive (such as Pink, 2011; Warr, 2007). The idea began to simmer that workers could be nudged into doing things in a specific way, like consumers. In the first pages of *The Persuaders*, Packard marvelled at the 'large-scale efforts' in the 1950s that were being made, with what he saw as 'impressive success', to 'channel our unthinking habits', linking specific methods for channelling thinking to purchasing decisions and consumer habits. Marketing experts were starting to use concepts from psychiatry and methods of social sciences to identify how marketing was beginning a trek into the hidden self, or what happens below, behind and beneath people's levels of awareness. Attempts to penetrate a level of sub/unconsciousness for specific purposes of behaviour change were labelled 'the depth approach'. Soon it became accepted wisdom that people could be nudged into behaving differently.

In Britain, David Cameron's government set up the Behavioural Insights Team, nicknamed the 'Nudge Unit' in 2011. This Unit was to be a group of civil servants assigned the task of altering the perceptions people have about their choices, to lead them to make the best option easiest to choose. The use of public service announcements was a proven method since '5 a day' in several countries in the early 1990s, but 'nudge' takes it a step further. The 2015–2016 Behavioural Insights Team report indicates that simply telling doctors that they were prescribing antibiotics more than 80 percent of their peers led to a reduction of prescriptions deemed unnecessary by 3.3 percent (more than 73,000). Another example of a successful nudge suggested is the removal of the requirement for people to sign a consent form to allow their organs to be used after death for transplants. Given the medical service's shortage of organs, this could be a positive move, but some people could perceive the lack of explicit consent as a violation of rights. Nudge as a method has been met with some scepticism and reflects a commitment to actively bias people in ways that could easily be seen as 'creepy', which was the theme for the Design Culture Salon Series Four where I was invited to speak at the Victoria & Albert Museum in London in 2016 alongside researchers and practitioners who were interested in looking at design as linked to behaviour change. Nudge is a compelling instrument of design practice in politics, marketing, transport and urban planning propagated by Richard Thaler and Cass R. Sunstein. Methods to effect behaviour in workplaces have begun to reflect the nudge methodology but in even more creepy ways where technology plays an increasingly prominent role.

So physical health became associated with wellbeing and positive states of mind, and wellness initiatives began to introduce self-tracking as a method—such as the case presented earlier in this chapter, where BP America employees' morale was improved, and the company as well as workers themselves saved money on insurance premiums. Attempts to promote behaviour that will lead to physical health and internal happiness are now quite common in the modern workplace. But the behaviours required for this to happen require high levels of self-management and other forms of unpaid preparatory labour. Furthermore, the measure of 'physiolitics' as extracted from wearables data 'to improve performance' (Wilson, 2013), a physiological update of time and motion studies, could mean that all workers are expected to have an identical capability to self-optimise, as well as equal access to resources and thus to compete as though they are high performance athletes. High performance management takes on a new meaning.

The danger is that new management ideas introducing new technologies at work and behavioural incentives will come to dominate the debate surrounding the indisputable changes that technology has had on the world of work and serve to overlook the political economy of the accompanying shift toward precarity and unprotected work. Current quantified work activities attempt to measure quantified outputs in the ways scientific management did. The contemporary ideal quantified worker tracks all-of-life and shares this information with her boss (when she can figure out who the boss is). She is now expected to track aspects of work that are probably innumerable and expected to measure unseen labour or the preparatory work that is required to put oneself in the right bracket of performance now expected.

As outlined above, companies have taken a growing interest in such tools as daily activity tracking software and other wearable digital recording equipment such as Sensecam, Subcam sensecams, automas, memoto and audio-visual recorders. These products are used for first person perspective digital ethnographies, lifelogging, and self-tracking of both mental and physical activities in conjunction with productivity-related measures. This understanding of the utility of self-archiving devices potentially allows a re-interpretation of radical elements of monism endorsed by the affective and corporeal turns. As Chris Dancy claims, 'if you can measure it, someone will, and that somebody should be you'. In 2013, Mr. Dancy, or the 'Quantified Man' (Finley, 2013) (who I have interviewed for this book: see Chapter 5) was hooked up to up to five sensors, all day and night, and used Google Calendar to track all daily activities (see Figure 1.1). His pulse, skin temperature, and REM sleep are all measured constantly. He has a sensor in his toilet that looks for patterns between sleep and usage. Meanwhile, despite the increasing levels of interest in adopting wearables in workplaces, recent ADP UK (2015) research shows that more than half (52 percent)

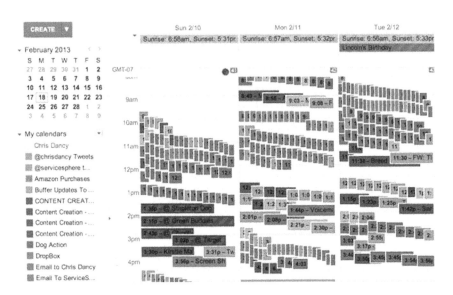

Figure 1.1 Chris Dancy's Google Calendar.

of employees have expressed concern with the amount of personal data that employers can access via the wearable technology used in work-places. Workers feel that devices may be used as tools to 'spy' on them (The Week, 2015). These attitudes towards privacy vary across countries, with 60 percent of German employees expressing reservations but only 36 percent of Dutch employees feeling this way. UK workers are the most hesitant to use wearables with as few as one in five feeling comfortable with this possibility (ADP UK, 2015).

Quantified workers are sought in white collar offices and dirty, dark and dangerous workplaces, art-houses and warehouses alike. Neilson and Coté ask, 'are we all cultural workers now?' given expressive value has become a key terrain of capture (2014). Management appears to take its foot off a paradoxical pedal, both removing explicit control over, but also guarantees of, work. The situation of the precarious worker is one whereby qualified, expressive, creative work is subsumed, where areas of activity formerly considered non-productive are increasingly incorporated in market economies, under the remit of the 'knowledge economy' and 'cognitive capitalism' (Boutang, 2011). With the elevation of workers across industries to 'entrepreneurs' this discourse arguably recognizes only one class: the managerial, entrepreneurial bourgeoisie.

According to Rose, the 'self-controlling self' of neoliberalism 'calculates about itself, and... works upon itself in order to better itself' (1996: 164), a process increasingly supplemented by machines that expand processes of workplace discipline (Moore and Taylor, 2009) and a process that is usually unpaid. Such processes are increasingly displaced from the enclosed workplace into the expanded spaces of home-based work, outsourced work, and the social factory. Psychological changes arising from precarity contribute to the formation of anxious selves who have internalised the imperative to perform, a two-part subjectification of workers as observing, entrepreneurial subjects and observed, objectified labouring bodies. Deleuze and Guattari suggest that in capitalism, only capitalists are subjects of enunciation whereas proletarians are subordinated to technical machines (1987: 457). With these provocations in mind, I now turn to look at the legal dimensions of the pursuits of tracking the quantified self at work.

Legal Landscape for the Quantification of Workers

The rise of tracking devices used in workplaces is significant because it merges traditions in productivity measurement starting from Taylor and the Gilbreths' projects and almost entirely new activities made possible by 'biosensing' (Nafus, 2016) devices that allow tracking of far more intimate and social aspects of work and increasingly, all-of-life. Human resources departments have used a variety of measurement software and measurement techniques which register workers' attendance, time spent at work and link this to payroll systems. Employees' days are scheduled through Outlook Calendars and we clock in and out of work using both swipe cards and embedded timeclock software such as Anuko and Kimai. Workers will want to know why monitoring and tracking is happening and what the data will be used for. The implications of new forms of measure are bringing corporealised data into appraisals and the possibilities of intensified workplace monitoring are very real. Both behaviour and workplace design change are central to this new regime; indeed, the reduction of the need for staff on the basis of data accumulation by wearable technology and other forms of monitoring are already evident in warehouse work. The collection of extensive personal data is contributing to an increasingly lucrative business, and the aggregation and comparison potentials of information about many users' experiences is seen as extremely valuable. It is no surprise that commentators have begun to look at the legal landscape surrounding quantifying workers.

Doctors have long been able to see patients' heartrates and X-rays of the insides of our bodies. Wearable devices are fully entrenched into fitness coaching where our step counts and heartrates are interesting and can be cross tabulated on dashboards to help us to assemble fitness plans. Use of fitness devices is also expected to inspire behaviour change. Few would claim that the possibility a device would inspire more physical activity is somehow insidious as far as behavioural change goes, or that provisions to help hospital patients with memory loss or physical necessity is questionable. More contestable, in legal terms, is the introduction of sensory technologies into workplaces for behaviour change and for the designation of a singular, idealised self as I will argue. The Senior Editor for *Computerworld* spoke to a commentator to the U.S. Equal Employment Opportunity Commission, named only as Ann Kelly, who stated that:

> I'm concerned about the proliferation of employee wellness programs that seem to be coming ever-more intrusive and coercive...If employers may lawfully discriminate against people on the basis of intimate, personal health matters, where will that end?
>
> (Hamblen, 2015)

The Information Commissioner's Office's (ICO, 2011) *Data Protection: The Employment Practices Code* lists the core principles of workplace monitoring as follows:

Core principles are:

- It will usually be intrusive to monitor your workers.
- Workers have legitimate expectations that they can keep their personal lives private and that they are also entitled to a degree of privacy in the work environment.
- If employers wish to monitor their workers, they should be clear about the purpose and satisfied that the particular monitoring arrangement is justified by real benefits that will be delivered.
- Workers should be aware of the nature, extent and reasons for any monitoring, unless (exceptionally) covert monitoring is justified.
- In any event, workers' awareness will influence their expectations.

Companies are at risk of non-compliance if 'line managers introduce monitoring arrangement without due authority'. Recommendations include:

3.1.2 Before monitoring, identify clearly the purpose(s) behind the monitoring and the specific benefits it is likely to bring. Determine – preferably using an impact assessment – whether the likely benefits justify any adverse impact.

Key points and possible actions include in 3.1.2:

- Identify which of your organisation's rules and standards are enforced partly or wholly through use of monitoring.
- Ensure that these rules and standards are set out in policies that are clearly communicated to workers.

3.1.4 Tell workers what monitoring is taking place and why, and keep them aware of this, unless covert monitoring is justified.

In key points and possible actions in 3.1.4, the recommendations tell employers to:

- Ensure that workers are aware of the nature and extent of any monitoring.
- Set up a system (for example by using the workers' handbook or via an intranet) to ensure workers remain aware that monitoring is being conducted.
- Tell workers when significant changes are introduced.

Importantly, the criteria also state that an employer should not 'use personal information collected through monitoring for purposes other than those for which the monitoring was introduced' unless:

a   It is clearly in the individual's interest to do so, or
b   It reveals activity that no employer could reasonably be expected to ignore (ICO, 2011: 65–7).

A company is advised to decide whether monitoring is justified by:

- Establishing the benefits of the method of monitoring
- Considering any alternative method of monitoring
- Weighing these benefits against any adverse impact
- Placing particular emphasis on the need to be fair to individual workers
- Ensuring, particularly where monitoring electronic communications is involved, that any intrusion is no more than absolutely necessary
- Bearing in mind that significant intrusion into the private lives of individuals will not normally be justified unless the employer's business is at real risk of serious damage
- Taking into account the results of consultations with trade unions or other representatives, if any, or with workers themselves (ICO, 2011: 63)

The Advisory, Conciliation and Arbitration Service (ACAS), which is widely used by lawyers and other employee representation groups like trades unions, lists the key advisory points about monitoring at work as follows (ACAS, 2017):

- Employers should have written policies and procedures in place regarding monitoring at work.
- Monitoring shouldn't be excessive and should be justified.
- Staff should be told what information will be recorded and how long it will be kept.
- If employers monitor workers by collecting or using information the Data Protection Act will apply.
- Information collected through monitoring should be kept secure.

ACAS lists the ways that employers monitor staff at work in various ways, including:

- CCTV
- looking at use of email or website visits
- listening in on telephone calls
- bag searches
- email and web monitoring

Regarding 'Covert Monitoring', the ACAS site indicates that:

> It's very rare that employers would need to carry out monitoring in secret without the staff being told they are being monitored. Employers must have a genuine reason to carry out covert monitoring such as criminal activities or malpractice. Monitoring must be obtained as quickly as possible, and only as part of a specific investigation. The monitoring must stop when the investigation has finished.
>
> (ACAS, 2017)

The codes of conduct listed here refer to more standard methods of surveilling employees, but now a boss can find out where you are, how you are, what you are doing, who you are talking to, what you are writing and how much sleep you have had. Data collected from a FitBit has also been used in a Canadian court as evidence in a personal occupational injury claim (Carter, 2015).

The availability of big data that is accumulated by workplace wearable devices is not itself a problem, rather is *how data is used* and how/whether management tells employees that they are using data, which leads to arising social tensions. Could collected data be explicitly used in workplace appraisals? In the factory setting, this is already happening. But as we will see in Chapter 4, there is no guarantee that management will be transparent with what data is being used, and how it is being used. There are few existing corporate codes of conduct regarding data collection at many points in factory work settings, and in many areas aspects of work are being measured in ways that go beyond previous standards, such as increasingly precise time and movement that are tracked in Amazon and Tesco warehouse floors, and now courier and food delivery companies' widespread tracking of delivery drivers with XDA/PDA handheld computers such as Palm Pilots and GPS. Collection of bodily data is a legal grey area. There have been significantly delayed legal responses to personal privacy in corporate data collection because corporate data reservoirs are largely unregulated (Cohen, 2015). Levy indicates that 'as a rule, law has been loath to get too involved in intimate domains' (2015: 679). Legal risks fall predominantly in the areas of how and where data is stored, personal and corporate security risks, data privacy and discrimination as relating to health when used in wellness initiatives as we will see in the chapters that follow. In terms of security and privacy, cybercriminals could hack wearable fitness devices' company servers and gain access to people's health information or to locations where an employer stores this and other employee data. In the United States, by law employers are usually not allowed to conduct medical examinations, as is the case in the 1990 Americans with Disabilities Act (ADA) guidelines. Data collection of workers' health is not identical to an examination but heartrate and blood pressure could be considered as such. Employers are not permitted to make employment decisions based on genetic characteristics so wearables gathering information about this could lead to significant tensions.

In June 2015, the US Equal Employment Opportunity Commission (EEOC) issued a proposed rule amending aspects of the ADA regarding how corporations collect data from workplace wellness programmes. The questions raised in response to the proposal were around data that companies are gathering from employees' wearable technologies relating to what exactly qualifies as simple health data and what may violate privacy concerns around more intensive medical data. Employees' steps may be defined as simple health information, but data on heart rate, a medical measure, would be considered too invasive according to this ruling. Public comments were invited at the EEOC's proposals to curb the use of employer surveillance over wearable data in wellness programmes (Mingis, 2015). EEOC spokesman James Ryan indicated that:

> If the information the employer is obtaining is considered 'medical information' (e.g., a person's heart rate over a period of time), then the information would be subject to the ADA's confidentiality requirements regardless of how the employer obtains this information. By contrast, information that would not be deemed medical information (e.g., how many steps a person takes per day, number of active minutes or calories burned) is not subject to the ADA's restrictions on disclosure.
> (Hamblen, 2015)

Timothy Collins, an employment lawyer for Duane Morris LLP states that:

> ...employers are up in arms about this proposed rule (...) wearables would be subject to the rule, especially if employers are handing them out for free and using them to gather data on the habits of workers.
> (Mingis, 2015)

Workers often use mobile devices on the consumer market for work, which puts these items into the category of BYOD, which stands for 'bring your own device'. Often, such personally owned devices do not meet PCI Data Security Standard compliance requirements. Bob Russo, general manager of Payment Card Industry Security Standards Council (PCI SSC) states that:

> Productivity trumps security (...); consider the salesperson in the field who has a better chance of closing business if they have immediate access to important data. Think he or she wouldn't do it? The likely thought process would be, closing business is in the best interest of the firm, and a security breach will never happen to me.
>
> (Armerding, 2013)

In many cases, wearable technology is worn for health and safety and professional data transmission reasons. Telephone maintenance workers wear armband computers when they climb telephone poles. Truck drivers can wear a 'smartcap' which looks like a baseball cap and has built-in sensors that detect drivers' levels of tiredness, preventing fatigue-related accidents. Some construction sites allow foremen to see workers' heartrates which allows risks to be spotted. Surgeons use voice activated systems to pass on information to doctors. Military fighter pilots use heads-up displays (HUD), transparent displays that present data that appears before one's eyes even when one moves the head.

While these technologies collect information about physical states of being to identify risk factors in already risk-laden and dangerous environments such as the battlefield and hospitals, companies are beginning to take on more interest and responsibility in their employees' mental wellbeing as well as physical safety which introduces even more legal questions. Happy and healthy employees are seen as good for business performance, but how far can employers go to check this?

Companies are then generally expected to be transparent with employees about the methods they choose to adopt to monitor them, outlining reasons to do so and the expected impact as well as benefits. Compliance will involve employers not using data for any other reason than the ones they outline to staff except in extreme cases. The codes of conduct suggested do not set out specifics for variable worker categories. Another obvious problem is that it is very difficult for workers to know what is being monitored if this information is not communicated, leading to the paradox of information loops where workers may feel they are forced to carry out sousveillance, or begin to watch the watcher by asking to see a code of conduct or, in more extreme cases, launching 'freedom of information' enquiries, 'subject requests' or grievances to find out. More technically inclined people may choose to look for other signs. For example, companies might use third-party remote desktop software like RealVNC, TightVNC, UltraVNC, LogMeIn, and GoToMyPC if they want to monitor the physical screen. This can be located by looking in a System Tray or the Windows Start Menu (Dachls, 2012). As worn, sensory technologies are relatively new on the human resources scene, however, it is not as clear how employees will be told about the use of data generated by these. Nonetheless, the codes set forward by ACAS and the ICO should be sufficient for general cover in any projects pursuing self- and other-tracking using the new kinds of technologies identified above. Whether there will be compliance, however, is yet to be seen.

Introducing Possible Conclusions

This book investigates what the new digitalised, quantified world of work means for workers. The introduction of technologies at the level of intimacy that self- and other-tracking allows, brings about questions of work/life integration; whether employers' advocacy of physical health overshadows concerns for mental and emotional health; and asks to what extent this changes the labour process, the employment relationship and people's experiences of work. Should your employer be given access to detailed information about your health and wellbeing? What happens when data is used to make judgements about you as a worker, whether by a physical manager or an online client such as seen in demand economy platform work discussed in Chapter 4? To fully comprehend and to theorise this trend, in Chapter 2, I outline a history of work design experimentation from industrial betterment to the current phase that I label 'agile management systems', to identify whether and to what extent tracking in workplaces is different to older methods of workplace measurement. Labour processes and designs of workplaces intended to improve workers' performance operated in each period but in many cases did not succeed. Subsequent chapters will look at how self- and other-tracking at work have begun to track what I call unseen labour, resulting in work intensification and exacerbated control over labour as capital gains with more absolute and relative surplus value.

In the next chapter, emphasis is placed on time-honoured scientific management, because its ideals have penetrated most eras of work design experimentation since Taylor's time. Scientific management, also called 'time study' and 'Taylorism', was extremely influential across Europe. While it started in the steel and bricklaying industries, its principles were integrated into the public sector. As recounted from a document published by the League of Nations in 1927 in Chapter 2, hundreds of research centres were set up to run experiments and to look at how this ideology was expected internationally to introduce a civilising influence as well as feed into the prevailing hope at the time for an interdependent and fully cooperative international system in the interwar period. This doctrine of standardisation, efficiency, separation between manual and mental labour and emphasis on the role of the expert engineer, was embraced internationally by employers' associations, education institutions and the state, but was ardently resisted by workers' representatives (the legacy of which we will see also in Chapter 4) because it was seen as the first steps toward mechanisation and automation.

Agility, as the latest work design regime, is similar in emphasis to scientific management, because its principles are influencing work beyond the technological production line in software where it originated (in a similar proliferation trend to scientific management). Agile's roots are in *kaizen* and lean production, capturing traces from the past. Agility is an era where both absolute and relative value is subordinated; unseen and seen labour is captured through measure; and concrete is made abstract. In these ways, numeration, as related to production and work intensification, is an age old method for control in workplaces and work, and are now prolonged to maintain neoliberal capitalist hegemony. However, quantifying the body and mind (as though they are separate) is one thing, but the trend now in quantifying workers' experiences of emotions and affective labouring to survive precarity is an increasingly visible feature in work design. Importantly, unseen labour is required in the current management regime called 'agile' work. Agility requires workers to align themselves with specific values and to be constantly prepared for change, because technology inevitably changes, simultaneous to taking more authority over human work, whether through algorithmic management or automation, intensifying management practices or self-management responsibilities.

To examine these claims, Chapter 3 identifies the precarious worker as they survive the era of agility. Who is this person? How can/do/will they (we) survive? Is their (our) work dignified, decent, or simply degrading? Contemporary precarity has once again revealed the material and corporeal aspects to human life despite its digitalised quantification. Advancing technology stares back at us in the fragments of temporal and spatial impossibilities as we struggle to identify our role in production. Along these lines of questioning, the tensions in the digitalised employment relationship are outlined empirically in Chapter 3. Using the empirical example of sensory technologies in workplaces in Chapters 4 and 5, we can see that there is more than an academic 'turn' in thinking about the material.

I identify how the international community has responded to the rise in precarious conditions and that the rise and types of agile, precarious, quantified work significantly impact women and vulnerable groups. With this in mind, I approach a philosophical landscape, aiming to contribute to the new materialist literature as it emerges from the corporeal and affective turns. I outline the emergence of this area of research from both feminist and orthodox Marxist literatures. To address Negri's claim that political economy has become de-ontological, I challenge Marxists to re-think assumptions about how life happens and where struggle occurs in their depictions of new materialism so that we can better understand how technology is being used to calculate the corporeal and the affective. Turning to the feminist new materialist and Marxist social reproduction literature, I foster an emerging dialogue between new materialism and my own discipline of international political economy to theorise issues around the quantified self at work. New materialism is not only an idea or a philosophical treatise but is lived, practiced, and agential and as Clough has indicated, it is a response to the technoscientific (2007: 3). To look at divisibility of labour as intentional practice I investigate theses in both poststructural and Marxist camps with an emphasis on a newly emerging area of 'new materialism'. Individual workers become accountable for attitudes and behaviours that are recounted by algorithm, leaving no room for qualitative depiction of affective selfhood within communities. I ask how workers can begin to resist the rise of control aspects in precarity, where even self-management is subordinated, where all of life is at risk of being subsumed, leaving a spectre of a non-realised self under conditions of the haunted.

Continuing this argument, Chapter 4 assesses the claim that monitoring and tracking of work is an *intentional* move toward capturing and controlling affective and emotional labour, accompanied with a more prescient place for technology as it begins to actually replace management. To highlight where precarity is emerging in our new digitalised world of work and I outline how and where precarious digitalised labour is emerging most acutely, and discuss ways this work is encouraged, monitored, policed and measured. The objective is to unravel the ethical implications around the use of algorithms and big data through indicating how they impact people. Measurement and quantification are never *neutral* exercises as they have historically been portrayed. To demonstrate these points, I look at workplace surveillance; electronic performance monitoring; and then, to metaphorically answer the most recent iteration of Ricardo's 'machinery question', I look at how automation and gig work requires unseen labour. Unpaid, affective and emotional labour is required in these contexts. Unseen labour includes, among other things, the creation of a digital personality and reputation management to algorithmically attract work. Sections of Chapter 4 also include information and empirical examples from discussions with people who are directly impacted in these contexts. Mags Dewhurst is the chair of Independent Workers Union of Great Britain and a gig work cyclist courier for CitySprint UK Ltd. Mags told me about the changes to her work over the past five years and the introduction of invasive new technologies. One anonymous warehouse worker who experienced top-down implementation of tracking devices told me how s/he and a colleague carried out everyday forms of resistance and discovered their data was not being used in the ways they had been told. I also include a short report of a car factory visit I conducted in 2016, where I was able to speak to workers, work council members and trade unionists about the impact that automation has had, where it has eliminated thousands of jobs over time.

Then, also in Chapter 4, I outline the case study of the Quantified Workplace project run by one company over the course of one year in the Netherlands, where workers were made precarious because they experienced a merge and acquisition, where one smaller company was absorbed by a multinational company. To manage the effects of the change, the company provided self-tracking devices and lifelogging tools to measure employees' unseen labour, identifying how people respond to change, and identifying whether management of change through healthy lifestyles impacts productivity.

Chapter 5 provides verbatim interviews with four individuals. All four are very experienced self-trackers and have valuable insights into the world of self- and other-tracking. Interviewees include Bethany Soule, the CTO for Beeminder, a productivity tracking software; one of the founders of the Quantified Self conferences in San Francisco, Robin Barooah; Chris Dancy, who is internationally known for his avid self-tracking and self-archiving; and one Master's student who tracks every second of his day to identify how productive he has been, who I saw speak at a Quantified Meetup in London in 2015. The final chapter then provides a conclusion and suggests next steps for research.

Note

1 Management is a term used to denote the relationship between capital and labour where structures are in place to exploit surplus value.

Bibliography

ACAS (2017) '*Being Monitored at Work*.' www.acas.org.uk/index.aspx?articleid= 5721 (accessed 02/02/2017).

ADP UK (2015) 'Putting Wearables to Work – New Technology Could Revolutionise the Workplace' *Personnel Today, Technology* 14/07/15. www.personneltoday.com/ pr/2015/07/putting-wearables-to-work-new-technology-could-revolutionise-the-workplace/ (accessed 02/02/2017).

Akhtar, P. and Moore, P. (2016) 'The Psycho-Social Impacts of Technological Change in Contemporary Workplaces and Trade Union Responses' in *Psycho-Social Risks, Stress and Violence in The World of Work* Special Issue (Biondi, A. and Guseva, V., eds). *International Journal of Labour Research* 8(1–2): 102–131.

Armerding, T. (2013) 'Can the New RIPAA Rule Cut PHI Breaches?' *CIO* 8/11/2013. www.cio.com/article/2381042/data-protection/canthe-new-hipaa-rule-cut-phi-breaches.html (accessed 03/02/2017).

Bain, P. and Taylor, P. (2000) 'Entrapped by the "Electronic Panopticon"? Worker Resistance in the Call Centre' *New Technology, Work and Employment* 15(1): 2–18.

Berg, J. (2016) 'Inclusive Labour Markets, Labour Relations and Working Conditions Branch' *Conditions of Work and Employment Series No. 74* (Geneva: International Labour Office).

Bergvall-Kåreborn, B. and Howcroft, D. (2014) 'Amazon Mechanical Turk and the Commodification of Labour' *New Technology, Work and Employment* 29(3): 213–223.

Berlant, L. (2011) *Cruel Optimism* (Durham, NC: Duke University Press).

Bersin, J., Mariani, J. and Monahan K. (2016) 'Will IoT Technology Bring us the Quantified Employee? The Internet of Things in Human Resources'. *Deloitte University Press*. http://dupress.com/articles/people-analytics-internet-of-things-iot-human-resources/#end-notes (accessed 02/02/2017).

Bhave, D. P. (2014) 'The Invisible Eye? Electronic Performance Monitoring and Employee Job Performance' *Personnel Psychology* 67(3): 605–635.

Boutang, Y. M. (2011) *Cognitive Capitalism* (Cambridge, UK and Malden, MA: Polity).

Burawoy, M. (1985) *The Politics of Production: Factory Regimes Under Capitalism* (London: New Left).

Campbell, D. (2015) 'Prof Bruce Keogh: Wearable Technology Plays a Crucial Part in NHS Future' *The Guardian* 19/01/15. www.theguardian.com/society/2015/jan/19/prof-bruce-keogh-wearable-technology-plays-crucial-part-nhs-future (accessed 02/02/2017).

Carter, J. (2015) 'Are Wearables at Work a Risky Business? Data Collected by Wearables is Now Being Used as Evidence in Court' *Techradar Pro* 14/11/2015. www.techradar.com/news/wearables/are-wearables-at-work-a-risky-business-1308722?src=rss&attr=all (accessed 03/02/2017).

Castells, M. (2000) *The Rise of the Network Society* (2nd ed.) (Malden, MA: Blackwell).

Cederström, C. and Spicer, A. (2015) *The Wellness Syndrome* (Cambridge, UK and Malden, MA: Polity).

Cheney-Lippold, J. (2011) 'A New Algorithmic Identity: Soft Biopolitics and the Modulation of Control' *Theory, Culture & Society* 28(6): 164–181.

Clough, P. T. (2007) 'Introduction' in Clough, P. T. and Halley, J. (eds) *The Affective Turn: Theorising the Social* (Durham, NC and London: Duke University Press): 1–33.

Cohen, J. (2015) 'Code and Law between Truth and Power' *LSE Public Lecture* 11/03/15. www.lse.ac.uk/newsAndMedia/videoAndAudio/channels/publicLecturesAndEvents/player.aspx?id=2972 (accessed 03/02/2017).

Corden, J. (2013) 'Investigating One's Diet' *The Royal Society Repository* 06/11/13. http://blogs.royalsociety.org/history-of-science/2013/11/06/investigating-ones-diet/ (accessed 02/02/17).

Dachls, A. (2012) 'How Can I Tell If I'm Being Monitored at Work and What Can I do about It?' *Lifehacker.* http://lifehacker.com/5894689/how-can-i-tell-if-im-being-monitored-at-work-and-what-can-i-do-about-it (accessed 02/02/2017).

Davies, W. (2016) *The Happiness Industry: How the Government and Big Business Sold Us Well-being* (London: Verso Books).

Daws, R. (2016) 'Adopting Fitness Trackers in Businesses Saves $1000 per eEmployee' *Wearable Tech* 19/10/2016. www.wearabletechnology-news.com/news/2016/oct/19/adopting-fitness-trackers-businesses-saves-1000-employee/ (accessed 02/02/2017).

DeLanda, M. (2006) *A New Philosophy of Society: Assemblage Theory and Social Complexity* (London: Continuum).

Deleuze, G. and Guattari. F. (1983) *Anti-Oedipus: Capitalism and Schizophrenia* (Minneapolis: University of Minnesota Press).

Deleuze, G. and Guattari, F. (1987) *A Thousand Plateaus: Capitalism and Schizophrenia* (London: Continuum).Dyer-Witheford, N. (2015) *Cyber-Proletariat: Global Labour in the Digital Vortex* (London: Pluto Press).

Finley, K. (2013) 'What if Your Boss Tracked Your Sleep, Diet, and Exercise?' *Wired.co.uk* 18/04/13. www.wired.com/2013/04/quantified-work-citizen/ (accessed 05/02/2017).

Fotopoulou, A. and O'Riordan, K. (2016) 'Training to self-care: fitness tracking, biopedagogy and the healthy consumer' *Health Sociology Review* 26(1): 54–68.

Frey, C. B. and Osborne, M. A. (2013) The Future of Employment: How Susceptible are Jobs to Computerisation? (*Oxford Martin School Working Paper*).

Fuchs, C. (2014) *Digital Labour and Karl Marx* (London: Routledge).

Gandini, A., Pais, I. and Beraldo, D. (2016) 'Reputation and Trust on Online Labour Markets: The Reputation Economy of Lance' *Work Organisation Labour and Globalisation* 10(1): 27–43.

Gibbs, S. (2015) 'Is "Corporate Wellness" the Big New Thing That Will Keep Fitbit Ahead of the Pack?' *The Guardian* 19/06/15. www.theguardian.com/technology/2015/jun/19/is-corporate-wellness-the-big-new-thing-that-will-keep-fitbit-ahead-of-the-pack (accessed 20/02/2017).

Gill, R. C. and Pratt, A. (2008) 'In the Social Factory? Immaterial Labour, Precariousness and Cultural Work' *Theory Culture & Society* 25(7–8): 1–30.

Greenhill, A. and Fletcher, G. (2013) 'Labouring Online: Are There New Labour Processes in Virtual Game Worlds?' *Journal of the Association for Information Systems* 14(11): 672–693.

Guéry, F. and Deleule, D. (2014) *The Productive Body* (Hants: Zero Books).

Hamblen, M. (2015) 'Programs Are Used to Weed Out Workers Who Raise Premiums, One Attorney Says' *Computer World* 19/06/15. www.computerworld.com/article/2937721/wearables/wearables-for-workplace-wellness-face-federal-scrutiny.html (accessed 03/02/2017).

Haraway, D. (1991) 'A Cyborg Manifesto: Science Technology and Socialist-Feminism in the Late Twentieth Century' in *Simians Cyborgs and Women: The Reinvention of Nature* (New York, Oxford: Routledge): 127–148.

Hardt, M. and Negri, A. (2000) *Empire* (Cambridge, MA: Harvard University Press).

Hatfield, I. (2015) 'Self-Employment in Europe' *IPPR* 04/01/15. www.ippr.org/publications/self-employment-in-europe (accessed 16/02/17).

Hennigan, A. (2014) 'Goodbye to the Gimmick and in with the Year of Truly "Wearable" Tech?' *Hospitalitynet* 06/02/14. www.hospitalitynet.org/news/4063931.html (accessed 02/02/17).

Holts, K. (2013) 'Towards a Taxonomy of Virtual Work' *Work Organisation, Labour and Globalisation* 7(1): 31–50.

Hutton, W. (2017) 'If Teresa May Gives in Over Self-Employment Row, She's Not Serious about Tax Reform' *Guardian* Budget 2017 12/03/17. www.theguardian.com/commentisfree/2017/mar/12/theresa-may-self-employment-row-not-serious-about-tax-reforms.

Huws, U. (2014) *Labour in the Global Digital Economy: The Cybertariat Comes of Age* (London: Monthly Review Press).

ICO (2011) *Data Protection: The Employment Practices Code.* https://ico.org.uk/media/for-organisations/.../the_employment_practices_code.pdf (accessed 08/03/17).

International Data Corporation (IDC) (2016) 'IDC Forecasts Worldwide Shipments of Wearables to Surpass 200 Million in 2019, Driven by Strong Smartwatch Growth and the Emergence of Smarter Watches'. www.idc.com/getdoc.jsp?containerId=prUS41100116 (accessed 02/02/17).

Jarrett, K. (2016) *Feminism, Labour and Digital Media: The Digital Housewife* (New York: Routledge).

Jeske, D. and Santuzzi, A. M. (2015) 'Monitoring What and How: Psychological Implications of Electronic Performance Monitoring' *New Technology, Work and Employment* 30(1): 62–78.

Jiff (2016) 'Jiff Challenges Myths on Workplace Wearables' *Jiff® Inc.* 21/12/2016. www.jiff.com/press-news/jiff-data-challenges-myths-workplace-wearables/ (accessed 02/02/17).

Kelly, K. (2007) 'What is the Quantified Self?' http://quantifiedself.com/2007/10/what-is-the-quantifiable-self/ (accessed 12/8/2015).

Knights, D. and Willmott, H. (eds.) (1988) *New Technology and the Labour Process* (London: Palgrave).

Kohll, A. (2016) '8 Things You Need to Know about Employee Wellness Programs' *Forbes* 21/04/16. www.forbes.com/sites/alankohll/2016/04/21/8-things-you-need-to-know-about-employee-wellness-programs/#1ec78c4d610c (accessed 02/02/2017).

Leon, A. P. (2015) *Machines* (Charlotte, NC: Information Age Publishing).

Levy, K, E.C. (2015) 'Intimate Surveillance' *Idaho Law Review* 51: 679–93.

Lindsay, G. (2015) 'We Spent Two Weeks Wearing Employee Trackers: Here's What We Learned' *Fact Coexist*, 22/09/15. www.fastcoexist.com/3051324/we-spent-two-weeks-wearing-employee-trackers-heres-what-we-learned (accessed 03/02/2017).

Lindzon, J. (2014) 'What Industries are the First to Introduce Wearables at Work?' *FastCompany* 09/29/14. www.fastcompany.com/3036331/what-industries-are-the-first-to-introduce-wearables-at-work (accessed 03/02/2017).

Lupton, D. (2012) 'M-Health and Health Promotion: The Digital Cyborg and Surveillance Society' *Social Theory & Health* 10(3): 229–244.

Lupton, D. (2013) 'Understanding the Human Machine' *IEEE Technology and Society Magazine*, Winter: 23.

Mance, H. (2016) 'Telegraph Installs Then Removes Motion Trackers from Staff Desks' *Financial Times* 11/01/16. www.ft.com/cms/s/0/48537dce-b88c-11e5-bf7e-8a339b6f2164.html#axzz46TaWA1UK (accessed 03/02/2017).

Mandel, E. and Novak, G. (1970/2014) *The Marxist Theory of Alienation* (Atlanta, GA: Pathfinder Press).

Massumi, B. (2002) *Parables for the Virtual: Movement, Affect, Sensation* (Durham, NC: Duke University Press).

Mingis, K. (2015) 'The Takeaway: Feds Eye New Rule for Workplace Wearables' *CIO* 19/06/15. www.cio.com/article/2937731/wearable-technology/the-takeaway-feds-eye-new-rule-for-workplace-wearables.html#follow (accessed 02/02/17).

Mohan, A., Ara K., Pentland A., with Olguin, D. and Waber, K. (2009) 'Sensible Organisations: Technnology and Methodology for Automatically Measuring Organisational Behaviour' *Systems, Man and Cybernetics, Part B: Cybernetics IEEE Transactions* 39(1): 43–55.

Moore, P. (2006) 'Global Knowledge Capitalism, Self-Woven Safety Nets, and the Crisis of Employability' *Global Society* 20(4): 453–473.

Moore, P. (2009) 'UK Education, Employability, and Everyday Life' *Journal of Critical Education Policy Studies* 7(1): 243–273.

Moore, P. (2010) *The International Political Economy of Work and Employability* (Basingstoke: Palgrave Macmillan).

Moore, P. (2011) 'Subjectivity in the Ecologies of P2P Production' *The Fibreculture Journal* FCJ-119. http://seventeen.fibreculturejournal.org/fcj-119-peer-to-peer-production-a-revolutionary-or-neoliberal-mode-of-subjectivation/ (accessed 03/02/2017).

Moore, P. (2015) 'Tracking Bodies, the Quantified Self and the Corporeal Turn' in Van Der Pijl, K. (ed) *The Handbook of International Political Economy of Production* (Cheltenham: Edward Elgar) 394–408.

Moore, P. and Piwek, L. (2015) 'Unintended Consequences and the Dark Side of the Quantified Self' *Sustainable Societies Network Commissioned Paper* 15/06/2015. https://phoebevmoore.wordpress.com/2015/06/15/unintended-consequences-the-dark-sides-of-quantifying-selves/ (accessed 03/02/2017).

Moore, P. and Piwek, L. (2017) 'Regulating Wellbeing in the Brave New Quantified Workplace', Employee Relations 39(3): 308–316.

Moore, P. and Robinson, A. (2015 DOI, 2016 Print) 'The Quantified Self: What Counts in the Neoliberal Workplace' *New Media & Society* 18(1): 2774–2792.

Moore, P. and Taylor, P. A. (2009) 'Exploitation of the Self in Community-Based Software Production – Workers' Freedoms or Firm Foundations?' *Capital & Class* 33(1): 99–120.

Nafus, D. (2016) *Quantified: Biosensing Technologies in Everyday Life* (Cambridge, MA: MIT Press).

Nield, D. (2014) 'In Corporate Wellness Programme, Wearables Take a Step Forward' *Fortune* 15/04/14. http://fortune.com/2014/04/15/in-corporate-wellness-programs-wearables-take-a-step-forward/ (accessed 02/02/2017).

Neilson, B. and Coté, M. (2014) 'Introduction: Are We All Cultural Workers Now?' *Journal of Cultural Economy* 7(1): 1–11.

Neuringer, A. (1981) 'Self-Experimentation: A Call for Change' *Behaviourism* 9(1): 79–94.

O'Connor, S. (2016) 'When Your Boss is An Algorithm' *Financial Times* 08/09/16. www.ft.com/content/88fdc58e-754f-11e6-b60a-de4532d5ea35.

Office for National Statistics (ONS) (2017) *UK Labour Market: Feb 2017.* www.ons.gov.uk/employmentandlabourmarket/peopleinwork/employmentand employeetypes/bulletins/uklabourmarket/feb2017#summary-of-latest-labour-market-statistics (accessed 02/02/2017).

Office of National Statistics (ONS) (2016) 'Part-Timers Contribute to Strong Growth in Self-Employment' *ONS.gov* 13/07/16. www.ons.gov.uk/news/news/parttimerscontributetostronggrowthinselfemployment (accessed 16/02/17).

Parliamentary business (2015) 'The Self-Employment Boom: Key Issues for the 2015 Parliament'. www.parliament.uk/business/publications/research/key-issues-parliament-2015/work/self-employment/ (accessed 03/02/17).

Peaucelle, J. L. (2000) 'From Taylorism to Post-Taylorism: Simultaneously Pursuing Several Management Objectives' *Journal of Organisational Change* 13(5): 452–467.

Pennic, J. (2016) 'Infographic: How Wearables Are Revolutionizing Healthcare' *HIT Consultant* 04/08/16. http://hitconsultant.net/2016/04/08/how-wearables-are-revolutionizing-healthcare/ (accessed 02/02/2017).

Pink, D. (2011) *Drive: The Surprising Truth about What Motivates Us* (New York: Riverhead Books).

Poster, W. R. (2011) 'Emotion Detectors Answering Machines and E-Unions: Multi-Surveillance in the Global Interactive Service Industry' *American Behavioral Scientist* 55(7): 868–901.

Power, B. (2016) 'Why John Deere Measures Employee Morale Every Two Weeks' *Harvard Business Review* 24/05/16. https://hbr.org/2016/05/why-john-deere-measures-employee-morale-every-two-weeks (accessed 03/02/2017).

Rackspace (2014) 'Wearable Technologies Can Boost Employee Productivity By up to 8.5%' *Goldsmiths University of London News* 22/09/14. www.gold.ac.uk/news/homepage-news/wearabletechnologiescanboostemployeeproductivityby upto85.php (accessed 24/11/16).

Quantified Self Bay Area Meetup Group (2017) Homepage. www.meetup.com/quantifiedself/ (accessed 03/02/2017).

Rose, N. (1996) *Inventing Our Selves* (Cambridge: Cambridge University Press).

Ruckenstein, M. (2014) 'Visualized and Interacted Life: Personal Analytics and Engagements with Data Doubles' *Societies* 4(1), 68–84.

Spence, E. (2013) '2014 Will Be the Year of Wearable Technology' *Forbes* 11/02/13. www.forbes.com/sites/ewanspence/2013/11/02/2014-will-be-the-year-of-wearable-technology/ (accessed 24/11/16).

Taylor, F. W. (1911/1998) *The Principles of Scientific Management* (Mineola, NY: Dover Publications).

Terranova, T. (2000) 'Free Labor: Producing Culture for the Digital Economy' *Social Text* 18(2), 33–58.

The Week (2015) 'The Rise of Workplace Spying' *The Week* 05/07/15. http://theweek.com/articles/564263/rise-workplace-spying (accessed 16/02/17).

Till, C. (2014) 'Exercise as Labour: Quantified Self and the Transformation of Exercise into Labour' *Societies* 4(3): 446–462.

Tractica (2016) 'Enterprise Wearable Technology Solutions' White Paper Published Second Quarter 2016 in Partnership with Enterprise Wearable Technology Summit East.

Verma, P. (2014) 'How to Jumpstart Your Corporate Wellness Program with Big Data' *Forbes* 20/11/2014. www.forbes.com/sites/castlight/2014/11/20/how-to-jumpstart-your-corporate-wellness-program-with-big-data/ (accessed 09/07/15).

Wajcman, J. (2015) *Pressed for Time: The Acceleration of Life in Digital Capitalism* (Chicago, IL: University of Chicago Press).

Warhurst, C. and Thompson, P. (2006) 'Mapping Knowledge in Work? Proxies or Practices?' *Work, Employment and Society* 20(4): 787–800.

Warr, P. (2007) *Work, Happiness, and Unhappiness* (Mahwah, NJ: Lawrence Erlbaum Associates Inc.).

Whitney, L. (2016) 'Fitbit Still Tops in Wearables, but Market Share Slips' *C/Net* 12/02/16. www.cnet.com/uk/news/fitbit-still-tops-in-wearables-market/ (accessed 02/02/17).

Wilson, H. J. (2013) 'Wearables in the Workplace' *Harvard Business Review* 10/09/13. http://hbr.org/2013/09/wearables-in-the-workplace/ar/1 (accessed 02/02/2017).

2 Labour Processes from Industrial Betterment to Agility
Mind, Body, Machine

Machines are tools of quantification and division, compartmentalisation and potentially control. Machines, in the narrative presented in this book, have functioned as catalysts for quite dramatic changes throughout work design history, perhaps most influentially, during the period of scientific management. We are now living and working in the era of the so-called Fourth Industrial Revolution, which is 'characterized by a fusion of technologies that is blurring the line between the physical, digital and biological spheres' (Schwab, 2016), where we increasingly work alongside, with and against machines, in both cognitive and manual workplaces. Technology has become an increasingly prevalent partner in employment relations since well-known industrialists Taylor and the Gilbreths busily devised schemes to understand workplace productivity as linked to specific, measured human behaviour. These industrialists searched for scientific methods to depict perfect bodily movements for ideal productive behaviours through technologically informed work design. The separation of the mind from the body became a technique for control that has continued throughout the ages. Looking at work design's recognition of the body and the mind and at the use of technologies for control over possible labour uprisings, this chapter outlines a history of work design experimentation and resonant managerial ideologies, from industrial betterment through to the contemporary period of the agility management system characteristic of Industry 4.0.

Management methods reflect assumptions about the mind, the body and the machine and their role within each historical period's labour process and corresponding work design models. In each historical bloc, capital attempts to separate the manual from the mental to ensure class subordination or otherwise to attempt to obscure class and to identify inventive ways to measure and then profit from the surpluses in other forms of corporeal and affective, reproductive labour. In each historical era, I look at methods to exploit the surplus value of workers and at the requisite labour processes pursued. I note the rise in the use of technology for quantification as quantification is increasingly used to capture new avenues of labour. The historical discussion in this chapter sets the scene for me to prepare for discussions asking whether technologies can be appropriated for democratic workplaces and avenues for social change, or whether they may lead to a dark side of decreasing labour power.

History of Work Design Experiments and Labour Processes

Marx named 'labour process' as the production of use values, referring to the transformation where raw materials and labour power are used for profitability and the creation of commodities to be sold on markets. In Section I of Chapter 7 of *Capital* Volume I, Marx wrote that 'the elementary factors of the labour-process are (1) the personal activity of man, i.e., work itself, (2) the subject of that work, and (3) its instruments' (1867/2015: 127). While man's labour 'effects an alteration' in the material that s/he works upon, the product absorbs the appearance of the final product, where the product is a 'use-value' and where 'the process disappears in the product'. The product is itself a use-value, or 'nature's material adapted by a change of form to the wants of man'. In that sense, labour becomes materialised (but not necessarily 'seen'). The movement of labour becomes something fixed in the product. Marx gives the example of the blacksmith's work where the labour is done by a blacksmith and the product is 'a forging' (1867/2015: 128). The labour process involves the capitalist's consumption of the blacksmith's labour power, where the capitalist's primary target is to reduce inefficiencies, seeing that 'the means of production are used with intelligence, so that there is no unnecessary waste of raw material, and no wear and tear of the implements'. The forging, in this analogy, is also the property of the capitalist (*Section I* 1867/2015). A labourer is the property of the capitalist when the labourer has nothing to sell but her own labour. In that sense, Marx states that the 'product of this process belongs, therefore, to him [or her], just as much as does the wine which is the product of a process of fermentation completed in his [or her] cellar' (brackets included by present author) (Ibid.). The grapes have their flavour and ability to ferment to offer; the worker has her labour power. In that sense, labour power is itself a commodity that is purchased by the capitalist, albeit at a rate that allows the capitalist to earn a profit.

To gain as much as possible from the work performed, it is in the capitalist's interests to obscure the labour itself in the labour process and to keep it invisible, or what I call 'unseen'. Quantification of work, the subject of this book, may appear to reveal work's true nature by giving numeration and perhaps a timeframe, but the process of abstraction works to detract from the qualified experience of labour and invisibilise suffering and the non-denumerable. Technology is the 'instrument of labour', which Marx calls a 'thing, or a complex of things, which the labourer interposes between himself and the subject of his labour, and which serves as the conductor of his activity' (1867/2015). This can be mechanical, chemical, or physical. A key argument in the present text is that mechanics in the labour process and technology as an instrument of labour have become increasingly powerful. Management has always looked to technology to abstract labour, but now, technology itself has begun to play the role of management. A labour process, in its ideal sense, is fuelled by the agency of labourers within it. As agency is detracted from workers by machinery and what Marx talked about in his time as 'modern industry', production processes are at risk of no longer being labour processes at all. Marx stated in the *Grundrisse* that 'the production process has ceased to be a labour process in the sense of a process dominated by labour as its governing unity' (Marx, 1973/1993: 693) as there is no reference to the worker's craft or skill that is seen to be directly linked to production. So, the 'man/product relation gives way to the machine/product relation and jobs and tasks are treated as the residuum of the machine/product link' (BLP, 1977: 2; Davis and Taylor, 1972: 12 and 300–301, cited in Littler: 22).

Labour process theory today focuses on labour power's ongoing transformations in the context of capitalism (Thompson and Smith, 2010) and looks for ways the capitalist extracts value from labourers in settings Marx could only have imagined with the help of a very good fortune teller. The early debates in labour process theory began with a pamphlet in 1977 published by the Conference of Social Economists, *The Labour Process and Class Strategies*. Two articles stood out as framing the early debates, one by the Brighton Labour Process Group (BLPG) which looked at Gorz and Braverman; and one by Andy Friedman (Thompson, 2010: 7). The BLPG, Thompson states, identified the laws of the capitalist labour process as being (i) the division of intellectual and manual labour, (ii) hierarchy or hierarchical control and (iii) the fragmentation/deskilling of labour (Thompson, 2010: 9). Thompson argues that the BLPG version labour process is not the only contributions that labour process has made, and notes that 'what actual labour process (and other) research' has done is to reveal and valorise other areas of labour, including tacit knowledge and skills (Thompson et al., 2000, cited in Thompson, 2010: 9) and socially necessary labour time. Labour process theory, then, has shown how emotional and corporeal labour is captured by capitalist processes (Bolton, 2005; Witz et al., 2003; Wolkowitz, 2006, cited in Thompson, 2010: 9). Thompson's critique of BLPG is that there can be no 'immanent law' separating manual and mental labour, given the pursuits of labour capture in these non-material areas, as was seen in the late 20th and early 21st century (the period I call 'agile'). Labour process theory is distinguished from critical management studies which is seen as 'postmodern', where the labour process debates are seen to address the 'material' and are mostly Marxist.

Labour process theorists are critical of scientific management for its drive to take qualitative areas of work and force them into quantified straightjackets (Braverman, 1974/1998; Newsome et al., 2013; Thompson and Smith, 2010). Braverman is well known in labour process circles for taking up the concept of labour power and historicising it, to reflect the working conditions people faced during the period of scientific management.

Braverman (1974/1998) develops Marx's thesis on labour process and reproduction of labour by elegantly emphasising the fact that 'skill and knowledge are expropriated from the direct producer and placed in the hands of management' (Littler, 1982: 22). Braverman emphasised the role of the machine in dividing mental from manual labour and the people who are selected for both, a division that advanced significantly in the period of scientific management as I demonstrate below. Littler argued that more advanced technologies allow science to be 'harnessed to the labour process' (Littler, 1982: 22). This process both 'compounds and complements' Taylorism because it requires a separation of conception and execution under the guiding principles of managerial control, which are deskilling and fragmentation of work, and through the creation of an apparatus of 'conception' or the methods to control labour themselves. This apparatus of methods, of course, requires its own producers; Braverman indicates that a cadre of administrators (managers and technical personnel, clerical workers) has arisen to ensure strategies are put into place. Braverman shows that 'conception – the planning, coordination and control of work – is itself a labour process and subject to the same separation of conception and execution' (Ibid.); this created a cadre of administrators (managers and technical personnel, clerical workers), jobs and work that is itself being automated or substituted and managed by algorithm.

Braverman argued that workers are even more acutely estranged from our own labour in these processes and claims that our subjectivities, histories, even potentials and pre-existing skills, must be pushed aside, since the 'new relations of production' (Braverman, 1974/1988: 39), which is one that introduces a range of technologies into the labour process and works to alienate labour power. We must surrender our personal interests, Braverman says, in this labour process (Ibid.). Indeed, 'subjectivity is destroyed or rendered ineffectual' (Littler, 1982: 22). Building on my 2010 argument, and developing Braverman's points, I argue that any authentic or self-selected type of self-hood and subjectivity is not permitted (see Subjectification section in Chapter 3). The reasons for its abstraction, mawkishly but aptly put, are that labour power, once it informs person-hood, will contain elements of resistance to capital. So perhaps it is no surprise that there are only specific subjectivities considered available in the new Industry 4.0 world of work which must be aligned with labour processes: the entrepreneur, the 'doer', the 'go-getter'. In our current work design experimentation phase of agility management systems outlined below, because technology advances and changes constantly, humans' subjectivities are expected to be constantly adaptable, flexible, change-able. We are expected to embrace the specificities of idealised subjectivities and identify ourselves through a process of subjectification, consuming an identity of affective flexibility, and adopting it in full. Skills such as 'adaptability' and demonstrating the right 'attitudes' are sought by employers (Rubery and Grimshaw, 2001). Now, management has set out to measure tacit skills more precisely and 'revolutionise the technical process of labour' (Marx, 1867/2015: 360), to capture the absolute (the time it takes to get something done and intensity of the work) and the relative (the level of productivity demonstrated) surplus value, providing the conveyor belt from formal to real subjection of labour to capital (Ibid.).

Workplace quantification is an aspect of subjectification which leads to the 'modification of individual conduct, not only skills, but also attitudes' (Foucault, 1988). Subjectification takes a particular form in neoliberalism where subjects self-define in terms of their status for the external quantified gaze. However, Rolnik argues that in the neoliberal period, the same individual is now split into both of these components, the entrepreneurial self and the self-exploited proletarian (Rolnik, 2011: 48). As split selves, with an inner manager exploiting an inner worker, workers are induced to quantify and regulate our affective labour to remain subjects of and to capital.

Labour process theorists identified management strategies to acutely quantify and divide labour (both socially and personally) also building on Hyman's paper in the first edition of *Work, Employment and Society*. Here, Richard Hyman indicates the ways that 'numerical control' and the use of 'computer-based technologies were not merely to displace traditional skills, but also to monitor and hence discipline the remaining workforce' (1987: 37). The selection of, and now, imminent resignation to, technology and its predictable unpredictability, 'is a social and political and not merely technical question' (Ibid.). Hyman refers to Murray, whose paper in *Marxism Today* in 1985 indicates that 'computer programmes in the 1980s were written to organise new systems of production, but also to control labour, rather than to emancipate it' (Ibid.).

In other work, labour process theorists Bain and Taylor (2000) argued that call centre surveillance, while real, is not necessarily internalised by workers. Critiquing Fernie and Metcalfe's Foucauldian argument that workers' absolutely internalise the imperative to perform and do not recognise their exploitation, and moving away from Braverman's arguments about the self in technologised labour processes, Bain and Taylor argue that workers' subjectivities are not (but should be) accounted for in research that totalises the call centre workers' experience, which also ignores trade unions and worker resistance. These and other labour process studies are foundational for making the argument that one must cross disciplines to theorise the political economy of quantifying work. Overall, the emphasis on numeration seen in labour process research makes it an appropriate resource for looking at quantified work today. As Noble pointed out in the 1970s, the introduction of numerically controlled machines to work was deliberately designed to be a 'valuable means of taking the intelligence of production and thus control of production, off the shop floor' (Noble, 1978: 337, cited in Hyman, 1987: 37). Along these lines, later chapters in the present book look at the introduction of more intimate and pervasive numeration techniques as reflecting a strategy to control workers in ways similar to those seen in previous eras. However, I also argue that numeration is being introduced in increasingly creative methods with a range of new, sensory technologies that have only recently been available to firms.

It cannot stop there, however, because I have committed to a philosophical argument to address critiques that labour process researchers do not look at ontology but rather, make assumptions about the hierarchies of minds over bodies. I deal with the point that Thompson makes in 2010, i.e. that studies of management have tended to fail to look at political economy and thus to carefully look at the impacts of work and labour processes on humans and our lives. Bringing new materialism to the discussion and through looking at quantified work and its agile work design context, the theoretical framework for this book addresses these limitations. Specifically, by bringing the new materialism question to the proverbial table, I invite discussions of ontology, to identify where power relations in work begin and to indicate how labour power can be affected for resistance. I execute this in the next chapter. But first, I look at labour processes leading up to the quantified precarious self at work, by looking to history for clues as to how we have arrived in the era of quantified agility.

Labour processes within each period of management and work design, also called job design, rely on assumptions about the rate of divisibility between minds and hands, and have engaged with technology and machines at varied levels. Littler argues that the capitalist organisation of work occurs at three macro-levels: 'the division of labour and technology, the formal structure of authority and surveillance, and the relation of job positions to the labour market' (Littler, 1982: 41–2). At the micro-level, work and organisational psychologists have noted that dominant characteristics in work design research over time have been those that are seen to be motivational, the principle being that jobs are enriched or made more motivational if specific characteristics can be observed (Morgeson and Humphrey, 2006). There are two other types of characteristics increasingly researched in work design literature: interpersonal and social aspects, and contextual characteristics, but the tools and equipment and work conditions still appear as the least researched and understood (Ibid.: 1323). Because of this, there is little background understanding for the introduction of new technology and management practices in workplaces that document and monitor both the arena of the social for the use of social media and lifestyle initiatives and the physiological, where sensory devices are designed to promote good health and happiness and are used in workplaces to promote this as part of productivity.

Work or *job design* refers to the 'way that a set of tasks, or an entire job, is organised'. Job design helps to determine:

- What tasks are done?
- How the tasks are done
- How many tasks are done?
- In what order the tasks are done (CCOHS, 2002)

Work design accounts for any and all factors affecting work and 'organises the content and tasks so that the whole job is less likely to be a risk to the employee', involving such things as:

- Job rotation
- Job enlargement
- Task/machine pacing
- Work breaks
- Working hours

Over time, work design has been explicitly oriented to reduce workers' stress and to address problems like work overload, repetitiveness, isolation, limited control over work and excessive work (CCOHS, 2002). Research has begun to look at the benefits of 'job crafting' (Grant et al., 2010; Wrzesniewski and Dutton, 2001), where workers are explicitly involved in organising and designing work. Grant and Parker trace the history of work design in *The Academy of Management Annals* (2009) and find it to be based in the discipline of organisational psychology. These authors comment on a relatively recent dearth in investigation, speculating that researchers had started to believe most issues in work design had been dealt with already (Grant and Parker, 2009: 317). These psychologists state that global shifts from manufacturing to service work and the rise of the knowledge economy alter the nature of work and change viewpoints on work design. They look at relational perspectives, where it is clear that work is more socially embedded than ever, where interdependence and interactions between clients and recipients of services and co-workers are central to work. The other emerging viewpoint these researchers point to is the 'proactive' perspective, where employees take 'initiative to anticipate and create changes in how work is performed, based on increases in uncertainty and dynamism' (2009: 317). They are describing agility, though they do not use this term explicitly, perhaps because the concept has been introduced in non-academic management circles and then developed in industrial relations research rather than organisational psychology. In a special issue in *Journal of Organisational Behaviour* the following year, Grant (et al) collected several articles that reflect changes to work resulting from globalisation and the shift to service work mentioned above. According to Grant (et al), practitioners and management design work in order to: 'promote employee performance and well-being' (2010: 145). Researched over the previous thirty years, they comment that:

> ...research on job design has played a critical role in building a bridge between theory and practice. Prominent theories such as the job characteristics model (Hackman & Oldham, 1976, 1980), socio-technical systems theory (Trist, 1981; Pasmore, Francis, Haldeman, & Shani, 1982),

action regulation theory (Hacker, 2003), and the interdisciplinary work design framework (Campion & McClelland, 1993) have stimulated much of the research in the field. As a result, researchers have accumulated extensive insight about the diverse task, knowledge, and physical characteristics of jobs; the psychological and behavioral effects of job design; the mediating mechanisms that explain these effects; and the individual and contextual factors that moderate these effects (e.g., Fried & Ferris, 1987; Humphrey, Nahrgang, & Morgeson, 2007; Parker & Wall, 1998).

(Grant et al., 2010: 145)

Research contributing to theories on work design has been relatively comprehensive, but Grant and colleagues stated in 2009 and 2010 that theories must be updated to account for workplace changes. This includes increases in labour force participation, where women as well as aging and more educated populations enter the increasingly diverse workplace. People are now responsible for more emotional work and are involved in global operations and resultant cultural and social interactions, experiencing more flexible work methods 'from virtual teams to telework' (Grant et al., 2010: 146). Customer management is increasingly important, where business clients and individual customers 'know what they want, what they want to pay for it... customers such as these don't need to deal with companies that don't understand and appreciate this startling change in the customer-buyer relationship' (Hammer and Champy, 2001: 216). Hammer and Champy write that these changes require an entire reengineering of corporations, which involves a 'reeingeering team'. The new world of work (which I label below the world of agile work), involves a range of new types of responsibilities including extreme empathy. All these changes are 'associated with increased unpredictability and uncertainty' (Grant et al., 2010: 146) which I argue is directly linked to our contemporary phase in technologically driven 'agility'.

Management theories and specific work design methods over time have tended to prioritise 'performance' over all else, to achieve the best productivity and to get as much work out of workers as is possible. I now turn to look at how management has used technology to make this happen. Barley and Kunda (1992) outline historical blocks of 'industrial betterment' to 'organisational culture and quality' methods and here I rely on their categorizations for my own account. These authors indicate that managerial changes tend to assert 'normative' and 'rational' ideologies alternate over long time periods, linked to long wave technological/economic cycles associated with periods of labour activity. For each period, there is a 'surge' stage associated with a particular rhetoric that emphasizes specific aspects of work and what is most important as well as what is expected to facilitate productivity (such as machines). These surges are followed by a challenge to the dominant rhetoric where the surge for the emerging paradigm begins (and thus replaces the previous era), along these periods:

1st wave: Industrial Betterment 1870–1900
2nd wave: Scientific Management 1900–1923
3rd wave: Human Relations 1925–1955
4th wave: Systems Rationalism 1955–1980
5th wave: Organisational Culture and Quality 1980 – 'ongoing' (Barley and Kunda, 1992)
6th wave: Agility Management System (2001–present) (my designation)

These 'waves' of managerial ideology in work design alternate between control and consent (Barley and Kunda, 1992; Ramsay, 1977), where normative and rational frameworks and communal and individualistic tropes inform work design attempts, corresponding with periods of economic expansion and contraction that I do not outline here. Rather, I focus on the expectations for subjectivities as they consider divisions or compatibilities of workers' minds/bodies for labour; and the ways that technologies are used to control the labour process.

Barley and Kunda's periodisation stops at the 5th wave, but given the article was published in 1992 these authors would not have written about 'agility'. The current dominant model is one of agility, so I have prescribed the 6th wave in this way. Figure 2.1 demonstrates the breakdown of ideologies and influences for each work design period.

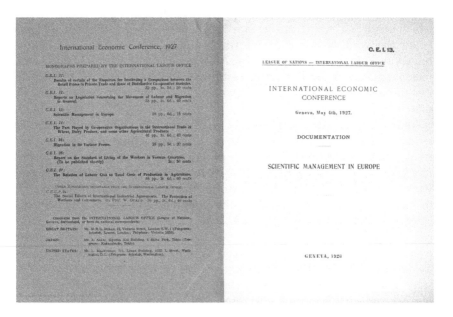

Figure 2.1 Unseen labour capture, 1800s to present.

Industrial Betterment

Scientific management, which is perhaps the most referenced period in labour process research, was preceded by the period of 'industrial betterment'. Industrial betterment was a period of *normative* management. At least in the United States, there had been little attention paid to employee welfare and working conditions before the civil war. Industrialists had ignored Robert Owen and James Montgomery's recommendations for 'welfare capitalism' and 'industrial betterment' in the first half the 19th century, but then started to listen to a handful of clergymen and intellectuals who recommended the 'principles of cooperation' and 'industrial partnerships' in the 1870s, to improve workers' 'mental and moral qualities of the working-people' (Gladden, 1876: 44–50, quoted in Barley and Kunda, 1992). The industrial betterment model included classes for workers and families, social clubs, benefits, profit sharing schemes and the like, a foreshadowing of the work/life integration models so familiar today. The YMCA was founded as a way to encourage and provide spiritual guidance for industrial workers and provide respite from work that would not include drink. Industrialisation in the late 1800s required a large number of workers and one of the reasons given for the normative appeal to workers' sentiment and personal happiness was the technical difficulty of managing individuals.

Owners of large corporations enjoying mass manufacturing enabled by new technologies looked to immigrant labour to fill the need. European workers brought notions of socialism and the rise in unionism, which led to labour unrest. Employers began to take increasing responsibility for, or at least notice workers' out of work activities and even sought to 'Americanise' them and bring them into Protestant values. This was both a precursor for Weber's Protestant Ethic of Capitalism arguments and reminiscent of reformist values of the 1600s. Nonetheless, the mix of values during this period of Christianity—work loyalty and the hints of socialism brought by immigrant workers who needed to be disciplined— may explain the introduction of scientific management, Barley and Kunda speculate (1992). The violent Pullman Palace Car Company strike of 1894 led to significant criticism of 'betterment' programmes. Pullman had provided more welfare programmes for workers than any other company, but critics began to point out that this may only have been done to prevent dissent rather than authentically care for workers. Professor of Economics Richard T. Ely at Johns Hopkins wrote for Harpers New Monthly Magazine in 1885 that Pullman was a 'gilded cage' for workers, 'a benevolent, well wishing feudalism which desires the happiness of the people but in such a way as shall please the authorities' (Ely, 1885: 466, quoted in Barley and Kunda, 1992). Even industrial and mechanical engineers began to query the methods of industrial betterment, which led to a severe loss of credibility.

Scientific Management

Industrial betterment's wane may have been what led to a shift in the management ideology and work design methods toward a more rational control oriented model, scientific management, which lasted for about twenty-five years at the beginning of the 20th century. Frederick W. Taylor and Lillian and Frank Gilbreth celebrated science and technology in work design and quite explicitly portrayed the mind in contrast to the body. This division is inherent to Taylorist scientific management where managers and consultants busily looked for ideal movements of manual workers to achieve what Marx had identified to be 'no unnecessary waste of raw material' (Marx, 1867/2015), if that raw material is the movement of humans' very limbs. While handling a pig-iron, Taylor writes in *The Principles of Scientific Management*, is 'so crude and elementary in its nature that the writer firmly believes that it would be possible to train an intelligent gorilla so as to become a more efficient pig-iron handler than any man can be'. However, he stresses, 'the science of handling pig iron is so great and amounts to so much that it is impossible for the man who is best suited to this type of work to understand the principles of this science' (Taylor, 1911/1998: 18). Scientific management required separation of unskilled and skilled labour categorised in terms of manual and mental labour, and Taylor was quite scathing in his accounts of the less-able human who, he argued, would be best suited for manual work. Taylor was also convinced of the need to separate play from work (which is very different to subsequent participative management methods we will see), indicating in *The Principles* that it is a 'matter of ordinary common sense to plan working hours so that the workers can really "work while they work" and "play while they play", and not mix the two' (1911/1998: 44).

Two other industrialists in the early 1900s were also devising schemes to understand workplace productivity as linked to human physical movement as well as physiology: Frank and Lillian Gilbreth. Frank Gilbreth, upon entering the construction industry, was intrigued to discover that every bricklayer went about laying bricks with a different set of motions. Reading the biography Lillian Gilbreth wrote about her husband in the archives at the British Library, I learned that Mr. Gilbreth was from an established family where his siblings went into various professions. Because he was not good at writing and languages, Mr. Gilbreth was given a job in the bricklaying industry. Reading between the lines, I also came to the conclusion that it seems likely that Frank Gilbreth was dyslexic and possibly autistic, conditions that were not fully recognised during this period. Based on his perceptions of the inefficiencies and diverse methods that each bricklayer used, Frank set out upon what he and Lillian called 'The Quest of the One Best Way' (which is also the name of the biography Lillian wrote). Looking at micro-movements by using a series of technological devices including a spring driven camera, an electric motor-driven camera, and a michrochronometer, which was an instrument for measuring very small intervals of time, the Gilbreths looked for the 'best way' to lay bricks that would lead to the least fatigue—research that soon became known as *motion and fatigue studies*. The Gilbreths also measured workers' heart rate using a stethoscope and stopwatch—a foreshadowing of the heart rate measures we see in the construction industry today, wearable technology that is used as a risk aversion strategy where an employer can spot worker's heart rate rising abnormally and can warn a worker to 'take it easy' (Hughes, 2015). A 'therblig' (Gilbreth spelled backwards) was the name these two gave the system of analyzing the body's basic movements and using technology to isolate movements into discrete units and quantify their outputs. Therbligs were a presage for much more recent types of data analysis that could inform workplace design based on technological readings.

In 1905, the psychologist William McDougall wrote an article on 'a new method for the study of concurrent mental operations and of mental fatigue' using similarly creative technologies. McDougall was against behaviourism and is known for his theories of instinct and social psychology. McDougall cited Külpe in the first line of the 1905 article, stating 'the discovery of a reliable measure of the attention would appear to be one of the most important problems that await solution by the experimental psychology of the future' (1905: 435). McDougall wrote about the Messrs Diedrichs of Göttingen University who designed an apparatus to measure individuals' capacity to carry out mental work, which consisted of a cylinder covered with sheets of paper containing red dots, mounted on a steel axis that was rotated regularly by clockwork. People in various states of fatigue and under the influence of drugs were asked to mark spots with a stylograph, as they passed. Their precision was recorded and linked to subjects' various states of intoxication and fatigue. The apparatus was intended as a 'study of the onset and passing away of fatigue, drugs, rest, etc. upon capacity for mental work' (McDougall, 1905: 439).

In a similar timeframe to the work that was being done elsewhere, but unknown to the Gilbreths in the early days, Taylor started working at Midvale Steel Company. As general foreman, Taylor quickly became convinced that the greatest obstacle to cooperation between workmen and management is the 'ignorance of management as to what really constitutes a proper day's work for a workman' (Taylor, 1911/1998). He asked the plant to invest in research to identify the 'fraction of horse-power, or foot-pounds of work that one first-class man could reasonable perform in one day' (Ibid.). Taylor selected two strong, able-bodied, so-called 'first-class' men, and carried out experiments for several years to identify exactly how much work was needed and which movements were the best, to carry out specific tasks.

While Taylor's work was similar to Lillian and Frank Gilbreths', Taylor focused on time and measurement and prioritised efficiency and productivity more predominantly than the Gilbreths. The Gilbreths looked more closely at motion, and emphasised the physiological by looking at fatigue and the need for rest. Taylor was becoming well-known in industrial circles through consultancy work and quickly became an internationally respected specialist; his talks and research were in high demand. Frank Gilbreth was invited to one of the several-hour lectures Taylor held in his home in the 1920s. Gilbreth introduced the concept of *motion* to Taylor after the lecture, which led to collaborations that were soon known as 'time and motion studies' and later, 'scientific management'. 'The Principles of Motion Economy' from scientific management, seen as 'helpful in work design' (Barnes, 1937/1980: 174) were generally split into three areas: those related to the use of the human body; the arrangement of the place and area; and as related to the design of tools and equipment. The experiments informing these techniques were also informed by 'human factors engineering' research in the early part of the 20th century and are most obviously applicable to factory production environments, although later research looks at Taylor's work as continuing to hold significance.

The ideas of scientific management were not necessarily new, but Taylor successfully systematised a range of concepts designed to increase and control industrial production through widening the function of management and coordinating elements of his system. Taylor believed that there was a science to his system and that, perfectly implemented, the system would lead to prosperity for all. He set out to look at each component of production processes, to experiment with machines and methods of work as well as materials, and was very committed to using measuring instruments in investigations, using stop watches to measure the length of time a worker took to finish a task. There were four basic categories of scientific management: research, standardisation, control and cooperation. Standardisation was ideally set so that all practices, classifications and qualities would be prescribed and tools and equipment, methods of accounting and wage rates all comparable. Control was an important factor in reaching the 'full potential' of the production process, and management was given more authority by

> planning the work to be done, routing it through the factory, and scheduling each machine or group of machines for its part of the job; providing the necessary materials and tools for the worker when he required them; and inspecting the finished product and even the workman's work methods.
>
> (Nadworny, 1955: v–vi)

This relationship between the worker and manager required 'a mental attitude', 'a condition of efficient common effort, a model of conduct, the result of the formulation of standards of purpose, facility, method and relationship' (Ibid.). Nadworny states that the most difficult thing to achieve in the employment relationship of scientific management was an appropriate 'mental attitude'.

In 1927, the League of Nations' International Labour Office published documentation from the 1927 International Economic Conference called 'Scientific Management in Europe' (see Image 1), a yellowing copy of which I found at the Trades Union Congress archives at London Metropolitan University in 2016. This report was printed in the interwar period, when nations were furiously seeking to set up interdependent organisations and establish a climate of cooperation to reduce the chances for any further wars. The Office interestingly advocated standardisation of industrial practices in this report, and scientific management is heralded as a field '*par excellence* for international cooperation' (1927: 14).

The document starts by stating that

> scientific management is the science which studies the relations between the different factors in production, and especially those between the human and the mechanical factors. Its object is to obtain, by the rational utilisation of these various factors, the optimum output.
>
> (1927: 5)

The Office reported that scientific management had already 'overflowed the limits within which it was originally applied by Taylor' and its recommendations and practices 'now cover all departments of the factory, all forms of manufacture, all forms of economic activity, banking, commerce, agriculture and the administration of public services' (Ibid.). The report notes that scientific management's purpose and nature are often simplified or confused with industrial efficiency or the elimination of waste, which are only a fragment of its scope. Practical applications for scientific management are sub-divided as follows:

Technique:
  I Production planning; choice of site and construction of buildings; arrangement of workshops, choice and lay out of equipment and raw materials, organization and maintenance of store-rooms; transport within the factory; supply of materials and tools.
 II Research and planning offices; routing, use of card indexes, classification, use of statistics and charts.
III Accountancy, costing; purchasing and sales departments; advertising.

Psycho-physiology:
  I Psycho-physiology of the individual:

   a   time study (by stop watch); motion study.
   b   vocational selection; vocational education; study of the functions of management.
   c   Fatigue study: attention, monotony, absent mindedness.

   d   Study of optimum material, working conditions: improvement
       of equipment, lighting, heating, ventilation, general workshop
       hygiene, as affecting the human factor.
   e   Occupational diseases; safety.
   f   Welfare (housing, transport, co-operative restaurants).

II Collective psychology

   a   Study of the different systems of wages payment, profit sharing and
       co-partnership.
   b   Industrial relations (study of the various theories and their practical
       application).
   c   Personnel department, workers' representation.
   d   Study of methods of collaboration inside and outside the factory,
       with a view to improving output.

III General Organisation of Production

   a   Study of methods for stabilizing production and employment.
   b   Standardization (normalization, unification, simplification).
   c   Elimination of waste.
   d   Horizontal and vertical combination: national and international
       industrial agreements, cartels, trusts, syndicates; actions by
       Governments, by public services, by employers' and workers'
       organisations.
   e   Specialisation; mass production and distribution; study of the gen-
       eral problems of the distribution of raw materials, the organisation
       of markets, transport power, and labour supply.

The report stated that the purpose for delineating these categories was
to harmonise activities under an umbrella of concepts that fueled this
management system. Its critics warned of its ideological overtones and
were concerned that its merits were not proven. But this report is quite
optimistic about it. Without irony, the report notes that the system was
itself a response to a scarce labour market during America's rapid industrialisation at the turn of the century. The improvement of machinery and
scarcity of labour led manufacturers to look for ways to reduce production costs. While the experiments originated in the United States, they
rapidly saw international influence. Its psycho-physiological research was
adapted in Britain and Germany. In Russia, Germany and Czechoslovakia, it quickly became the 'guiding principle of the national economic
system' (1927: 8). Austria created a central committee, the Zentralver-
band für wirtschafltliches Schaffen, at the suggestion of technicians, to
rationalise standardisation and waste elimination. In Belgium, a national
committee was set up for the purpose of studying scientific management. In Czechoslovakia, the report says, 'there has been since the war
an intensive campaign of research, instruction and propaganda for the

introduction and spread of rational organisation, on which the economic prosperity of the new State was considered by its leaders to depend'. One of its boot and shoe factories was showcased for successful application of scientific management principles. In Finland, rationalisation methods were in the areas of railways and agriculture. In France, the Society of for the Encouragement of National Industry, the Michelin Committee and the association of engineers were all looking at integrating American methods. Labour was hostile to the plans in France, but it was expected to 'develop rapidly' (1927: 9). Germany is recognised in this League of Nations report to be the most active and to hold the 'leading place in the movement'. Its 'Rechskuratorim für Wirtschaftlichkeit' was set up to centralise and direct institutions for scientific organisation. It carried out 'intensive propaganda' (1927: 9). Germany had already started to call the science 'industrial rationalisation' with branches of this movement being called 'standardisation, industrial concentration, mass production, and distribution' which were adaptations of scientific management. In Germany, workers' organisations were more favourable to the undertakings, and their 'new spirit, methods and practical measures' (1927: 9). Britain also enthusiastically embraced this new doctrine, putting emphasis on the social welfare dimensions. The nodes of activity were the National Institute of Industrial Psychology and the Industrial Fatigue Research Board. Labour was very skeptical of what they called 'Taylorism' (quotes in text). But, the report states, due to economic lag in Britain, it was very likely that 'in future there will be a wider adoption of scientific methods of organisation of production'. In Italy, the Enge Nazionale Italiano per l'Organizzazione Scientifica del Lavoro (ENIOS) was created to spread new methods across Italian industry. The 'Efficiency Institute' was set up in the Netherlands where municipalities and State administration had introduced related practices, with the help of consulting engineers. In Poland, the Warsaw Institute for Scientific management was founded in 1925 and carried out research in the area. The practical side again was directed by engineers. An enquiry was launched to identify any 'waste in industry', which attracted public attention.

In Soviet Russia, a Ministry was set up called SOVNOT to direct integration into railways, munitions industries, agriculture, banking and industry; and nearly 100 institutions for practical application, research and education were affiliated to the institution. Russia took steps also to establish cooperation with German specialists and there were agreements to standardize practice across countries. In Spain, the movement was headed by technicians and the Federation of Associations of Civil Engineers and vocational guidance experts. In Sweden, the Committee for Scientific Organisation was set up by the Federation of Swedish Industries, which was assisted by engineers and facilitated a 'most favourable reception' of standardisation (1927: 11). Finally, in Switzerland, the Swiss Friends of the U.S.A. (SFUSA) was set up and led by manufacturers and traders.

After two international congresses in Prague and Brussels, an International Committee for Scientific Organisation was set up to lead and coordinate activities across countries. While each country had adapted scientific management in local context and national temperament, it 'tends to become a powerful means of creating uniformity in the conditions of industrial production' (1927: 12). Despite this, it was strongly believed that the principles would be positive for workers, where, if it

> tends to economise and improve the distribution of human effort, by thus securing the putting of the right man in the right place, it causes the reduction of fatigue, the improvement of health, and an increased feeling of professional dignity.
>
> (1927: 13)

The 1927 report is very positive about its possibilities and praises the Russian, German and Czechoslovakian governments for funding research centres and initiatives. The International Labour Office even set up an International Management Institution in Geneva with the XXth Century Fund of Boston, Massachusetts and the International Committed for Scientific Organisation. Scientific management was seen as a solution for many problems, from workers' fatigue to national economic slowdown.

As the Europeans had picked up, Taylor and his disciples proselytised scientific management with the conviction that science would perfect the foibles of human experience and that exact measurement would both eliminate any unnecessary waste of spent time and human effort as well as any possible loss of expenditure for a company. But implementing scientific management was not the smooth process that the Europeans seemed to think it had been in the decades preceding the League of Nations report. Its journey became disrupted when the implications of separating work design from execution were identified not with the asserted mutual gains of rising productivity, but with work intensification, deskilling and displacement. Trade unions started to suspect something was not right with scientific management, and in August 1911 the Molders Union held the first walk-out protest to what was also called 'time study'. That same year, the United Textiles Worker President expressed fear that it would be used as a 'speed up programme' and ultimately, to automation. Ted F. Silvey, Education Officer of the AFL-CIO was very vocal about the risks that automation posed to workers in the 1950s, and this was preceded by concerns about these trends in allowing technology to play an increasingly prominent role through measuring productivity.

The International Association of Machinists gave the first full statement on scientific management on 14 April 1911, stating that they did not see the necessity of introducing a system that embodies 'drastic measures' and 'undemocratic principles' including 'elimination of workmen who cannot attain the maximum efficiency' and the possible elimination of the 'average man' (Nadworny, 1955: 58–9). Littler writes that Taylorism's 'emphasis on compliance and obedience to management in the pursuit of the common interest, could be mobilized as an ideological attack on the nascent trade union movement' (Littler, 1982: 42–3). As a response to rising dissent, Lillian Gilbreth published a series of articles in the periodical the Iron Age (1915, in Price, 1992), criticising unions for thinking that scientific management confused humans with machines. Gilbreth's articles looked at the 'human element' of scientific management, claiming that its prescriptions were intended to improve and train workers rather than to 'destroy skill' as unions suspected (Price, 1992). Stark suggests that the fallacies in scientific management, even on its own terms, were that it placed too much power in the hands of the knowledge workers, or engineers, where engineers' ideology rather than capitalist managers (Stark, 1980: 102–103).

Management in companies where the Taylors and Gilbreths consulted *also* began to question methods used, asking whether humans were in fact at the heart of their interests, or was it mechanisation and work intensification? Gramsci pointed out that Taylor expressed a 'brutal cynicism' about workers. Taylor required workers to develop the best 'automatic and mechanical attitudes, breaking up the old psycho-physical nexus of *qualified* professional work, which demands a certain active participation of intelligence, fantasy and initiative of the worker, and reducing productive operations exclusively to the mechanical, physical impact' (emphasis added) (Gramsci, 1971: 303).

Human Relations

Scientific management was seen perhaps as a 'fad' at first, but it received a large amount of press and interest from many corners. However, it fell out of fashion when trades unionists and managers alike began to critique its effectiveness and question its legitimacy. The next 'wave' of management attempts is called 'human relations' and lasted from around 1925–1955. The industrialists, Gramsci noted, realised that

> "unfortunately" [quotation marks in text], the worker remains a man and even that during his work he thinks more, or at least has greater opportunities for thinking... not only does the worker think, but the fact that he gets no immediate satisfaction from his work and realizes that they are trying to reduced him to a trained gorilla, can lead him into a train of thought that is far from conformist.
>
> (Gramsci, 1971: 610)

Management reverted to some of the soundings of the 'betterment' period by remembering the human side of work and by introducing more welfare oriented offerings intended to capture workers' work outside the typical differentiation regime of mind *vs* body and life *vs* work. This time, however, officers were not called 'welfare secretaries'. Instead, they were called 'personnel managers'. Barley and Kunda (1992) talk about this period as being grounded in 'normative control' rather than 'rational' which had dominated scientific management. These authors note that experiments to improve work were not based in the terminology around communalism or 'improved workingmen' as they were in the industrial betterment period but instead focused on entitlements and better working conditions. This period is associated with research conducted at the Harvard Fatigue Laboratory, set up in 1927 by Lawrence Henderson in consultation with Elton Mayo. Mayo famously offered preliminary cutting edge research on physiology and work. The intention of the laboratory was to research the 'group psychology, the social problems, and physiology of fatigue of normal man... not only as individual factors in determining physical and mental health, but more especially to determine their interrelatedness and the effect upon work' (Tipton and Folk, 2014: 43). Elton May became known as the father of the human relations period. He was convinced that work experiences were not purely dependent on the environment and physiological features for the manual worker, which was the conviction in Taylorism. Instead, Mayo began to look to psychology, sociology and anthropology for answers. The first applied psychology text was published by Hollingworth and Poffenberger and the *Journal of Applied Psychology* was launched during this period of work design. Some elements of Taylorism remained, such as the commitment to testing and analysis, but 'ergonomists' of the Gilbreth influence looked at the environmental and physiological aspects of work. At the tail end of this period, psychiatrists started to look at depression more closely. While it was a recognised medical disorder before the 1950s, studies were limited and focus was placed on cures rather than prevention. In the late 1950s, psychologists began to think about techniques to boost positivity through behaviour, a change from the more passive understandings of depression and the psychosis that it was seen to have stemmed from, rather than as related to life and circumstance, such as working conditions.

In the lead-up to the school of human relations, Mayo famously ran the Hawthorne Studies starting in 1924, seen as the experiment that gave industrial sociology a disciplinary category (Smith, 1987). In these much-critiqued studies, Mayo led a project where researchers interviewed several young women about their experiences of work. Mayo's main conclusion, or the Hawthorne Effect, was the recognition that people are able to impact an 'experimental situation', led management to accept the idea that 'workers should be treated as responsible beings' which should be the 'proper basis for industrial cooperation and increased efficiency' (112). Studies led sociologists to challenge conventional wisdom by

> placing a new emphasis on social as compared with economic satisfaction; on the need for co-operation in the workplace rather than

conventional discipline and on the case for research in social skills to match the accepted emphasis on technical skills.

(Ibid.)

More recently, Lemov reminds us that in the period of human relations, personnel management looked for not just obedience, but cooperation (Gillepsie, 1991, cited in Lemov, 2017). Lemov importantly indicates that the Hawthorne Studies were also run precisely to sabotage and undermine strikes (2017).

Meanwhile, Ford had been very influential in setting up the assembly line model of work in the United States. His work design methods involved paying workers a wage high enough to allow workers to purchase the products they made; offering language classes for migrant workers; assigning as much work as possible to machines. His techniques appeared to assuage some of the fears trade unionists had put forward that automation would deplete jobs by changing the discussion to some extent and focusing on the consumption power of workers. The argument goes that machines take work from humans giving them more free time to spend with family and learn new skills. The role of the machine was portrayed as positive by management but feared by workers and their representatives. In any case, Fordism was not the everlasting panacea its inventor had intended. Workers organised wildcat strikes in 1941 because the company would not recognise unions. Workers organised anyway, and Ford fired eight of the independent union 'members'.

Systems Rationalism

The next period of work design experimentation is called 'systems rationalism', lasting from 1955 to 1980. Groups of physicists, mathematicians and statisticians called 'operations research teams' had been set up during the Second World War to look for methods for logistical problems using early computers. These teams were so effective that after the war they were asked to inform industry and the Operations Research Society and Institute for Management Science, which were set up to look for ways to apply quantitative methods to management. During this 'rational' control block, managerial discourses once again turned to the search for an 'orderly body of knowledge' (Luthans, 1973: 67, cited in Barley and Kunda, 1992) to appropriately inform management. Researchers sought 'idealised principles' and 'functions' that could be universally applied. So while Taylor and the Gilbreths looked for correct practices for work and management, researchers in operations research sought idealised processes, introducing a level of abstraction that has not disappeared. Management became a process of objective setting, planning and forecasting, driven by targets and calculations, with the goal of designing the perfect structure to facilitate this. Drucker proposed management by objectives (MBO) in 1954 but it was not popularised until 1965 when Odiorne introduced a manual with step-by-step instructions to implement this system.

Systems rationalists did not enjoy a figurehead in the way scientific management did, but camps of researchers emerged with various titles in this arena including 'management science, process theory and contingency theory' (Barley and Kunda, 1992: 378). While they held different names, what these work design gurus had in common was their opposition to the 'human relations' movement and their conviction that planning and forecasting was the way to get the most out of workers and to build the best company. The cognitive was prioritised over the corporeal in these discourses. Systems rationalist researchers were undeniably informed by scientific management and even heralded it as 'the most powerful contribution America has made to Western thought since the Federalist Papers' (Drucker, 1954: 280). Scientific management flourished during the period of mechanical industrialisation and adapted many concepts from engineering in this area, but systems rationalists looked to electrical engineering and computer science, devising organisational models that resembled computer programmes using terminology such as 'input/output interfaces' and 'subunits'. Henry Gantt's now well-known Gantt Chart, developed much earlier, is seen to have influenced such experiments as the Critical Path Method, the Programme Evaluation and Review Technique developed during this period. Organisations were visualised using boxes and lines and managers simply had to know how to draw the best one. However, no precise workforce design models emerged. Indeed, Barley and Kunda note that 'employees were largely absent in texts written by systems rationalists' (1992: 380). The research relied on a supposed objective truth that humans are rational beings and that employees would simply behave as instrumental actors in the workplace. Human behaviors in workplaces were expected to model the performance and terminology derived from early computers.

Hyman writes that during this period, systems of management were not implemented with much rigour in Britain. This period was one of 'unscientific management' (Hyman, 1987: 26) where firms knew a lack of 'effective personnel policies to control methods of negotiation and pay structures', where firms had no conception of basic industrial relations. Perhaps as a result, trade unions had a stronger hand than they do today (Ibid.). There was hope that this period would see a rise in the 'rediscovery of the labour process' (Ibid.), seeing the workplace as one where class struggles could see some success. Hyman discusses management strategies to prevent this from happening. After all, the systems rationalist period is one that was led by ex-military groups, and 'strategy' is a concept that emerges from the role of a military commander. Upchurch outlines that strategies may have been seen as a method to quell the emerging dissent such as the resistance to technologies of containerisation which led to job losses in Pentonville in the 1970s (Upchurch, 2016). However, in a similar way to scientific management, the era bled into the next one which heralded the human experience far more intently.

Organisational Culture and Quality

The next phase of work design is called 'organisational culture and quality', dated from 1980 to the 'present', which in Barley and Kunda's understanding would have continued into the early 1990s, since the article outlining these periods was published in 1992. The organizational culture and quality phase revamped normative forms of management and critiqued rationalism for its likely exacerbation of anomie and even its prohibitive impacts on productivity. 'Values' became the driver for employee loyalty and workers became integrated subjects in new and inventive ways. This was the beginning of the post-industrial, knowledge economy, an era when management sought to identify how knowledge work could be measured and used for profit (Warhurst and Thompson, 1998). This phase includes the belief in a 'spirit' of capitalism so named by Boltanski and Chiapello who were interested in the moral relationships that develop between workers and work (2005: 9). Boltanski and Chiapello updated notions of a capitalist spirit by looking at changes in work expectations in the 1960s. A new work ethos emerged as a way for capitalism to metaphorically respond to its critics in the wake of the movements of 1968. During this period of civil liberties and desire for equality, young people were reported as resisting alienating work. This grass roots change was seen to result in companies struggling to attract new workers, and so they started to look for ways to convince applicants of the meaningfulness of work beyond the vulgar generation of profit. Companies became seen as arenas to provide for the possibility of self-development at work (Boltanski and Chiapello, 2005: 63–4).

The new spirit of capitalism in the organisational culture and quality period is one that brings the human into the equation was still individualist, but the recipe for correct productive behaviours moved from the church into the workplace. Morality and ethics were re-labelled as initiatives in knowledge based industries, and opportunities for productive self-development and improvement became secular. A range of new characteristics within working life quickly emerged. A level of work autonomy was available to those avoiding outright casualization, but this was only in exchange for intensified work programmes and responsibilities (Ibid.: 43). So, the work/life and mental/manual divisions are less distinctive than in the previous period, but still matter a great deal. Knowledge is perceived as the most important resource and its capture has the greatest importance.

Under this new 'spirit', work took on a 'more human orientation' by enabling workers to hold productive desires as linked with selfhood. Managing workers works best if people are treated as 'self-organized, creative beings' (Ibid.: 75). The removal of explicit authoritarian controls alongside opportunities for self-development allows workers to share in the vision of the organisation and to associate with, and emulate the organisation's values through personal branding (Ibid.: 78). Managers are asked to behave like business athletes, pros, or coaches, who inspire workers with specific personal qualities (which are probably not critical or resistance oriented). This is along the lines of the homogenising criteria that has begun to infiltrate 'agile' systems. Managers, in the new spirit of capitalism and quality organisational cultures, help others to develop the right skills and idealised potential (Kelly et al., 2007: 78–9). Managers are expected to play the roles of missionaries, champions of company values. Even heroes and workers must have an emotional commitment to their work and managers, missionaries, as pointed out by Ulrich (1984: 126, cited in Barley and Kunda, 1992):

> The manager who attempts to change the organisational culture must assume... the role of a missionary. If the manager is successful in converting key personnel to the new set of values, then appropriate symbolic change should follow... As with any new proselyte, organisations which are converting their cultures can be helped in this process by institutionalising new rituals, symbols, languages, and heroes. This will take the form of memos and directives from top management... and reward systems which praise those who serve the new values.

In the 1980s, employees were encouraged to embrace the brand and image of their company and to align personal identities with the norms of their employers. The firm must aim to 'promote employee identification with corporate efficiency as a personal value' (Zoller, 2003: 194).

During this post-industrial, knowledge economy phase, the idea is that knowledge should be removed from the worker and contained by management, commercialised and capitalised upon, and mainstream discourses believe that organisations will need to modify modes of management and recognise that knowledge is the new factor for production and profit, displacing other forms like land and capital (Warhurst and Thompson, 2006: 788). During this period, the OECD (2001) indicated that 'symbolic resources are replacing physical resources, mental exertion is replacing physical exertion and knowledge capital is beginning to challenge money and all other forms of capital' (cited in Ibid.: 788).

Agile Management Systems

The next phase, which I have called the period of *agile management systems*, continues today (at the time of writing, 2017). It is within and about the agile period that most of this book's arguments exist. Agility gives workers no choice but to be, as the name implies, 'agile', or flexible and adaptable to a world of work that is incessantly changing. This phase is new in that it was introduced in 2001 by a group of software developers and new because of the new technologies that it both accommodates and encourages the use of, in terms of self- and other-tracking. In our new world of work, management seeks to obtain more information than ever before about workers at both work and in life, in ways hardly imagined during

Taylor's and the Gilbreths' lifetimes. This occurred simultaneous to intensifying workloads for those in work through idealised precision and using algorithmic management to make work more precarious. Interestingly, during this work design phase, management has also put 'wellbeing' at the centre of the employment experience, so it holds normative overtones as well as precision techniques for work scrutiny seen in quantification techniques.

Agility, as a period of experimentation is new, but is also, of course, a product of its preceding periods of work design history. It has been useful to look at the history of work design to remind ourselves that while 'agility' is a feature of the present and of neoliberal conditions, it is built on the assumptions and persuasions of several periods of history. Agility both intensifies management responsibilities seen in the era of scientific management and escalates the role of the engineer and technician, also seen in Taylor's recommendations. The primary difference between scientific management and agility is the even-greater emphasis placed on technology, to the point that we are symbolically asked to 'serve' the machine, as I outline in the next chapters. Efficiency and productivity gains are still prioritised in the agile phase, with a parallel desire to maintaining wellbeing and health of workers (akin to the Gilbreths' interest in fatigue and rest). It is partly because new technologies for tracking and monitoring have been introduced that management can further control work at ever-intensified levels, even as traditionally non-routine professional work is increasingly divided into discrete piecework that often can be done by machines and artificial intelligence (Ford, 2015), building on Braverman's observations in factories (1998).

There is now a growing literature on agility in academic work, management advisory literature and even work by the Chartered Institute for Personnel Development (CIPD) to lay a framework to discuss how workers' bodies and minds are portrayed during this phase. Findings indicate that we are expected to be adaptable and changeable, both physically and mentally. It is precisely because technology is expected to change and develop, that we are expected to follow suit; so, symbolically we are following the machine's footsteps. Furthermore, machines are likely to become increasingly important in the employment relationship. Agile, as will see, promotes both a paper-less workplace and one that relies on data and externalised and technologised management systems. It is perhaps the most invasive into the body and mind as tracking becomes increasingly detailed. The seeming paradox is that agile systems rely on teamwork, but team-based management starts to bleed into technological management. Even self-management holds a tinge of management control (see discussion of this by Parker, 2014 below). Now, I identify suggestions for how to pursue a debate that reflects the current context empirically outlined in case studies and interview discussions in future chapters. We work under conditions of agility and precarity and here I outline how 'agility' is reflected in this new world of work.

Getting Smart about Agility

We increasingly work with machines in 'agile' environments, in both the cognitive and manual workplace. The introduction of new technologies of measure may reduce labour costs but also creates increased stress. Agile production was introduced in 1991 (Sanchez and Nagi, 2001: 3563), focussing on principles for more frequent, simplified, self-organised team-based software development and delivery. It is now known for promoting specific principles in iterative development, self-organising teams, customer inclusion and adaptability to change (Rico, 2010). Highsmith notes that 'agility is the ability to both create and respond to change in order to profit in a turbulent business environment' (2002).

Agile has been popularised and used in an increasing number of companies and industries despite warnings from the CIPD in 2014 about incorporating agility without discernment. In 2001, a group of seventeen software developers, fed up with bureaucracy and obstacles to technological development, wrote their ideas for how an ideal production team should operate, calling it the Agility Manifesto:

> We are uncovering better ways of developing
> software by doing it and helping others do it.
> Through this work we have come to value:
> Individuals and interactions over processes and tools
> Working software over comprehensive documentation
> Customer collaboration over contract negotiation
> Responding to change over following a plan
> That is, while there is value in the items on
> the right, we value the items on the left more.

The manifesto reflected other IT workers' sentiment as they felt the waterfall system used in factories was ineffectual for software development (The Agile Movement, 2008). Agile approaches 'help teams respond to unpredictability through incremental, iterative work cadences and empirical feedback. Agilists propose alternatives to waterfall, or traditional sequential development' (Ibid.) used in factories.

Agility requires a 'group work design' model because 'individual roles are interdependent and there is a need for collective working' and 'sociotechnical systems principles were early influences on group work design' (Parker, 2014: 666). Parker, who has published extensively on job and work design, states that attention has been given to group autonomy in recent work design research. Studies in organisational psychology show group autonomy leads to job satisfaction and organisational commitment (Maynard et al., 2012; Parker & Wall, 1998, cited in Parker, 2014: 666). The 'inputs' for an 'input-process-output' model are group led work design, group composition and contextual influences; 'processes' involve intermediary group states and group norms that become attributes; and 'outputs' are what Parker calls 'team-member affective reactions' (Ibid.). Affect is not an alien term in organisational psychology. Where it is used, affect usually refers to positive shared emotions. Often, in any case, group work has an effect on psychological empowerment (Maynard et al., 2012, cited in Ibid.). However, Parker also points out that group work does not always lead to positive outputs. At times, people may feel it is an 'insidious form of control' (Ibid.: 66). Workers appear to rigidly impose values on themselves, and initially excited and energetic participants start to feel burdened.

The organisation of the agile workplace involves a process by which a product backlog, or an 'evolving, prioritised queue of business and technical functionality that needs to be developed into a system' (Schwaber and Beedle, 2002) feeds into a decision to call a 'sprint'. Sprint is the period within which a product is intended for development or an increment in the process which will be achieved, usually around thirty days. At the 'sprint meeting', all stakeholders, including 'customers, users, management, the product owner and the scrum team' decide on the goal and the functionality of the goal and decide who will do what to make that increment happen (Ibid.). Then a team is organised to carry out the project, designating who holds scrums to report back on work to ensure they are all up to speed on what is happening with the team and also that they are all contributing. Ideally, there are fewer than eight people in a team. The scrum is a regular team meeting where the development team is self-directed and self-organising, with authority to work on a 'sprint' in any way they collectively decide. If a scrum team decides to meet daily, they will usually meet for fifteen minutes and answer three questions: 'what have you done since the last scrum?', 'what will you do between now and the next scrum?' and 'what got in your way of doing work?' Meetings are beneficial because they are seen to 'improve communications, eliminate other meetings, identify and remove impediments to development, highlight and promote decision-making and improve everyone's level of knowledge' (Ibid.). Scrum introduced three main roles for team meetings: product owner, team and scrum master. Hierarchy is shunned in agile environments as out-of-date. The 'scrum master' is important, but s/he is not a traditional manager. As one such qualified 'master' indicated, they are 'there to make sure that the process runs smoothly'. Agile is meant to be very different from a 'bonus driven culture...' because that kind of culture 'takes people's eyes away from what they should be doing and they lose focus' (interview with one qualified Scrum Master 2016, transcript below).

After the Agile Manifesto was written in 2001, companies in all industries began to recognise the value of operational agility where workers and management have the 'ability over time to respond quickly and effectively to rapid change and high uncertainty' (Joroff et al., 2003: 294). Agile is a 'co-evolution of workplace and work'; an adaptation of *kaizen*, or 'continuous improvement' (Danford et al., 2008); 'neither top-down nor bottom-up: it is outside-in' (Denning, 2015). Agile relies on the conscious co-evolution and improvement of work which happens through 'experimentation, integration and disseminated learning' (Joroff et al., 2003: 294) via just-in-time communication, rear-view mirror checking, continuous improvement and resource maximisation (Cooke, 2010). Agile emphasises the reduction of waste, another similarity to scientific management. While the latter was supposedly designed to be a process whose results would benefit all, it was obvious that management had more say in what would happen, since they were the ones who held all cognitive skill. Workers are expected to fully co-create our workplaces in agile conditions. Ultimately, in much of the literature on 'agile', authority is given to clients as decision makers, because it is a type of total quality management systems. Critically, Lazzarato points out that the techniques of participative management styles seen in related systems are a 'technology of power, a technology for creating and controlling the "subjective processes"' (1996).

Agile has often been used as a replacement term for 'lean' production, but it differs in that it is considered a necessary response to the complexity of constant change in unpredictable environments (Cooke, 2010). In 2012, Wang et al. depict a term, 'leagile', stating that agile software development often uses lean approaches. In particular, *kanban* has been used in agile, which has to do with flow-based, continuous systems, contracted to 'time-boxed agile processes', these authors report (Wanga et al., 2012).

Skills: Self-Tracking Agility

Having discussed the tenets of agility, we now look at how workers might self-track and thus self-manage the process, which is inherent for its operation and success. Perhaps obviously, agile workplaces require agile workers. However, agile work requires extensive unseen labour.

As stated, agility assumes that changes to the workplace are inevitable because technology inevitably changes. Agile reflects older management systems, but it is different because the relationship between workers, management and machines is reformed. Where technology was used in scientific management to facilitate work efficiency, in agility innovations in technologies themselves are dominant and work competencies must catch up with these. Workers are expected to self-manage the impact of constant change through emotional management and affective control. Managing change thus becomes an all-of-life responsibility, where wellbeing is a worker's remit. Corporate wellness programmes are made available to help workers' resilience to constant, inevitable change and do not consider methods to prevent change or instability. So specific skills to manage change are expected.

Agile eliminates the traditional manager and puts the customer as manager, requiring the worker to self-manage this process (Denning, 2015).

Even managers are expected to 'fall in love with the customer'. For management to embrace agile, they need to be touched and inspired at a

> ...deeper emotional level through experiences and leadership storytelling that enable them to embrace a different set of attachments, attitudes, values and understanding about how the world works.
>
> (Denning, 2015)

Agile is a form of total quality management *and* a high-performance work system, which are both oriented around the 'high road' approach, where companies invest in human resource quality as a primary means to be and remain competitive (Ramsay et al., 2000; Tata and Prasad, 1998). Total quality, as a philosophy, inspires management to set a vision, to infuse all systems with this vision, and to involve and empower employees. High performance practices involve the introduction of employee involvement programmes. In the following chapter, the company running the project communicated a vision of the ideal agile workplace and set up systems to make this happen, fully involving workers by setting them as subjects in an office experiment, reflecting total quality and high performance systems. Agile differs from total quality and high performance because it was invented by technology experts to address immediate problems they faced in working with and developing new technology.

Agile was a grassroots model in its earliest stages, but the CIPD notes that it is being explicitly incorporated by management into many workplaces (CIPD, 2014). It has been appropriated into mainstream management terminology, work design research and job descriptions. Agile appears as a very modern model for production, but perhaps the first company to show how agility could be used in manufacturing was Toyota. Just-in-time, later called the Toyota Production System (TPS) was developed from 1948 to 1975. It allows for constant change in demand and technology, and tries to anticipate requirements as they develop. TPS means workers are encouraged to experiment with their work, challenging associations with rigidity and routine in factory work. Several interfaces are needed to carry out and measure this work, which could include self-tracking. However, performance management oriented around self-tracking should not be implemented without an understanding of the work people really do (Joroff, 2003: 299). The differences between JIT and agile are that more intimate worker tracking is inherent to agile while the relationship between humans and technology is advanced, with technology leading.

Agile, of course, requires agile workers: agile in the sense that they are prepared for constant change and prepared to make personal changes; always on the move and mobile; but also, always trackable. Workers' unseen labour involves the constant personally generated reproduction of a company's image by aligning it with our own identities, preferences and hobbies (Land and Taylor, 2010). Work, identity and life blur together and it is increasingly difficult to log out, switch off, and tune out (Gregg, 2011). Agile workers 'struggle to be left alone rather than to be included, a type of refusal that would have looked strange to their Fordist predecessors' (Fleming, 2015: 83). The workplace characteristics of agile are intensified within a digital economy where the corporeal is no longer separable from either the mind, or the machine (Moore and Robinson, 2016).

The CIPD's *Getting Smart about Agile Working* report in 2014 noted that companies aiming for the agile system overlook workers' personal experiences of agility transformations, do not train appropriately for it, and rely on a casualised, precarious workforce. Even within agile organisational environments geared for ongoing rather than intermittent adaptation to market demands, the simultaneous 'level of sophistication in designing and implementing smart and agile working practices' is not evident (2014: 2). This CIPD report shows that it may not even be appropriate to focus on 'the now' in, for example, public sector jobs or at least not in the same way that is needed in technology services. Focus on output, or work performed, rather than hours and physical presence in offices is not a panacea for work casualisation. The report showed that 90 percent of agile organisations offer 'some sort of flexible working, with part-time working and flexi-time being the most commonly used' (CIPD, 2014, 15). Sixty percent of companies looked at in the CIPD report hold formal policies on flexible workplace practices; however, if they have one, it is most likely to be about homeworking (47 percent) and mobile/remote working (35 percent). Given the expectation for constant workplace change in agile models, companies have been less willing to provide consistent training. The report showed that half of most HR departments stated that this was due to costs. While over half of organisations use multi-skilling, fewer have the scope for rapid re-training. The private sector is most likely to provide rapid training while the public sector tends to offer secondments and job rotations. Of course, the quantified self at work can be resisted by the refusal to track and quantify activity as part of work (as is seen later in this book), and by finding ways to hack quantification through organising across platforms and other forms of resistance.

The use of temporary and atypical (precarious) workers discussed in Chapter 3 is increasingly widespread in agile conditions. Accordingly, the CIPD indicates that casualised workers are not widely in support of the incorporation of agile (CIPD, 2014). In the empirical findings in subsequent chapters, I demonstrate that workers were expected to obtain affective self-awareness and self-management as part of the shift to agility of work or self-management, but there are usually no benefits or perks associated with doing so. Agile is seen to give workers more control over changes to the workplace, but forgets that this control leads to work intensification and does not necessarily lead to raising income or status or possibilities to self-manage outside prescribed methods. Nonetheless, companies continue to seek out agility in processes and systems and for unprecedented ways to prepare workers for it.

Conclusion

Here I have outlined the lineage of work design experimentation as labour processes that aim to capture the body, soul and mind of workers and to identify the best ways to inspire productivity, always placing the mind in control of the body and always neglecting to consider worker agency. Outlining the employment relationship from the period of industrial betterment to organisational culture and quality, I postulate that we are now in a renewed period of an eclectic work design experimentation whereby workers are told they have agency and that they can and should take full control of their work, personal lives and wellbeing, but are simultaneously expected to self-manage and self-track even in teamwork contexts; and are surveilled, measured and quantified at increasingly intimate levels. The agility drive is both normative because of the personalised aspects it introduces, and rational, because of its reliance on metrics. It also relies on communalism with the group work ethos and individual competences of self-motivation and drive. Research on quantified work is not abundant, but of what there is, research does not focus on the conditions of workers who are being quantified or on their direct experiences of it. Instead, it looks at the processes and the phenomenon and does not investigate the assumption that quantification must involve optimisation of the corporeal.

These discussions set the foundation for the next chapter where I begin to outline a possible ontological framework where labour processes can be more acutely identified and interrogated to recognise the corporeal and its measure viewed through the lens of new materialism. I introduce seemingly disparate theoretical approaches in new materialist research, from feminist post-structuralism to Marxism and international political economy research, arguing that bridges across these arguments can be formed by focusing on labour processes which involve new attempts to capture affective and emotional labour, the empirics of which I explore in more detail in Chapter 4. These discussions allow me to theorise, to delineate research questions, and to pursue the project of identifying what is at stake for workers, quantified.

To conclude, I provide transcripts from an interview that I conducted with a certified Scrum Master (SM) in 2016, who provided me with exceptional insights into agility.

Interview with Scrum Master

PM: What are some of the key features you see in an agile company?

SM: So, there's a whole lot of different things that get tied up into this, which is what makes it so interesting for me, 'cause I actually come from a social science background as well and psychology and sociology really interest me, but yeah, knowledge work always deals with stuff which is complex, as opposed to complicated. Someone very eloquently on Friday put it, the difference between us is putting a man on the moon is complicated, right, it's really hard, but once you've done it, you've got to reproduce the whole process! Bringing up a child is complex, you can bring up your first child brilliantly and that doesn't mean your second child is going to be brought up as well, because every day is different and every interaction is different, it's not a reproducible process. Knowledge work is not a reproducible process, so if somebody comes to you and go, if we want to implement a customer relationship management system, that's going to be different for every single company you do it at, because you've got different people there, a different culture there, different products you're selling. Likewise, putting together a legal document, well, you're applying some knowledge but it's not a reproducible process because every deal is different, every situation is different and again, sales deal, a sales deal putting together is a complex process.

So, the best way of, you can only manage a complex environment, you can't solve a complex problem, so having something which is iterative and experimental reduces, sorry, increases the probability that you will succeed, because rather than doing something which is, like, massive in one go, so if you've got a pen and paper on you, I'll just scrawl on this, so I mean, a traditional software development process and I would actually say this is a traditional project management process, taking it beyond, is that what you do is you kind of go along like this, just not really doing anything and then right at the end, you just have this big bang deliverable here. If there are any problems, you find out all of the problems here and all the while, you've got money tied up in this and if it goes wrong at this point at the end, then you haven't realised any of the value from this, you've got no way of understanding whether it's the right thing or not. An iterative process suggests, okay, right, we're going to spend this amount of money and then we're going to throw it out there and see what people think and then we're going to do another one and we'll throw it out there and see what people think and so on and so forth.

PM: How do companies work to be agile?

SM: So, with a company, say you're just getting feedback all the time and so you might get lots and lots of little things going on here, where people go, this is terrible. The other thing you often see is, well, if this is point A and this is point B and we think at the beginning we want to be, you know, at B, the journey never is a straight line and actually with this, what sometimes happens is, well, you know, you suddenly find out that really where you wanted to be at was C. If you're planning to be at B from the get go and you're not giving yourself any learning opportunities, you're in the wrong place.

Right, so that talks totally in terms of, you know, come up with a theory, test that theory, learn from it, change the theory, right, so there's this three step process all the time inside how businesses work, so for example, Groupon, I believe they started out as some guys basically doing some sort of political social network to do engagement and put people into politics, learnt very quickly that wasn't going to make them any money, so they set up a deal with a pizza company that was below them, in the office below them or the shop downstairs or whatever, threw out a completely static website with an email address for people to actually apply for vouchers for this pizza place and the rest is history. So, you know, there are lots and lots of examples of companies who've started out going here and they've gone, actually, this isn't going to work, we go off this way completely.

PM: Part of the Agility model, I think, isn't it...

SM: Yeah.

PM: So in terms of working with software development there, and if it starts with this kind of, well, so you're saying that there's a kind of an evolution history with Just-in-time and those kind of keeping customer focussed are looking for, I mean, throughout the period of time that you've kind of predicted it would take, being quite flexible, also listening on some feedback, all those kinds of things that allow you to be a lot more, yeah, plausible in terms of your outlook and what your final destination is at some sort of predetermined?

SM: No, I mean, it isn't, because if you knew what your final destination was in a complex scenario then it wouldn't be complex.

PM: Exactly, that makes perfect sense actually, so in terms of scrum and you talked about it a little bit before, I'm curious about how the role of the scrum master maps onto your, I mean, it does that, does it ever require kind of big changes and you've sort of alluded to this earlier, flat management structures or I guess elimination of hierarchies?

SM: Okay, so a scrum master, in its purest sense, should have no authority whatsoever, because there's a conflict in that and that's what very few companies seem to get, right, you'll see jobs advertised of scrum master, slash, development manager or scrum master, slash, project manager. The scrum master is there really, well, in my opinion anyway and you ask 10 different people this, you'll get 10 different answers, right, so I can only give you my opinion, the scrum master is there, in my opinion, purely as a master of ceremonies, so in the same way as a master of ceremonies at an event isn't really, has no authority over the people there, they're just controlling the flow of the event, that's it, so they're there to make sure that the process runs smoothly. You know, they'll intervene and what have you where necessary, but they haven't got any authority as such to fire people or any of that and the moment they do have that authority, well, then actually, this essence of a self-organising team, which is what a scrum team is meant to be...

PM: Right, is necessary for it to work, I guess.

SM: Well, you know, you hire the right people and get out their way at a management level, the skill in the management part of it is to hire the right people, so hire motivated, you know, great people, who can get along and co-operate, collaborate, it's all about the collaboration.

PM: Yeah and it's necessary in knowledge work.

SM: Yeah, well, exactly, so I mean, you know, in what you do, I guess, you know, you get, I suppose you get a level of mentoring for the people who are within your hierarchy but I would imagine and I don't know this for a fact, but I would imagine a lot of the hierarchy is actually, there's an HR function but the most of it is kind of an academic sort of, well, mentoring.

PM: Well, you're right, I mean, collaboration requires, as you say, a kind of constant communication and thinking through possibilities, otherwise how can knowledge be kind of forwarded, does it work, I have no idea. [Laughter]. In fact, no, last year I was working in sectors outside of IT, and where the term originates, to what degree is institutional change a prerequisite for organisations to benefit from agile, it might be...?

SM: I mean, that's absolutely huge. The problem is, again, that, so there's another thing that I'm quite into, which is this notion of lean change management, there are a lot of consultancies out there who are pedalling this one size fits all change process and I don't know, I think large companies, like massive organisations, tens of thousands of employees, they've got a real headache with this because it's really difficult to get that number of people to change and it also depends on where the change comes from. So, again, I'll do another scrawling, you know, if this is the hierarchy, you've got a bunch of different ways that the change can happen, so this is middle management, this is, I don't know, just, I'll put W for workers, I don't want to put any loaded statement in there and this is C-suite, okay, so of the C-suite goes off here, right, you end up with basically an organisation that looks like this, right?

The C-suite is miles ahead and it's got to drag the entire organisation behind it, so that's top down change and then you can end up with a situation where the middle management want to, decide to try to do something and you end up with this kind of situation occurring, the middle management has gone off, left the C-suite behind and I mean, likewise, if you've got bottom up change, then, you know, these people will get left behind and you can get variations of this and so, you know, it's a real problem.

PM: I can see it.

SM: So, how on earth, with an organisation of 10,000 people, where you've got some massive egos sitting in the C-suite, I mean, they wouldn't be there if they weren't massive egos, some people who are wannabe massive egos in the middle and some people who just want to get their head down and work, how do get all of those people, you know, basically to understand what's going on? This can also happen at a departmental level, so if IT goes, we're going agile, well and their main client is, I don't know, sales and sales go, no, we're not, we have to have fixed deadlines, we want fixed budgets, we want fixed scope, how are you going to deliver that for us, it's a big, big headache. Again, the problem is that, what happens is, companies will go, so there's a very large bank in this country whose CEO, I believe, went, we're going agile, so just hired loads and loads of agile coaches, we're going agile, well, that's exactly this, right, you know, the C-suite has decided that's going to happen, make it so.

The great view of the lean change model is we're actually applying experimental goodness to change, so okay, we might have a vision which is, we want the organisation to go and become agile, how do we do that, what problems are we going to face, what's the smallest, minimum viable change that we can apply to the organisation to begin this process? The way that I liken it, again, is like, if you have a millpond, right and you grab a handful of gravel and you throw it into the millpond, doing massive change to an organisation is a bit like that, well, which ripple had the biggest effect, I don't know, 'cause I threw like fifteen pieces of gravel into this completely flat millpond. Likewise, if you grab a massive rock and throw it into the millpond, all the water flies out of it and then you're left with employees leaving en masse, mass discontent...

PM: We all have a story that we know about where that's kind of happened, right, yeah.

SM: Yeah, whereas if you just drop one stone in at a time, you can see how effective it is and that might not be fast enough for some people but, you know, the companies that are best at this, everybody looks at where they are now and not how they got there, they go, well, they started as two guys in a room trying to sell blow up beds, right, you know, for a couple of nights and ended up as Airbnb, right, well and they just had that idea. Well, no, they didn't. They did a lot of change and a lot of, just micro experiments and they ended up as Airbnb, yeah.

PM: In what conditions would you say agile works best?

SM: So the most successful project I've ever encountered with agility was with, I was a development manager and I had three developers who were working with me, I was very outside of the project, they were just a very well gelled team, who got on very well with each other and that doesn't mean it was all fine and dandy, I mean, they could have a raging argument with each other, but they were friends afterwards, they were that well gelled really and they had a really engaged and talented product owner, who was a marketing person, but a talented and clear individual, very clear in her vision of what she wanted from the product and yeah, there was also a tester involved in this as well. It was a four or five month project, they had a hell of a deadline, they didn't think they would make it and without doing any overtime they paced it and got it delivered ahead of time. The output from it, because they were constantly delivering something for the product owner to view, well, you know, led to something which was I believe of great value. I mean, we ended up getting some really good responses from, well, actually, Clare's ultimate boss sent us a very pleasant email about it, so you know and I believe it's quite an important function to them now.

Where I've seen it go wrong is where companies have had, or rather the project has had very little engagement, so this idea of like, well, I'm going to send somebody off by proxy to engage with this and yeah, it just ended up in this death march project which just happens to have every two weeks something happening. It's like the team almost ended up forgetting that they should be delivering a product that everybody can view at the end of it, yeah, that's kind of, can be depressing when that happens. This stuff's really hard, it's not easy, it sounds easy, it sounds deceptively easy but it's really hard.

PM: What makes it hard to do this, or are there things that you've seen that you'd say those would tend to make things more difficult? Actually that's part of one of my questions, I mean, you talked about obstacles and...

SM: So, organisational inertia, that's one hard thing, massive misconceptions in the way that humans work, so people going into this kind of commander control mentality, which is fine if you've got to run across a minefield or someone's firing a machine gun at you, but when you need to see the bigger picture and try to understand what the possibilities are, that's really, really problematic. Yeah, I mean, you know, traditional project managers deciding to put their oar in really at inopportune moments and there's a whole bunch of reasons why this stuff fails. It ultimately comes down to some of the Tayloristic kind of views on how we should do work and that being, you know, I mean, even things like bonus driven culture, that sort of stuff, it takes people's eyes away from what they should be doing and they lose focus. I mean, another one is like, oh well, if they do more, if they work on more things at once they'll deliver more work, that's been proven completely to be wrong, but it's something that we have as a bias, when I say we, the human race, let's multitask.

PM: [Laughs] I try to multitask...

SM: Yeah, but it's impossible, we can't actually multitask, we context switch all the time and in switching contexts, we slow ourselves down, if you just get the job done and then move on to the next thing, but I mean, we're all guilty of it, you know, but there's so much science to back up that...

PM: Yes, it's absolutely this, isn't it?

SM: So you were asking about the play camp thing as the second part of that, so this is a slightly different thing, I mean, there is a level of like the agility part in it, in that a good scrum master will also be a good facilitator, because a lot of the ceremonies, they require facilitation and that's really the role of the scrum master in that, is to make sure that a good conversation occurs which leads to actionable outcomes, so the retrospective is one thing that they do, where you have a look at what went well and what didn't go so well and what you want to change and all that kind of stuff and ideally, you'll come back from that with something concrete.

So, a bad retrospective will have someone come back going, oh well, documentation was a problem, alright, well, give us a specific example of that, no, no, just documentation, oh well, how do you fix documentation as a problem? If you say, well, you know, Bert didn't update the documentation on this date and that led to this, you can then start to kind of do a route course analysis of why that was the case and actually come out and say, alright, well, that means next time we're going to do this, is everybody into this, right, great, we're going to do that, that's great.

PM: Yeah.

SM: Sure, but there'll be something concrete you can do, rather than next time better documentation, well, what does that mean, so the reason I give that as an example is I've seen that occur in scrums and you know, next time, what comes up, oh well, documentation was a problem, well, why didn't you fix it, you said last time, well, we thought we had, it's not, you know…

PM: You need to be more specific.

SM: Yeah, good old smart kind of specific measurable, actionable and all that kind of business, realistic time, and so in doing that, I got into, well, how else can you improve those sorts of processes, 'cause it's horrible, every two weeks, looking at why everything went wrong, you know. From time to time, you need to do something fun and pat yourself on the back and go, well, it went really well, you know, how did it go really well, how can we carry on doing that stuff and mixing it up as well. Some people will just do this one particular thing where they go, it's called Stop, Start, Keep or Stop, Start, Continue, there's very different versions on it, so it's like stop the bad stuff, start some new ideas and continue doing the good stuff and again, I've seen scrums run where they do that every two weeks and it gets really boring.

So, having a load of things in your toolkit which can spice that up and improve creativity leads you to looking at some of these things like innovation games, so innovation games originally was set up by a guy called Luke Hohmann, who, he wrote a book about, it was really to do with how product people can engage and be more creative and it kind of got big, because he comes from a background of the Agile community, it sort of got picked up by this unintended audience, I guess and yeah, it's become quite a big thing. The Lego I've used with, well, I've used with charities and with executive teams and so on.

That originally actually came out of Lego themselves, so the late nineties, Lego were in real trouble, they had an existential problem and they brought in a load of management consultants to help them try to figure out the way through and various different things happened and it led to them bringing in the guy who's head of Lego's educational division, a guy called Robert Rasmussen and they ended up coming up with this Lego serious play thing. Basically, they came to the realisation, well, all the tools we need are in front of us, so they had this process where basically they'd take you through learning how to build metaphors, so you can have a conversation in a safe environment, which is creative and has some constraints to it, basically a facilitator will pose a question and it's usually a very open ended abstract question, 'cause if there was an easy answer you wouldn't be using Lego to try to model it, everyone goes away and builds and then they come back and everyone who's built tells the story of their model.

So, you might ask a question like what is trust and everyone then goes off and builds trust and then explains what trust is to them and this demonstrates, you know, I'm talking to you, what I have in my head is probably quite different to what you're hearing, 'cause of life experience and so on and so forth and then from that, you can actually build a shared understanding, so you can then go, right, well, what's the essence of what you think trust is and you can go, right, well, this is the most important thing, and it means this and you can negotiate it into a shared model and then everybody goes, alright, well, so to us this is what trust is for our team.

PM: It's interesting and it really gets people to think about it and talk about what they mean by it and so it forces them to bring the life experience in and talk at a different level.

SM: Well, additionally, it takes away this situation where you have in a meeting, where, you know, either some bigwig at the front will just be going, blah, blah, blah, blah and it turns into like the Charlie Brown teacher kind of thing, all you're hearing is that kind of trombone noise going on and there might be, you know, one or two people who are vaguely interested and everyone else is on their smartphone or at the back, just trying to hide and hoping they don't get asked a question. Then they get asked a question and they're disengaged and they don't really have an answer, so they just make something up on the spot, they haven't really thought about it and that's like a really uncollaborative, uncooperative way of working. So, this buys you space to think and it then means that, well, the aim is that most people are models. The thing is, because it's about the model, not the person as well, that's where the safety comes into it.

PM: I see what you mean, the communication is happening anyway, regardless of what people are doing, that's perfect.

SM: Yeah and that's where that's come from and the reason I got into it was actually the guy that we brought into scrum training, one of my very good friends got invited along to this demo session, he came back raving about it, so I then was at a conference about playfulness at work in Antwerp a couple of years back, I got a chance to try this and I was like, yeah, I'll give this a go, so I signed up with Robert Rasmussen, who's one of the guys who started it, he runs training courses and learned like a four day training course, quite intense, yeah and you know, I've run a few sessions since then, yeah, you know, well, a friend who lives not far away from here, we set up a meet-up group in London so we could kind of practise this stuff, so yeah, it's interesting. One of the things that really interests me is group dynamics and well, just getting large groups of people to co-operate and collaborate and you know, I guess that's what really drives me.

PM: If you had to say that there kind of a couple or two or three major things that have happened over time in terms world of work, what are the reasons agility has become something that's seen as quite a useful model that works well, so what are some of the bigger changes in work?

SM: Well, I think it's both, so it used to be that technology was really expensive, I mean, it's still expensive but, I mean, I'll give you an example of this, so disk space, right, the very first PC I ever owned, which was in about 1992, I'd had computers before that but I'm talking actual IBM compatible with Windows on it PC that I owned, I think it had 250 megabytes of disk space on it, I mean, that's just laughable nowadays, right? So back then, when people were building big database systems, they would worry about the exact length of every single column of data within it, because they had to because disk space was so expensive, so if they made, I don't know, a two million row table, two bytes bigger than it needed to be, that suddenly scales massively, they'll run out of disk space really quickly.

So now, people are still conscious of it, but they don't need to be as conscious as they were before, they have other concerns they need to worry about. Now, with things like Cloud technologies and just platform based development, we can build something and just throw it out there, you don't have to worry about ordering, you know, fifteen racks in from Dell or whoever and getting that into the CIS admins and getting them to tie that in with their other workload and then install and you know, maybe they might even have to build a new server in to put that in, all that stuff, it's now at the point where you can just go, alright, well, we'll just rent this stuff off Amazon or Microsoft and there's some cost and set-up involved in that, but the lead time, theoretically, has gone down quite a lot and so you end up with a situation where you can have continuous delivery. That wasn't possible twelve, thirteen years ago or, I mean, even, you know, eight years ago, that wasn't possible and it's becoming increasingly possible.

There's also an attitude as well, so you know, I've gone through, I remember when, like the first time I went on the internet, I differentiate that from the worldwide web because they're different things, I think I was about eight years old, I was round at a friend's house, he had a Commodore 64 and he was downloading music that somebody had written, it's like you play, you know, a music file that the computer would then play, what's it like, Napster or Spotify or something, this is kind of, and they had these message boards, so you could go and communicate with people and this was wonderful stuff but really slow and then I remember, you know, the web kind of really coming into being and so on and so forth. There are kids now who are of, well, where are we talking, I mean, if you were born in like 1992, how old would you be now, I mean, you're going to be working age, right, so your whole existence, the internet has been there, so the web has been there...

PM: Yeah, so they've never lived without it, exactly.

SM: They're completely digitally native and so their whole approach to it is they don't have this kind of experiential inertia to say that this isn't possible. They don't get why certain people might think that's impossible, 'cause that's not their life experience, whereas if you're coming towards the end of your IT career and you might be in some sort of middle management or even senior management position, you'll remember when people were having to, you know, write machine code to get stuff done, where people would have to do punch cards and rent time on the mainframe and all this sort of stuff.

PM: MS-DOS, I remember MS-DOS, I've used it.

SM: Well, exactly, so I mean, you know, pre-graphic user interface, so there's some very, very different frames of reference.

PM: So it provides possibilities for new ways of working that didn't exist before.

SM: Yeah, because people come in and go, well, why and you go, you know what, I don't know and it's great because they're able to challenge, because they haven't got this experience which is telling them...

PM: Yeah, mind block.

SM: Yeah, this block, yeah, they haven't got this kind of bind that's stopping them thinking about the possibilities.

PM: So, if you were to say agility is, this is what it means, what it is, how would you say, well, sort of sum it up, to give, these are the main components to Agile as a fair...

SM: Again, you'd get different answers from if you were asking a bunch of different people. The one thing that I do, I believe the Agile Manifesto, when they first were starting to come with it, they threw out a bunch of different ideas, so like Lightweight apparently was one of them, but they were like, well, hold on, that's not going to, nobody's going to take that seriously, right?

PM: Well, this is fifteen years ago too as well, right?

SM: Yeah and the other thing that I read and I can't remember who it was that said it, is that if they were to go back today, they might actually have called it the Adaptive Manifesto, but then there was a problem with the word adaptive, 'cause it suggests the manifesto itself adapts, which is not really the reason why that wouldn't work, but really... so it's about the ability to adapt, that's what it really comes down to and it's having a lightweight framework in there to help you adapt, it's deceptively simple.

PM: What are the obstacles to agility?

SM: Not knowing why you're doing it. People go, we want to become agile, why?

PM: Yeah, you can't just sort of say, well, this is like a bandage that does...

SM: Yeah, I mean, how do you know you've become agile? You know, say we want to spend $15 million on us becoming agile, give it to me, I will go to a desert island for a month and then send you back a certificate saying, congratulations, you've become agile, without having clear goals, KPIs, all those kinds of things, then how do you know you're achieving and you know, you've got to ask yourself the question why. It's just one of those quite common things, people will hear something, oh, we've got to go and do this, otherwise we're going to get eaten by our competitors, well, okay, maybe that's a good reason, you know, we're going to go and become agile so that we don't get eaten by our competitors, alright, but what does eaten by your competitors look like? Right, you want to retain market share, you want to expand into certain new markets, is that what you're aiming to do, I mean, there's a lot of absence of focus of the goals and what you're trying to achieve and really, the whole reason to do anything has got to be the output, the outcome, so if you're not concerned about the outcome from the get go then you are deemed to fail and there's nothing you can do about that, so...

Bibliography

The Agile Movement (2008) *Agile Methodology.* http://agilemethodology.org/. (accessed 03/07/17)

Bain, P. M. and Taylor, P. (2000) 'Entrapped by the "Electronic Panopticon"? Worker Resistance in the Call Centre' *New Technology, Work and Employment* 15(1): 2–18.

Barley, S. and Kunda, G. (1992) 'Design and Devotion: Surges of Rational and Normative Ideologies of Control in Managerial Discourse' *Administrative Science Quarterly* 37(3): 363–399.

Barnes, R. M. (1937/1980) *Motion and Time Design and Measurement of Work* (Canada: John Wiley and Sons).

Boltanski, L. and Chiapello, E. (2005) *The New Spirit of Capitalism* (London: Verso).

Braverman, H. (1974/1998) *Labour and Monopoly Capital: The Degredation of Work in the Twentieth Century* (New York: Monthly Review Press).

Cameron, A., Dickinson, J. and Smith, N. (2013) *Body/State* (London: Ashgate).

Canadian Centre for Occupational Health & Safety (CCOHS) (2002) *Job Design.* www.ccohs.ca/oshanswers/hsprograms/job_design.html (accessed 03/07/17)

Chartered Institute for Personnel Development (CIPD) (2014) *Getting Smart about Agile Working.* www.cipd.co.uk/knowledge/strategy/change/agile-working-report. (accessed 03/07/17)

Champy, J. and Hammer, M. (2001) *Reengineering the Corporation: A Manifesto for Business Revolution* (Boston, MA: Nicholas Brealey Publishing).

Cockburn, A. (2002) *Agile Software Development* (Upper Saddle River, NJ: Pearson Education, Inc.).

Cooke, J. L. (2010) *Agile Productivity Unleashed: Proven Approaches for Achieving Real Productivity Gains in Any Organisation* (Cambridge: IT Governance Publishing).

Danford, A. M., Richardson, P., Stewart, P., Tailby, S. and Upchurch, M. (2008) 'Partnership, High Performance Work Systems and Quality of Working Life' *New Technology Work and Employment* 23(3): 151–166.

Denning, S. (2015) 'How to Make the Whole Organisation Agile' *Forbes* 22/07/15. www.forbes.com/sites/stevedenning/2015/07/22/how-to-make-the-whole-organization-agile/#696ddb2b135b. (accessed 03/07/17)

Drucker, P. (1954) *The Practice of Management* (New York: Harper).

Fleming, P. (2015) *Resisting Work: The Corporatisation of Life and is Discontents* (Philadelphia, PA: Temple University Press).

Ford, M. (2015) *Rise of the Robots: Technology and the Threat of a Jobless Future* (New York: Basic Books).

Foucault, M. (1988) *Technologies of the Self: A Seminar with Michel Foucault* (eds.) by Martin, L. H, Gutman, H. and Hutton, P. H. (London: Tavistock).

Gramsci, A. (1971) *Selections from the Prison Notebooks* (London: Lawrence and Wishart).

Grant, A. M. and Parker, S. (2009) 'Redesigning Work Design Theories: The Rise of Relational and Proactive Perspectives' *The Academy of Management Annals* 3(1): 317–375.

Grant, A. M., Fried, Y., Parker, S. K. and Frese, M. (2010) 'Putting Job Design in Context: Introduction to the Special Issue' *Journal of Organizational Behaviour* 31(2/3): 145–157.

Gregg, M. (2011) *Work's Intimacy* (Hoboken, NJ: Wiley).

Highsmith, J. (2002) *Agile Software Development Ecosystem* (Boston, MA: Addison Wesley).

Hollingworth, H. L. and Poffenberger, A. T. (1917) *Applied Psychology* (New York: D Appleton).

Hughes, M. (2015) 'How to Adapt Your Recruitment and HR Strategy to Wearable Technology' *IT ProPortal* 03/08/15. www.itproportal.com/2015/08/03/how-to-adapt-your-recruitment-and-hr-strategy-to-wearable-technology/ (accessed 10/02/2017).

Hyman, R. (1987) 'Strategy or Structure: Capital, Labour and Control' *Work, Employment & Society* 1(1): 25–55.

International Labour Office (1927) Scientific Management in Europe. *International Economic Conference Documentation* (Geneva, 04/05/1927).

Joroff, M. L., Porter, W. L., Feinberg, B. and Kukla, C (2003) 'The Agile Workplace' *Journal of Corporate Real Estate* 5(4): 293–311.

Kelly, P., Allender, S. and Colquhoun, D. (2007) 'New Work Ethics? The Corporate Athletes Back End Index and Organizational Performance' *Organization* 14(2): 267–285.

Land, C. and Taylor, S. (2010) 'Surf's Up: Work Life Balance and Brand in a New Age Capitalist Organization' *Sociology* 44(3): 395–413.

Lazzarato, M. (trans Colilli, P and Emery, E.) (1996) 'Immaterial Labour' in Hardt, M. and Virno, P. (eds) *Radical Thought in Italy: A Potential Politics* (Minneapolis: University of Minnesota Press): 133–147.

Lemov, R. (2017, in production 03/07/17) 'Hawthorne's Renewal: Quantified Total Self' in Moore, P., Upchurch, M. and Whittaker, X. (eds) *Humans and Machines at Work: Monitoring, Surveillance and Automation in Contemporary Capitalism* (London: Palgrave).

Littler, C. (1982) *Development of the Labour Process in Capitalist Societies* (London: Heinemann Educational Publishers).

Marx, K. (1867/2015) *Capital: A Critique of Political Economy Volume 1, Book One: The Process of Production of Capital* (Moscow: Progress Publishers: proofed by Blunden, A. and Clayton, C. 2008, Harris, M. 2010, Allinson, D. 2015).

Marx, K. (1973/1993) *Grundrisse* (London: Penguin Books).

McDougall, W. (1905) 'On a New Method for the Study of Concurrent Mental Operations and of Mental Fatigue' *British Journal of Psychology* 1(4): 425–445.

Moore, P. (2010) *The International Political Economy of Work and Employability* (Basingstoke: Palgrave Macmillan).

Moore, P. and Robinson, A. (2015 DOI, 2016 print) 'The Quantified Self: What Counts in the Noeliberal Workplace' *New Media & Society* 18(1): 2774–2792.

Morgeson, F P and Humphrey, S E (2006) 'The Work Design Questionnaire' *Journal of Applied Psychology* 9(6): 1321 – 1339.

Nadworny, J. (1955) *Scientific Management and the Unions 1900–1932: A Historical Analysis* (Cambridge, MA: Harvard University Press).

Newsome, K. Thompson, P. and Commander, J. (2013) 'You Monitor Performance at Every Hour: Labour and the Management of Performance in the Supermarket Supply Chain' *New Technology, Work and Employment* 28(1): 1–15.

Parker, S. K. (2014) 'Beyond Motivation: Job and Work Design for Development, Health, Ambidexterity, and More' *Annual Review of Psychology* 65: 661–691.

Price, B. (1992) 'Frank and Lillian Gilbreth and the Motion Study Controversy, 1907–1930' in Nelson, D. (ed.) *A Mental Revolution: Scientific Management Since Taylor* (Columbus: OH: Ohio State University Press): 58–76.

Ramsay, H., Scholarios, D. and Harley, B. (2000) 'Employees and High-Performance Work Systems: Testing inside the Black Box' *British Journal of Industrial Relations* 38(4): 501–531.

Ramsay, H. (1977) 'Cycles of Control: Worker Participation in Sociological and Historical Perspective', *Sociology*, 11: 481–506.

Rico, D. F. (2010) 'Lean and Agile Project Management: For Large Programs and Projects' in Abrahamsson P. and Oza, N. (eds) *Lean Enterprise Software and Systems. Lecture Notes in Business Information Processing*, Vol. 65 (Berlin, Heidelberg: Springer): 31–36.

Rolnik, S. (trans. Holmes, B.) (2011) 'The Geopolitics of Pimping' in Raunig, G., Ray, G. and Wuggenig, U. (eds) *Critique of Creativity: Precarity, Subjectivity and Resistance in the "Creative Industries"* (London: MayFly): 23–40.

Rubery, J. and Grimshaw, D. (2001) 'ICTS and Employment: The Problem of Job Quality' *International Labour Review* 140(2): 156–192.

Sanchez, L. M. and Nagi. R. (2001) 'A Review of Agile Manufacturing Systems' *International Journal of Production Research* 39(16): 3561–3360.

Schwab, K. (2016) 'The Fourth Industrial Revolution: What It Means, How to Respond'. www.weforum.org/agenda/2016/01/the-fourth-industrial-revolution-what-it-means-and-how-to-respond/ (accessed 02/02/17).

Schwaber, K. and Beedle, M. (2002) *Agile Software Development with Scrum* (Upper Saddle River, NJ: Prentice-Hall, Inc.).

Serres, M. and Latour, B. (1995) 'Third Conversation: Demonstration and Interpretation' in Serres, M. with Latour, B. (eds) *Conversations on Science, Culture, and Time* (Ann Arbor: University of Michigan Press): 77–123.

Smith, J. H. (1987) 'Elton Mayo and the Hidden Hawthorne' *Work, Employment and Society* 1(1): 107–120.

Stark, D. (1980) 'Class Struggle and the Transformation of the Labour Process' *Theory and Society* 9: 89–130.

Tas, J. (2016) 'Where Are Wearables Heading?' *HuffPost Tech* 21/04/16. www.huffingtonpost.co.uk/jeroen-tas/where-are-wearables-heading_b_9747314.html (accessed 10/02/2017).

Tata, J. and Prasad, S. (2010) 'Cultural and Structural Constraints on Total Quality Management Implementation' *Total Quality Management and Business Excellence* 9(8): 703–710.

Taylor, F. W. (1911/1998) *The Principles of Scientific Management* (Mineola, NY: Dover Publications).

Thompson, P. (2010) 'The Capitalist Labour Process: Concepts and Connections' *Capital & Class* 34(1): 7–14.

Thompson, S. and Hoggett, P. (2012) *Politics and the Emotions: The Affective Turn in Contemporary Political Studies* (London: Continuum).

Thompson, P. and Smith, C. (2010) *Working Life: Renewing Labour Process Analysis* (London: Palgrave).

Tipton, C. M. and Folk, G. E. (2014) 'Contributions from the Harvard Fatigue Laboratory' in Tipton, C. M. (ed.) *History of Exercise Physiology* (Champaign, IL: Human Kinetics Publishers): 41–58.

Upchurch, M. (2016) 'Into the Digital Void?' *International Socialism* (152) 07/10/16. http://isj.org.uk/into-the-digital-void/. (accessed 03/07/17).

Wanga, X., Conboyb, K., Cawleyc, O. (2012) 'Leagile Software Development: An Experience Report Analysis of the Application of Llean approaches in agile software development' *The Journal of Systems and Software* 85: 1287–1299.

Warhurst, C. and Thompson, P. (2006) 'Mapping Knowledge in Work? Proxies or Practices?' *Work, Employment and Society* 20(4): 787–800.

Warhurst, C. and Thompson, P. (1998) 'Hands, Hearts and Minds: Changing Work and Workers at the End of the Century' in Thompson, P. and Warhurst, C. (eds) *Workplaces of the Future* (London: Macmillan): 1–24.

Wrzesniewski, A. and Dutton, J. E. (2001) 'Crafting a Job: Revisioning Employees as Active Crafters of Their Work' *Academy of Management Review*, 26: 179–201.

Zoller, H. M. (2003) 'Working Out: Managerialism in Workplace Health Promotion' *Management Communication Quarterly* 17(2): 171–205.

3 Precarity 4.0

A Political Economy of New Materialism and the Quantified Worker

Precarity is the purest form of alienation where the worker loses all personal association with the labour she performs. She is dispossessed and location-less in her working life and all value is extracted from her in every aspect of life. Because precarious workers are constantly chasing the next 'gig', spatial and temporal consistency in life is largely out of reach. Precarity is symptomatic of the fall in wage share as Fordism gave way to financialised accumulation (Bengtsson and Ryner, 2015; Somavia, 2008); the rise in self-employment (Hatfield, 2015; ONS, 2016, 2017); automation (Frey and Osborne, 2013); the fall of the dot.com bubble and repeated global economic crises. In the first chapter, I outlined the rise in self-employed workers, where in the UK, statistics in 2016 and 2017 indicate that the rise in national employment figures and economic growth are dependent on self-employment. In the UK alone more than 900,300 people worked on zero-hour contracts in 2016, which is a number that rose from 747,000 by 20 percent in 2016 alone. The global rise in economic and social inequality in advanced countries has 'pernicious effects' on societies, 'eroding trust (and) increasing anxiety and illness' (Wilkinson and Pickett, 2009).

Today, most workers experience some form of precarity with severely weakened job contracts, indebtedness, austerity and the rolling back of the welfare state. Both warehouse and knowledge workers' offices are target areas for new self-tracking devices and other uses of technology to measure work. Insecure work has increased by 27 percent from 2011 as of time of this writing in early 2017, and evidenced by and leading to the following experiences:

- Wages can fluctuate without warning
- Workers have access to fewer rights
- Workers in these jobs frequently miss out on key protections like sick pay; and
- This type of work often means being at the mercy of bosses who can withdraw hours or even take you off the job with no notice (Klair, 2017)

There are around eighty million people working in what optimists call the 'sharing economy' in the USA and twenty-three million in the UK. While these ventures started as grass roots start-ups, they have scaled upwards and the movement is led by global corporations backed by venture capital including such megaliths as AirBnB and Uber (Balaram, 2016). Revenues from the sharing economy across Europe are projected to exceed 80 billion euros and facilitate 570 billion euros by 2025 (PWC, 2016). Five sectors of the sharing economy across Europe (peer-to-peer accommodation, peer-to-peer transportation, on-demand household services, on-demand professional services and collaborative finance) generated four billion euros in revenues and facilitated twenty-eight billion transactions in 2015 (PWC, 2016). The early enthusiasm for the possibilities of the 'sharing economy' obscures the experiences of the workers fuelling these engines. The sharing economy is also called the peer-to-peer economy and gig economy. It is in these post-Fordist spaces that we find the crowdworking and platform work empirically discussed in the following chapter. People working in insecure conditions are forced into a relationship of flexible 'reciprocity' between workers and management (where it exists as an entity) and alongside the emergence of crowd sourced working spaces, they continue to be subject to ongoing privatisation, and shrinkages in welfare states (Berlant, 2011: 192). The precariat cannot be understood by once-conventional standards of living. Precarity is an 'epochal recomposition of capital and labour' (Brophy and de Peuter, 2007: 177; c.f. Van Veen, 2010) which uses disposability to re-subordinate workers (Bourdieu, 1998: 85; Federici, 2008; Lorey, 2010), and it is often contrasted with Fordism in the literature. Corporate, corporeal colonisation of precarity and unseen labour is endemic in post-Fordist management techniques. People also feel precarious because management have become more aggressive; for example the New Public Management techniques in post-Thatcher Britain have led to intensified work and the 'rise in stress, bullying and mobbing in the workplace' (Hardy, 2016). A 2004 NIDL CGIL Associazione Nuovo Welfare survey on the typologies of new work demonstrates that 42.5 percent of casualised workers talk about job flexibility as 'synonymous with fewer rights' and 24.6 percent as a 'necessary evil'. The data shows that the rise in flexible work has led to people living at home for longer and being required to share accommodation, where 35.8 percent of respondents to the NIDL CGIL survey saying that they lived with family, 32.5 percent with a partner and 12.7 percent living alone; 71.6 percent of those surveyed did not have children. The unpredictable hours inherent to precarity is the antithesis to sociality and any possibilities to 'construct sociality itself' (NIDL CGIL 2004, Chiara@CW, 2004; cited in Tari and Vanni, 2005).

In this chapter, I endeavour to set a framework for a renewed (critical) political economy of precarious, quantified work, through interrogating the corporeal and affective turns which have informed the emergence of new materialisms. Renewed debates on materialism have emerged in both feminist poststructuralism and Marxist circles, resulting from a reaction to the glut of cultural studies research that, for too long, focused on narratives and discourses rather than investigations of the ontological and the material. The material that feminist new materialist researchers identify is based in a monist ontology which clashes with orthodox Marxism and with mainstream political economy research where they are steeped in Cartesian binaries. Nonetheless, I look for traces of coherence between investigations in new materialisms and, ultimately, I look to the Marxist social reproduction literature for possible intersections. Critical political economy research can benefit from a radical new materialism that ties loose ends across the disciplines together for a clearer understanding of exploitation in digitalised work and to inspire discussions about resistance and emancipation.

Quantification is the latest management systems method to contain workers' resistance to capitalist labour relations. New methods to quantify unseen (emotional and affective) labour are part of this contemporary labour process. Concrete labour, as depicted in Marx's writings, is performed with intention and with personal value. The capitalist's goal is to earn profit by removing personal value from work and by owning our performance, outputs, and increasingly, our conscious and unconscious motivation and dispositions. The capitalist actively seeks to change concrete work and life into something abstract where management owns all tools of measure. Time and quantification are abstract concepts that increasingly control aspects of working life. New attempts, as shown in the following chapter, to transform concrete to abstract labour involve management authorised quantification of previously largely inaccessible aspects of our conscious lives with the use of sensory tracking technologies and automation, where machines offer purely abstracted labour.

In the following chapters I present interviews with people who experience urban precarity in Britain, the USA and the Netherlands, all of whom are in some way involved in the quantified work movement or have experienced workplace modifications resulting from tracking and monitoring technologies. In Britain, I have gained interviews with workers in the gig economy and warehouses, one quantifying student and several self-employed freelance creative and digital workers. At the Quantified Self Expo in San Francisco in 2015, I interviewed Bethany Soule, the entrepreneur behind the self-tracking productivity app called Beeminder, about her own experience using the app for extreme productivity. I spoke to Chris Dancy, the 'mindful cyborg' who has also been called the 'most connected' man on the planet, who told me about his feeling that he, himself, has become a sensor. In the Netherlands, I interviewed around thirty employees whose unseen labour was tracked over the course of a year. The element of precarity these employees experienced was brought about by the merger of a smaller company with a larger one, reflecting the conditions of constant engagement in agile workplaces that I argue *all* working people now face. We are all expected to be agile; in other words to expect the 'market' and technology to dictate our lives.

In this chapter, I set the theoretical and philosophical groundwork for interrogating a critical political economy of the quantified, precarious self. I theorise what it means for workers to be asked to both endure unprecedented levels of surveillance whilst simultaneously being asked to measure our own productivity, health and wellbeing as well as to permit others to track this information in the context of agility. Workers are expected to align subjectivities according to these conditions—in the office, our homes and on the streets, in everyday and every night working lives, in the biopolitical terrain of subjectivities and power struggles.

Precarity 4.0

The idea of precarity started with the practices and goals of the autonomist movement whose foundations were in the *operaismo* (workerist) communism. These movements were active responses to Fordist conditions of mass assembly, and the new forms of control of deskilling, dividing and preventing self-management, predominantly observed at the FIAT factory in Turin and protested by left wing authors in the *Quaderni Rossi*. The workerists were opposed to traditional forms of resistance and trade union politics, in particular those of the Comunisti Italiani (Union of Italian Communists), which developed a reputation for conservative, religious overtones and Puritanical views on sexual behaviour and family values (Wright, 2002: 125). Indeed, these movements rejected traditional union organisational mechanisms and related class consciousness.

Depending on how it is read, Fordism and factory styles of management in the 1950s and 1960s resulted in a completely oppressive system of rule, but the romanticisation of conditions of the factory during Fordism might also be seen as stable and reliable and resulting in several technological innovations. The workerist and autonomist movements' view is that precarity has dramatically challenged capitalism, has successfully reversed the dynamic between its defenders and its dissenters (Tronti, 1971), and that capitalism now picks up the pieces after situated tumult. However, it is not clear whether the intention is to remove capitalism, or just to reverse the power dynamic. Informatisation or the full automation of factories was, for early autonomists, a way to *reduce* work; but this has been actively transformed into fractalisation, or the fragmenting of time-activities through tracking technologies, the transformation from concrete to abstract labour.

'Precarity' refers to the state of being that results from unstable and non-standard work, being underemployed and hyperemployed. Authors who have written about precarity hold varied interpretations for how its conditions affect people and whether these conditions are empowering or disempowering. Precarious work is contingent, insecure, flexible, can be illegal casualised, temporary, piecework, fractional, project, sessional, intermittent, freelance, unstable, uncertain, unpredictable, or risky (Gill and Pratt, 2008; Kalleberg, 2009; Tari and Vanni 2005) and is often conducted by workers who are over-qualified for the work they are doing, and so underemployed. This is the most relevant international threat to decent and dignified work, and *precarite* is the root of all problematic social issues in the 21st century (Bourdieu, 1998).

Precarity 'draws attention to both "the oppressive face of post-Fordist capitalism", and the "potentialities that spring from workers' own refusal of labour" and their subjective demands' (Neilson and Rossiter, 2005 cited in Gill and Pratt, 2008: 10). The lack of stable waged labour can give rise to an affective condition that is predicated on social insecurity and can infect subjectivities with perpetual unrest and anxiety. When written about in celebratory terms, precarity can also lead to a shared subjectivity that replaces a need for the traditional view of 'class' (Hardt and Negri, 2000); when understood from a managerial lens (albeit under a different label such as 'the liberated worker' under northern European programmes of flexibility) it can also be perceived, as a dramatically individualised form of subjectivity. The precarity movements in Italy sought 'flexicurity' where welfare would protect workers and allow people to have flexible work arrangements (Tari and Vanni, 2005) and expect 'securities and rights in the midst of flexibility, of uncertainty' (Raunig, 2004).

The precarity of the modern worker is central to understanding the quantified self at work. Workers are compelled to squeeze every drop of labour-power from our bodies, including work that is mostly unseen, such as attitudes, sentiments, and thoughts. Hardt and Negri argue that much like earlier forms of capitalism which taught workers to 'act like machines', the current wave of technologies mean that, 'as general social knowledge becomes ever more a direct force of production, we increasingly think like computers' (2000: 94–5). This introduces unprecedented possibilities for stress, which management would like to track. Machines largely self-manage, do not complain, do not call in sick and do not make mistakes (interview with factory workers 2016), but the effects of technological change on humans' psychological and physical health are significant. A line of subordination in this labour process goes from the economic system to the ego-ideal or subjective image, to the mind, to the body. In effect, each person is commanded (or seduced) to use their mind to subordinate their body to the ego-ideal, and hence to the economic system. Capital encourages universal communication, and machinic devices appear to facilitate this communication—but only in quantified terms. Thus, anything that cannot be quantified and profiled is rendered incommunicable – meaning it is marked and marginalised, disqualified as human capital, denied privilege, and precarious.

Precarity is a life condition whereby resources for the most basic necessities, as well as access to career development, careers and jobs, are (an imposed) scarcity (Shukaitis, 2006). Life is 'contingent on capital and therefore precarious' (Mitropoulos, 2006). Life is precarious because people are treated as though there is no difference between them, and therefore their unpaid labour is dispensable. While there are problems with the way the 'precariat' has been identified—as though it would develop a homogeneous class consciousness as alluded to in Guy Standing's thesis (2011)—rates of unprotected work (Davies, 2005, 2006; Harrod, 2006) in the knowledge and high tech industries are well known, but work in traditional sectors is where the majority of increases in insecure work are located (Klair, 2017). Precarious life conditions very rarely lead to happiness and fulfilment, but often involve underemployment, anxiety, mental health issues and sickness. Precarity is associated with reduced welfare and informal, flexible contracts (Berlant, 2011: 192), enabled by lean, just-in-time production, telepresence and outsourcing (Berardi, 2009: 75–7; Virno, 2004: 56–9). It can be defined as a work regime of 'non-self-determined insecurity, of all areas of life and work, as well as to the possible invention of new forms of resistance and the chance of newly forming as "precariat", "cognitariat", "affectariat"' (Raunig, 2004), which leads to dependence on capital for survival (Mitropoulos, 2006), disposability (Lorey, 2010), and a 'hell of the absence of guarantees' (Guattari and Negri, 1990: 76).

The precarity movement from 1960s Italy has been picked up in the early part of the 21st century by the generation of creatives and other types of affective labourers, and spread across Europe. Precarity campaigners are happy to talk about liberation by not working, not via flexibilisation or casualisation as it is now deemed in mainstream diatribes. Already under great strain, precarious workers are pressured not only to survive unstable life conditions, but also to socially reproduce the capitalist future for themselves and everyone else (largely for free). Authors who celebrate entrepreneurialism in effect condone precarity as liberation propagate similar sounding perspectives, but are now ideologically in tension with the autonomist movement. Franco Berardi (Bifo) (2009) explains early overlap in workerist and autonomist overtures with new management rhetoric of wellness and liberation, by outlining the way that capitalism has appropriated many of the radical possibilities 'preached' by San Precario. San Precario is an effigy who first appeared in 2004 and is seen as the patron saint of precarity. The effigy has been used in many protests and reflects the movement from its origins, where the rejection of work was linked to revolutionary motives.

European responses to precarity and precarisation are embodied in EuroMayDay, at which time thousands of activists converge to protest the offenses of management and the lack of fair government responses to precarity. This is a transnational movement protesting neoliberal working conditions throughout the year, as well as on the traditional workers' day of the 1st May. At these events, San Precario often appears: indeed, the San Precario Network organises the events at the Euro Day. This effigy is a transgender saint, created in response to the realisation that 'no so a che santo vatarmi (I don't know which saint to pray to)' (Berardi, 2009: 25). Lorey notes that the interesting aspect of precarisation as a social movement:

> ...is not only the way in which under its auspices new forms of political struggles are tested and new perspectives on precarization developed; rather—and this is striking in relation to other social movements—it is how it has queered the seemingly disparate fields of the cultural and the political again and again.
>
> (Lorey, 2010)

The Potere Operaio's manifesto involves the refusal of work, but it has been appropriated through a rise in flexibilised work that claims to have liberating potential for all (rather than simply potential for those who would like it, which would better fit a consumerist model); informatisation of factories as a way to reduce work has become fractalisation or the fragmenting of time-activities whilst the separation of cognitive labour from the body leads to a form of subsumption. This managerial counter-attack is part of a cultural counterrevolution that assumed force after the spontaneous violent uprising in 1977 at Bologna University that started at a meeting of the fanatic Catholic group called Communion and Liberation. The movement quickly turned against unions, political parties, factory management, and fundamentalist religion. However, because of the absence of an explicit alternative to capitalism, the movement missed a historic chance for change. Capitalism is very good at re-inventing itself (Berardi, 2009: 77) and appropriation of concepts without providing an apparatus of support is particularly needed during times of economic crisis and rising unemployment.

As an appropriation of the overtures of the early automost and workerist movements, a range of management gurus began to preach that happiness is obtainable *through* work. Peter Warr (2007) reports that workers' happiness is inherent to increasing productivity in his text *Work, Happiness, and Unhappiness*. Dan Pink's (2011) *Drive: The Surprising Truth about What Motivates Us* tells us that workers want autonomy, mastery and purpose, and these are intrinsic motivational features that give people 'joy'. Davies outlines the history of the 'happiness industry', whereby governments consistently promote joy as a personal responsibility and find fault with individuals who seem to choose to not be happy and also supposedly choose to not work (2016: 106–137). The 'new economy' discourse, which idealises creative workers, is often a pretext for imposing precarity (Brophy and de Peuter, 2007: 177; Kapur, 2007: 163–4) or concealing labour exploitation (Dyer-Witheford, 2005; Neilson and Rossiter, 2005). Both the 'creative class' discourse, and the case for quantifying and measuring work as self-empowerment in any industry, depend on what Smail (2009) has criticised as 'magical voluntarism'; an ideology which elides the reality of class exclusions, blocks opportunities and structural decline by insisting on the miraculous power of each individual to be whatever they want to be with the corresponding assumption that what they 'want to be' is a localised variant on the neoliberal subject.

In concrete terms, this belief in compatibility with precarity leads to widespread depression as workers contrast their actual achievements with the myth of what they can achieve without wider social transformation away from capitalism (Fisher, 2014). This is the context for the introduction of quantifying wearables in the workplace to bridge the gap between workers' ego-ideal of managerial autonomy and the reality of psychologically debilitating precarious labour. Psychologically, the main effect of such quantification is raising anxiety. Although discourses on the creative industry celebrate a supposedly amorphous, autonomous force of creativity, in practice they strongly rely on quantification, 'enclos[ing] the knowledge and skill of workers and scholars as objectified knowledge and skill' (Raunig, 2010: 21). No wonder then, that capital seeks to quantify the fields of cultural production and consumption where work has long been underpaid and undervalued (Terranova, 2000). Critics deem such approaches a kind of gentrification and de-radicalisation of culture, promoting cultural markets at the expense of critical arts, public provision, and economic security (McRobbie, 2011; Mokre, 2011). In earlier periods, the cultural industry was limited to 'the rationalization of distribution techniques... [not] the production process' (Adorno, 2005: 100).

Sermonic messages of self-quantification for personal empowerment and improvement are characteristic of the annual Quantified Self Expos in California and the Netherlands, where people give testimonials about how tracking their personal lives has led to a significant change. The quantified self movement promotes a view of people whose ability to prosper is unrelated to traditional features of survival under capitalist conditions, such as an income and the ability to feed bodies. However, self-improvement without critique allows for a potential trap of work-life integration and overlooks the painful corporeal specifics of rising precarity, which is inherent to a supposedly agile labour process. Rather than troubling to find out about, or work to prevent the brutality of the everyday and every night lives of producers, happiness industry gurus promote messages that celebrate individualised and flexible work and portray the ideal of a privileged elite with access to the highest standard of survival and pleasure. The presumption is that people have a magical ability to prosper without the traditional features of social life such as a steady wage or secure future. Florida talks about the new precarious elite as an emerging 'creative class' (Florida, 2002), with access to the highest standard of survival and pleasure due to the freedoms of self-management. In the late 1990s and early 2000s, knowledge capitalism was celebrated as a space for self-fulfilled autonomous workers (Drucker, 1993) where technology would reduce hierarchies and control systems at work. However, the promises of joy and pleasure in the knowledge-based economy have largely been unmet. Instead, negative symptoms of precarity are rife.

Precarity is material and subjective and is a 'juncture of material and symbolic conditions which determine an uncertainty with respect to the sustained access to the resources essential to the full development of one's life' (Grupo de Investigación, 2005) rather than a historically specific set of events. The precariat, what Osawa and Kingston call the 'precarious proletariat' (2010), are living and breathing, productive and *re*productive labourers, individuals and groups who are oppressed by a wage labour system that renders them unwaged, underemployed, undignified, and subaltern. Precarity has had varied expression in different cultures. For example, lifetime employment was a given within the Japanese zaibatsu, an extreme contrast to contemporary workplaces and the rise of the precariat in Japan and across the world.

Precarity and Dignity

The rise in precarity observed above, in all of its indignity, triggered an international response. In 1999, Juan Somavia put 'decent work' in his election statements for the role of Director General of the International Labour Organisation (ILO), appealing for a global commitment to decency in labour relations. The choice of terminology is important because earlier key ILO documents had used the term 'dignity'. Guy Standing, who was a long-standing official at the ILO until around 1999, described work as dignifying with a story about meeting a young Jamaican man who said 'I want a work, not a job', indicating he was interested in 'an occupation which would lead to his being secure and respected in his community and family, with status, a sense of dignity and the possibility of self-improvement' (2005: 94). Standing's (2009) point was that a new framework concept should be Dignified Work. Standing advocated seven forms of work-related security. Building on Arendt's classifications between labour and work, Standing's point was that the concept of 'work' should replace 'labour' with all its baggage, and all forms of work would be included for support by the ILO.

The choice of the term *decency* for crisis reform is interesting, because it could be accused of overlooking the subjective dimensions of work (and thus class consciousness), which *dignity* does not do. Dignity, as linked with personality and status, is what is missing in the current precarious conditions workers experience, where they live in a spectre of the possible but not the probable. Capitalism reproduces itself via workers' subjectivities, and relations of production within gig work and unstable contracts rely on a digital lowest common denominator and what I call 'zero subjectivity', where life is hollow in its extreme commodification. Research has been conducted to assess *decent* work in the developing world, such as is seen in a series of surveys on home-based enterprises in Cochabamba, Bolivia;

New Delhi, India; Surabaya, Indonesia; and Pretoria, South Africa (Tipple, 2006). Australia's Fair Work campaign, Indonesia's Better Work initiative, and the Playfair movements are evidence of the international response to precarious work. Is decent work dignified?

As discussed above, in 2009, the ILO set itself the task to manage spiralling unemployment and the worst effects of the global recession, particularly on the poor, on workers in the informal sector, the young unemployed, and the weak middle class, who are all part of the precariat. The ILO promoted decent work as part of the formula for crisis recovery as a counterpoint to precarity. In 2011, the ILO organised the 'From Precarious Work to Decent Work' *Workers' Symposium on Policies and Regulations to combat Precarious Employment* to discuss the unacceptable rise in precarious work. ACTRAV (2012), the labour arm of the ILO tripartite structure, defines precarity as:

> Workers in precarious employment suffer from inferior working conditions in all aspects of work: security, predictability, health and safety, pay and benefits, and access to social security. The spread of precarious employment is part of what it is fair to call a worldwide corporate attack on the right to organize and bargain collectively, by shifting to subcontracting and individual contracts, attacking sectoral and national bargaining, and evading employer responsibilities by complicating what should in fact be a direct employment relationship with their workers.

The publication *Philosophical and spiritual perspectives on Decent Work* published by the ILO, World Council of Churches, and the ILO International Institute for Labour Studies, indicates that *decent work* has the potential to be a transnational ethic, or a 'global ethic... that allows us to interrelate the different religious, spiritual and ethical traditions among one another... provides, as it were, the hermeneutical keys that help one to move from one universe of ethical discourse or value discourse into another universe' (Raise, 2004: 17). In this ILO text, Peccoud indicates that 'work is a fundamental expression of intrinsic human dignity, which has both spiritual and material dimensions', and in all religious traditions, decent work is 'related to the dignity of man and woman to his or her capacity to earn a livelihood and live life abundantly' (2004: 34). Work should be fulfilling, should dignify the worker, and people should not be 'subordinated to work, or capital' (Ibid.). Decent work initiatives have not effectively battled the rise of precarious work, so perhaps what is missing from the formula is a more prominent role for 'dignity'.

The Universal Declaration on Human Rights popularised the use of the term dignity, or more precisely, 'human dignity' in development policy and international organisational decision-making circles. In Roman law, dignity was the right to possess status, to have an identity and even to have a personality. The concept is linked to worthiness, and a right to basic respect from others; it is what separates humans, institutions, and the state from animals, such as in the English Bill of Rights of 1689 which refers to 'the Crown and royal dignity' (cited in McCrudden, 2008). Simon Bolivar called slavery a 'shameless violation of human dignity', and after 1848 the French Republic claimed in one decree that slavery is 'an affront to human dignity'. Labour movement activists began to adopt the concept of dignity into their manifestos, but not without critique. In 'Moralising Criticism and Critical Morality, a Contribution to German Cultural History Contra Karl Heinzen' Marx had actually snubbed the term, claiming that it provided a 'refuge from history in morality' (Marx, 1847, cited in Ibid.) and Nietzsche—albeit from a rather different premise—chastises the dignity of man and of labour as being mere 'sentimental egalitarianism used to persuade those who toiled to continue to do so' (Ansell-Pearson and Diethe, 1994, cited in Ibid.).

By highlighting decent work, the international response to precarity overlooks the tie between precarisation and technology, where development is often portrayed as inherently improved by technological advances. Instead of improving societies, information and communication technologies may in fact 'exacerbate existing inequalities between men and women and create new forms of inequality' (United Nations Division for the Advancement of Women, 2005: 3) and women and girls are significantly affected within the global digital divide. The report *Because I am a girl: The state of the world's girls 2010: Digital and urban frontiers: Girls in a changing landscape* (Plan International, 2010) reports that women are the main victims of cyberbullying and online human trafficking. In Britain, domestic workers are increasingly tracked and monitored, which has led to stress and unpaid work (Moore and Hayes, 2017). Perceived cultural duties, and responsibilities and expectations of reproductive labour in effect double the workload of telemarketers in Brazil (Nogueira, 2009). Huws discusses eWork and the global division of labour in eServices, where local fallout in both the areas where investment happens and where work has disappeared affects young, female workers, who in developing areas receive wages that fall below subsistence levels (2014: 53–5). Alongside the growth of value-added work (such as data entry) in lower-cost countries such as the Dominican Republic, Madagascar and Sri Lanka, women tend to languish in lower-skilled positions while men occupy higher-skilled roles in systems design. Even in a supposedly developed country, *The Candidate* (2016) reports a study of 150 digital businesses in the United Kingdom where twice as many men are employed as women. One study by Harvard and Princeton academics shows that from 2005 to 2015, the percentage of women employed in 'alternative work arrangements' more than doubled, 'rising from 8.3 percent to 17.0 percent. The percentage increased by a more modest amount for men, from 11.6 percent to 14.7 percent'. In 2015, women were more likely than men to be employed in an alternative work (Katz and

Krueger, 2016). There are several studies by international organisations and academic researchers that look at, among other things, access to digital participation as linked to education and development in the global south; inequality of work in the ICT sector; research on the effect of digital monitoring on domestic work; and philosophical writings on the human experience with technology. However, data on the impact of heightened performance monitoring and other forms of quantified and digitalized labour on women specifically, and recommendations for improvement in the area of work and employment for women's empowerment, are worryingly limited.

In a special issue in the journal *ephemera* on digital work, King looks at the question of dignity in digital labour, first citing Kant's pre-capitalist presentation of dignity as a moral absolute, seeing the types of exchange relationships that were the signs of the emergence of capitalism as 'compromises to human dignity' (King, 2010: 288). Under these terms, anyone who is required to sell their labour and skills must survive indignity. Fast forwarding through history, the myth of the knowledge economy heralded during the Dot Com bubble introduced a brand of cognitive workers whose self-worth was not expected to relate to the exchange value of their labour, or at least not in a way that translated into remuneration. Dignity was available through the 'psychic opportunities for self-development' (Ibid.: 297) and the prestige associated with culture and digital work in trendy environments that cities bring. Dignity can be achieved through non-paid labour. Dignity, King writes, 'provides a benchmark against which to interrogate how human worth sustains itself when faced with the systematic compromises resulting from the sale of labour power as a commodity' (Ibid.: 289). However, I argue that intensively tracked and monitored work can never be dignified, because it requires extreme levels of alienation and transforms our work into something entirely abstracted from our own bodies and affectivities.

Digitalised precarious work is commodified according to increasingly granular measures of value, which puts abstract and living labour into direct antagonism with capital, and creates perpetually *undignified*, insecure and anxious working conditions. With this in mind, I now begin an investigation into how precarious bodies and minds can regain dignity through the possibilities for emancipation, by looking at a range of theses in political economy and philosophy. Colman (2014: 6) has reminded us that technologies inevitably transform working bodies and that the processes of change are both gendered and structurally violent. It can be concluded that technology can be used to seemingly neutralise and de-gender psycho-social violence in a range of ways that leads to work intensification and opens up a range of distinct areas for discrimination against precarious women workers.

Corporeal and Affective Turns and a Return to the Material

The undignified conditions of precarity have not gone unnoticed. As technology rapidly infiltrates bodies at work at an undignified level and as precarity is now the life condition so many people face, research in what might have been ontologically considered separate camps has begun to ask questions about the body and affect. 'New materialism', discussed in the next section, is identified in two philosophical 'turns': the corporeal and the affective, which investigates the absenting of bodies and neglect of research on technologies; research that is missing from most study of social sciences and humanities. It is within these 'turns' that I look, first to identify how we can resolve the incessant abstractions of concrete labour and the division of bodies from minds, which I argue prevents political subjects from reaching class consciousness and from realising emancipatory potentials in the quantified workplace. Do self-tracking devices in workplaces require individuals to 'fight for their own bondage as though it were freedom' and to appear as though they are 'proud of their own enslavement' (Deleuze, 1988)? Does self-tracking remove any possibility for affect and prevent people from mobilising in unison, to throw off such quantifying shackles? Or could these turns in research become associated with the rise of a possibility for a 'revolutionary virtual' which 'offers a zone of intensity or affect, a system of affective structures, which enable the Revolutionary Virtual and actualise Revolution' where social movements and management entities are simultaneously 'engaged through affective structures in enabling and disabling this Revolutionary Virtual' (Karatzogianni, 2012: 57)?

To theorise the quantified self in precarity I focus on a range of disciplines where attention has turned to discussions of the material and the corporeal, and technology in the labour process. I do this to ultimately assess how a dialectic of relations can have emancipatory affects and release pressures revealed for workers in Industry 4.0. A *corporeal* turn has been taken in feminist studies (Brush, 1988; Butler, 1993/2011; Federici, 2004; Grosz, 1987; Gunnarsson, 2013; Witz, 2000); in Jewish studies as reported by Kirshenblatt-Gimblett (2005) and Boyarin (1995); in geography (Anderson, 2011; Cooper, 2011; Goldstein, 2013; Longhurst, 2012; Orzeck, 2007); in social theory (Tamborino, 2002); critical geography (Harvey, 2000); and in environmental studies (Payne and Wattchow, 2009).

Not all scholars of the corporeal turn see the body as a separate entity to the mind, but they are predominantly committed to monist ontology. Unlike the corporeal turn, the *affective* turn is definitively monist. Spinoza, a dissident philosopher and lens grinder, first explored the concept of affect in the 1600s. Spinoza's radical ideas led to his excommunication from Judaism. He introduced the concepts of conatus and affect: ideas that much later inspired the affective turn. Spinoza is especially noted for rejecting the Cartesian mind-body split and resultant dualist ontology; instead insisting on a univocal continuum between mind and body. This 'turn' has been led by feminist and poststructuralist authors who call for a 'transdisciplinary approach to theory and method that necessarily invites experimentation in capturing the changing co-functioning of the political, the economic, and the cultural, rendering it affectively as change in the deployment of affective capacity' (Clough, 2007: 3). Clough invites research, in the introduction to her edited text, in the affective realm that recognises the effect that techno-scientific advancements have had on 'ghosted bodies and... traumatised remains of erased histories' emerging from the industrial era, and a consideration of 'self-reflexivity (processes turning back on themselves to act on themselves) in information/communication systems, including the human body' (Ibid.). The pieces in *The Affective Turn: Theorising the Social* (Clough and Halley, 2007) are focused on changes in the social sphere but see these as changes as taking place in ourselves, rather than constantly external as sociology and other disciplines often assume. The joining of bodies and subjectivities is not reducible to the personal or the psychological; therefore we can think of social change as starting with affect.

Inspired by Spinoza, Deleuze (1978, 1988, 1992), Colman (2008), Colman and McCrea (2005), Goddard (2011), Hardt (1999), Negri (1991, 1999), Deleuze and Guattari (1987) and many others, some of whom are listed here and some in the previous chapter, have contributed to the affective turn. The concept of affect has been developed by the feminist, autonomist and poststructuralist research of Deleuze (1978, 1988, 1992), Hardt (1999), Blackman and Venn (2010), Colman (2008), Colman and McCrea (2005), Gill and Pratt (2008), Massumi (2002), Thrift (2004), Gregg and Seigworth (2010), Berlant (2011), Clough (2007, 2008), Clough and Halley (2007), Blackman (2008a,b, 2011), Coleman (2012), Karatzogianni and Kuntsman (2012), and recently critiqued by Wetherell (2015). Affect has also recently been revisited in special issues of *ephemera* (2016) and *Organisational Studies* (2017).

The affective turn may 'be thought to emerge from the technopolitics of late capitalism, and the convergence of cyber, multimedia, information, and science studies with studies of the body, matter, being and time' (White, 2008: 181). It marks the 'intensification of self-reflexivity' in 'archiving machines' and in 'capital flows, including the circulation of value through human labour and technology; and in biopolitical networks of disciplining, surveillance and control' (Clough, 2007: 3). Beller states that 'the development of capital will be unthinkable without the simultaneous development of technologies for the modulation of affect and the capturing of attention' (Beller, 1998: 91). Affective labour is innumerable (Dowling, 2007; Hardt and Negri, 2000). Regardless, management is pursuing its capture with increasing intensity, because worker collapse resulting from the rise in precarity is increasingly likely.

Scholars writing about the corporeal and affective turns intend to resolve the issue of disembodiment in research, which is particularly vital for any analysis of the implications of quantifying the self when the self is considered a monist entity where body and mind are not separated and where quantification is antagonistic. Contemporary management attempts to control and measure affective and emotional labour are symptoms of endemic precarity.

Affect and Its Capture

The term 'affect' is sometimes used incorrectly as a fashionable euphemism for emotion or feeling. Instead, emotional labour is the visible production of affective labour. It can be understood as the correspondence between body and mind that is not instantly knowable in the way that emotion and affections may be. Affective labour becomes public, or at least made known to management who pay selective attention, through the quantified measure of emotions which were, in the case of the company project we studied, stress and subjective impressions of productivity. I use the term 'unseen labour' (Moore et al., 2017) to discuss affective and emotional labour to recognise the work that is done in these terrains as not being identical, but being intimately associated. Unseen labour leads to social reproduction in that it is work that reaches behind, below, and above the usually unproblematised behaviours at work. This type of labour involves the attitudinal aspects of work and involves workers' emotional expression or reactions, whether the producer's, client's or co-workers.

Precarity is rife in work that is affective and emotional. Silvia Federici's comments on 'Precarious Labour: A Feminist Viewpoint' confirms that there is a rise in fragmentation of work and experiences of work, but warns against homogenising workers' experiences by giving work that overlooks 'women's unpaid reproductive labour as a key source of capitalist accumulation' the label 'precarity' (2008). The intention in management techniques using self- and other-tracking is precisely *to capture* and to *prevent* full affectivity, precisely because the communities which form, and a deep consciousness about the 'self' outside of prescribed versions, could result in collective resistance. The power of affect is its refuge from both the knowable corporeal and the cognitive realms that are defended in Cartesian inspired Western philosophy. It is also powerful because it is at this level of affect that bodies have a radical impact on one another. This concept has inspired thinking about how social change occurs through the emergence of a multitude (Negri, 2002). Negri reasons that the singularity of affect is defensible because it 'poses action beyond every measure that power does not contain in itself, in its own structure and in the continuous restructurings that it constructs' (Negri, 1999: 85). At the same time affect is also universal, because 'affects construct a commonality among subjects' (Ibid.). So, 'as an entirely Spinozan thematic, we have above all that of the body, and in particular that of the power of the body' (Negri, 2002: 41); resolving as an ontological point that the mind is the idea of the body and body is the object of the mind. Action is permitted or prevented by affect; this is perhaps the most important aspect of this concept and has inspired a wealth of research. When management uses technologies of corporeal control they position the body against the mind with recognition of the unknown capabilities of embodied subjectivities; individualising and quantifiying subjectivity to prevent full affectivity and shared affinity across workers.

It is perhaps not a surprise that management systems have begun to seek to capture and control unseen labour because when workers become conscious of affect, or their power to act, they also become conscious of their ability to impact one another and to challenge abuses at work. This occurs through collaborative work, communication about working conditions and organising, which all start with affect. In that light, health care worker training is explicitly designed to modulate and regulate affect (Ducey, 2007). Gregg outlines the blockages to any affective communication induced by email and pseudo- intimacy in the office garnered by such activities as Secret Santas and other games that prevent affective relationships (Gregg, 2010). Cognitive behavioural therapy and related psychology highlight emotional and affect regulation for stress management at work and one group has provided the tools titled Affect Regulation (Psychology Tools, 2016). Indeed, Beller states that the development of *capital is not likely to proceed without the development of technologies for the modulation of affect* (Beller, 1998: 91, italics added).

Deleuze maintains that:

> Spinoza will be firm in telling us that what counts among animals is not at all the genera or species... What counts is the question, of what is a body capable? And thereby he sets out the most fundamental questions in his philosophy by saying that the only question is that we don't even know what a body is capable of, we prattle on about the soul and the mind and we don't know what a body can do.
>
> (Deleuze, 1978)

The body is not translated in the singular in Spinoza's work, neither from the mind nor from other bodies. Recognising the monist quality of the self and our dependence on another will facilitate solidarity and collective action. Negri calls the refusal to commit to the purely Galilean physical or spatial limitations or the metaphysical dimensions a 'unitary nexus' which is intended to presuppose class struggle, and the dialectic, because activity of the masses is foundational to social and political transformation. Deleuze notes that 'a body must be defined by the ensemble of relations which compose it, or, what amounts to the same thing, by its power of being affected' (Deleuze, 1978). His point is directly taken from Spinoza, indicating that bodies are both *affected* and *act*, but not in one sequence nor in a specific spatial context. This is not a moral question, Deleuze tells us, but:

> ...as long as you don't know what power a body has to be affected, as long as you learn like that, in chance encounters, you will not have the wise life, you will not have wisdom... A body has something fundamentally hidden: we could speak of the human species, the

human genera, but this won't tell us what is capable of affecting our body, what is capable of destroying it, the only question is the power of being affected.

(1978)

Spinoza's rejection of dualisms was an isolating claim when placed against Newtonian assumptions that inform most revelations in Enlightenment thought. Spinoza's claim that there is one substance or one essence of being rather than a separation between an immanent deity and the human violated religious principles of his time and caused his excommunication as already mentioned. This philosopher did not deny the existence of God, but did not recognise the separation between God and man; neither did he recognise the separation of mind with body/brain. In *Ethics*, Spinoza also pointed out the mistakes of those who perceive God to have the same characteristics as man and consider God to be a measurable and identifiable body with a mind and passions. Meanwhile, he noted, misguided theorists claim that man has been created *by God*. Spinoza asked: how can this be possible? If God is infinite, as these same theorists also claim, how can he be quantifiable and identifiable in particle form in the same way that man is (mis)understood? Further, these claims separate the corporeal/extended substance from the divine nature, and again state that the former is a creation by God. These binarisms are faulty, Spinoza noted, not in the tone of an atheist but with the insight of a philosopher who challenged spatial, temporal, quantifiable and otherwise measurable assumptions about the human experience of life common to modernity and now seen in the self-tracking movement. Spinoza further asserted that divisibility is purely a function and characteristic of imagination and intellect and that, though it is 'very difficult to do', if we fully make use of our intellect, we will see that 'quantity... [is] substance... infinite, one and indivisible... matter is everywhere the same' (*Ethics*). Attempts to quantify the precarity of human experience in contemporary life seal the divisions between the corporeal and the cognitive, alienating humans from one another except in externally approved scenarios.

The key unknown revealed in Spinoza's work is the exact capability of bodies: bodies that are influenced by one another; by cognitive responses to stimuli (as is detailed in the emotional labour literature); as well as in relation to affect, which is not identical to these registers. For Spinoza, the relationship between the body and the mind and vice versa is organic and does not have a temporal or a specific spatial context. What all bodies have in common is the capacity for movement, whether tangible or symbolic. The role of affect is not the same as the emotive responses to the representations we form based on corporeal experiences. It is seen in the enabling or disabling of our capacity to act, the power to act, puissance, as opposed to affections or emotions which are reactions to constituted environments and relations of power (pouvoir).

Descarte's dualism leads him to rate the body against the mind and in so doing, locates superiority in the mind, a point that Giancotti (1997) emphasises is impossible, since 'in reality and in perfection, in relation to another mind, its object, that is the human body, would have to be known more fully' for this comparison to be accurately made. Spinoza wrote that:

> [I]n proportion as a body is more capable than others of doing many things at once, or being acted on in many ways at once, so its mind is more capable than others of perceiving many things at once. And in proportion as the actions of a body depend more on itself alone, and as other bodies concur with it less in acting, so its mind is more capable of understanding distinctly.
>
> (1677/2003)

Spinoza warned us not to think that the body acts only when nature or the mind tells it to do so, by pointing out the active unconscious body, such as a sleepwalker who does things he/she would not dare to do when awake, or an animal (which he called a 'brute'), whose actions 'far surpass human sagacity' (1677/2003). Spinoza claimed that this 'is sufficient to show that the body itself, merely from the laws of its own nature alone, can do many things, at which the mind marvels' (Ibid.):

> PROP. VI. Everything, in so far as it is in itself, endeavours to persist in its own being.
>
> PROP. VII. The conatus, wherewith everything endeavours to persist in its own being, is nothing else but the actual essence of the thing in question.

To look at the corporeal and affective dimensions of cognitive and corporeal productivity that are part of the ontological investigation for the current book, we now turn to new materialist readings of the body and the mind. The previous chapter analysed labour processes throughout time to identify how technology appropriates labour and what kinds of subjectivities are expected in each time frame. Labour process theorists provide Marxist interventions which, like Marxist feminists including Jarrett (2015, 2016), are more willing to look at non-cognitive labour as value producing, and to consider ontologies, as well as philosophise about how processes occur. Althusser famously criticised Marxists for not looking at the theory of knowledge outside the binaries of classical economics. He claimed that dialectical materialism should be read differently, and that it is superior precisely because Marx looked at society as a whole, and looked at a very human structure and ideology. While Althusser saw humanism in much of Marx's work (which others had not done) and despite Spinoza's influence on Marx, Althusser himself did not explicitly address the concept of affect or the liberating possibilities these technologies introduce. To do so, I now outline the changing landscape of ontology we may need to inhabit in order to fully understand, as well as provide critique of quantification, particularly as its ontology begins to enter workplaces.

New materialism/Neo-materialism and Cross-Disciplinary Discussions

Starting in the first years of the new millennium, debates on materialism have been revived or labelled as something 'new' in a variety of disciplines and theoretical commitments. In both feminism and Marxist political economy, these debates are linked to corporeal and affective turns. These 'turns', as outlined above, are a response to the blind spots that emerged with the dominance of discourse analysis seen in constructivism and cultural studies. Materialism and the corporeal had been overlooked. Indeed, the affective and corporeal turns strove to address this gap in previous scholarship, and are part of the process of renewal in what has been termed 'new materialism'.

It is perhaps no coincidence that the intensification of interest in 'bringing the body back in' occurs as two global economic crises occurred in the late 1990s and again in the late 2000s. Work restructure, redundancies and an impenetrable job market for young people left millions wondering how they could pay rent or a mortgage. When someone feels like they are making a choice between buying lunch or a bus pass, s/he faces some of the most basic issues of the body, such as where s/he will sleep, what s/he will eat. The widening inequality gap is not a dry statistic; scholarly interest in the discursive has been affected by a growing panic over possible hunger. Unprecedented anxieties crept into the once seemingly secure middle class. People have been awoken, sensitised and politicised. The material has re-entered discussions. New materialism sets out to approach studies of life and knowledge in new ways that better reflect contemporary circumstances where survival is biological and production is often virtual.

Feminist New Materialism

New materialism is not one theory or one unified stance (van der Tuin and Dolphijn, 2010) but is an intellectual movement and approach, a field of enquiry to explore a monist way of being, with influences from Deleuze, Neitzsche, Berson, Proust, Kafka and others. The radical sense of materialism engenders immanent non-linear thought. It is seen to break from transcendental humanist thought and the ontological fallacies of Cartesian dualism, as well as the limitations in the discourse that was haunting research in cultural theory and political economy. Manuel DeLanda and Rosi Braidotti are credited with coining the term 'new materialism' in the late 1990s (their research in philosophy and postmodern feminism, respectively, used the term independently of one another). DeLanda's *Thousand Years of Nonlinear History* (1997) had earlier mapped the journey to study 'newness' in the material. Braidotti tested ontological assumptions in her *Metamorphoses: Towards a Materialist Theory of Becoming* in 2002. The 2010 volume *New Materialisms: Ontology, Agency and Politics* edited by Diana Coole and Samantha Frost (2010) set the scene with chapters by Jane Bennett, William Connolly, Rosi Braidotti and several others. Also in 2010 Iris van der Tuin and Rich Dophijn published 'The Transversality of New Materialism' in *Women: A Cultural Review.*

Braidotti encourages a renewed analysis of 'the embodied structure of human subjectivity after Foucault' (Braidotti, 2000: 158). As Spinoza wrote in *Ethics*, 'a human being consists of a mind and a body, and... the human body exists, as we are aware of it' (2003, Part II, Prop. 13 cor.). Feminist new materialisms introduce the concept of the 'abstract machine' (Deleuze and Guattari 1980/1987, cited in van der Tuin and Dolphin, 2010), or 'processes without form or substance that can be found in concrete assemblages of biology, sociology, geology, enabling cultural theory to move away from linguistic representationalism' (Ibid.). New materialism is a response to too much focus on representation and the reliance on language and communication in cultural studies, which overlook the complexity and breadth of human experience. New materialists from the affective and corporeal turns make the point that matter influences how things happen; simply put, matter is not just a collection of things to be acted upon. Braidotti writes about embodied memories and subjectivities with the aim to override monist dichotomies (Braidotti, 2000). New materialism is interested in dynamic and virtual generativity that is not causally linear, reductive or representationalist, with interest in de-territorialisations as opposed to counter-identities' that should break through naturalising tendencies of both sexist humanism and postmodern feminisms.

Enthusiasm for research on discourse and subjectivity in the field of international politics was driven by such authors as Laclau and Mouffe (1985), whose work in social constructivism looks at regimes of signs and of hegemonic strategies that include discourses of power. While the media and other actors' roles in manufacturing consent are intuitively convincing, these authors' research, along with social constructivism more generally, has been critiqued for being reductionist and not considering any actors in social change in focusing on cognitive processes. The emphasis on discourse neglects complexity and any non-linear theorisation noting relations of domination.

DeLanda critiques social constructivism for focusing too much on meaning rather than action, noting that limiting our discussions to categories, rather than actions and how they shape perception, are not as important as:

> ...unequal legal rights and obligations which are attached by government organisations to a given classification, as well as practices of

exclusion, segregation and hoarding of opportunities which sort people out into ranked groups. Thus, activists trying to change a given
category are not negotiating over meanings, as if changing the semantic
content of a word automatically meant a real change in the opportunities and risks faced by a given social group, but over access to resources
(income, education, health, services) and relief from constraints.

(DeLanda, 2006: 62)

New materialism, ontologically, from the feminist angle, is not only an idea
or a philosophical treatise, but is lived, practiced, and agential. Using the empirical example of sensory technologies in workplaces covered in Chapter 4,
we can see that there is more than an academic 'turn' in thinking about the
material. 'Material' is the term I use to encompass the corporeal and the
affective to emphasise their inseparability. The integration of sensory technologies into workplaces shows management's recognition of the material
aspect of work: affective, corporeal and potentially emancipatory. How
material emancipation may be defined is where things become interesting.
The dominance over how quantification is determined and how numeration
is deciphered as related both to production and time, are well-established
methods for control in work where capitalist hegemony is maintained.
Quantifying day-to-day productivity and work is one thing. Quantifying
the body as though it were inherently separate from the mind, is another.

Marxist Neo/New Materialism

We now look at Marxist materialism within international political economy research, to identify how and whether the new materialism emerging
from these circles intersects with feminist, Spinozian discussions. To begin this discussion, I turn to French communist theorist Althusser, who
distinguished between Marx's earlier and later work. Many orthodox
Marxists have only read his later work, but Marx's earlier work, such as the
Grundrisse and *Economic and Philosophical Manuscripts of 1844* look at
possibilities for a philosophy of social change which have largely informed
post-autonomist work.

Jeffrey Harrod began to refer to a 'neo-materialist approach' in the early
2000s in talks at the International Studies Association, which he later
published in 2006 in an edited collection by Matt Davies and Magnus
Ryner (Davies and Ryner, 2006). As discussed above, Laclau and Mouffe
(1985) contributed to the neo-Gramscian school of research from a social
constructivist perspective, but Jeffrey Harrod's engagement with Gramsci's
ideas comes from a different place. Harrod called for an updating of standard theses on materialism, looking for a 'neo-materialist' approach that
takes the most important activity of humankind - (productive work)' and
'observes that this involves different patterns of power relations, argues
that the world views of individuals are developed from or influenced by

these patterns, and that such world views are important to mobilization and political action' (2006: 40) . Harrod (2006) recalls a set of theses which he and Robert Cox devised (albeit in separate publications) on how power occurs in the global political economy; Cox referred to 'power, production and world order' and Harrod 'power, production and the unprotected worker'. Harrod points out that the focus on production is astute, but if it relies on Marx's theory of capitalism and production that focuses on alienation and surplus value it is overly narrow and looks too much like it could simply be called 'industrialisation'. Different modes of production contain their own exploitative relations and a theory of production should not be confined to anthropocentric histories such as feudalism or a currently non-existent form of pure communism. Rather, to explain what can be new in new (historical) materialism, Harrod turns to the work of Poulantzas and of Mao to show their deviance from a strict Marxist conceptualisation of class and power based on industrial modes of production.

Poulantzas was interested in a plurality of modes in social formations, but ultimately does not specify non-capitalist modes or dominant formations unless they were historic. On the other hand, Mao did. He identified renting peasants and small handcraft labourers within a class of the 'semi-proletariat' and self-employed artisans and owner peasants as petit-bourgeois in pre-industrial China. However, Mao neglected to look at household production in his 1926 pamphlet. He later corrected this in 1927 stating that,

> As for women, in addition to being dominated by these three systems of authority, they are also dominated by the men (the authority of the husband). These four authorities - political, clan, religious and masculine - are the embodiment of the whole feudal-patriarchal system and ideology, and are the four thick ropes binding the Chinese people, particularly the peasants.
>
> (cited in Harrod, 2006)

Despite neither Mao nor Poulantzas highlighting the significance of their interests in demonstrating power relations in alternative modes of production (and the obvious problems with overlooking Mao's own macabre practices during his time of rule), their theories pave the way for neo-materialism.

Harrod is clear that within different modes of production, there are unprotected workers who experience the world differently than the iconic industrial workers during the years Marx lived and wrote. Unprotected workers fall within six categories: subsistence peasants, renting peasants, the unemployed and casualised workers, self-employed, small enterprise workers and domestic labourers. Workers in each category experience varied power relations and so hold varied rationalities and consciousness as well as modes of resistance such as everyday forms of peasant resistance. These concepts are reminiscent of 'habitus' and urge research not to rely on a political economic framework of industrial capitalism alone. Harrod sees 'newness' as becoming necessary when we look at modes of production, since much of Marxist work is dependent on the industrial model (Ibid.). In particular, unprotected workers in all kinds of newer production scenarios must be acknowledged.

Separately, Paul Cammack published a paper in *Historical Materialism* in 2003 where he identifies 'new materialism', talking about this as an update of Marx's historic materialism. In Cammack's work new materialism is depicted in a strictly temporal and spatial sense. Cammack identifies capitalist expansion through the means of intensified multilateralism. What is 'new' is that the promotion of capitalism in rival states occurs at an international level (2003: 40–1). Thus, the newness in Cammack's version of new materialism is limited to a loose updating of a historical period and the scale of expansion. Marxist new materialists thus continue to work within an orthodox conceptualization of history. Despite using the same label for a seemingly new intervention in research, the texts published by Cammack, the debate he started with Taylor (2005) and Charnock (2008) and the work of Harrod do not explore their own assumptions at an ontological level as the corporeal and affective turn in feminist and other areas of inquiry do. While the small number of neo-materialist Marxists encourage a focus on global forces and production, they do not fully address questions of gender (Tepe-Belfrage and Steans, 2016). However, interpretations of a Marxist, human centric history relies on limited conceptualisations of the corporeal, with no concept of affect, and depends on the linearity of history. Where the new materialisms outlined differ is that Marxist 'new materialists' continue to work within these boundaries.

In 2013, Nick Srnicek, Maria Fotou and Edmund Arghand edited a special issue in *Millennium: Journal of International Studies* entitled 'Materialism and World Politics' which continued discussions on 'how does matter matter?' in the field of international politics. The introduction indicates that questions of matter have been overlooked for too long. While international politics and political economy researchers have put forward theses on the impending 'environmental catastrophe' (2013), asked questions of structure and agency, looked at technology and highlighted biopolitics and, to some extent, bodies, Srnicek, Foutou, Arghand and the other writers in the collection begin to look at the material bases for these questions. Editors indicate that 'the most common approach in International Relations has been to see material things as forming an inert backdrop for the play of social forces' (Srnicek et al., 2013: 397). In this issue, Connolly (2013) recalls what is human about social relations and highlights the 'fragility of things'; Barry (2013) calls for a renewed compatibility between actor-network theory and international relations; Cudworth and Hobden (2013) look at agency beyond the human, looking to Archer's work in primary and corporate agency; and Coole (2013) asserts that the new materialist ontology is one of immanence rather than transcendence.

Aside from this special issue, there is very little discussion of the ontological or recognition of the corporeal; unseen labour; or gender. More broadly, the issue with Marxist political economy versions of new materialism is that they neither clarify the physicality, affectivity or corporeality of unprotected work. Nor do they identify as Tepe-Belfrage and Steans (2016) indicate, the depths of suffering involved in relations of production and reproduction. The work of Smith and Lee (2015) argues that we must closely look at the impacts of corporeal capitalism Cohen (et al) provide a much needed analysis of body work, looking at overlapping categories of work that happens to bodies, on bodies; but also recognising the 'embodiment of labour and that of the body, emotions and sexuality are sites of commodification' (Cohen et al., 2013). Other critical political economy researchers have interrogated our assumptions in labour research and critiqued political economy for removing the body from any enquiry (Bruff, 2011, 2013; Davies, 2005, 2009; Fischer and Tepe, 2011; McFadden, 2015; Peterson, 2005; Pettman, 1997; Roberts, 2015; Smith and Lee, 2015) and Marxist feminist arguments in social reproduction have likewise worked in this area. But more work is needed.

Possibilities for Marxist Ontology

The Ancient Greeks, Democritus, Leucippus and Epicurus, looked for 'ontological truth of materials, speculating their inner workings and principles into extreme mathematics' (Gottlieb, 2016). Baruch Gottlieb states that we have over-speculated questions of materiality to the point that the 'objective is not philosophy but reliability, the mastering of measurable behaviour of materials in the service of human needs' (Ibid.) I would add, *some* human's needs. This becomes particularly relevant as machines take a more intimate and dominant role in the labour process and employment relationship, working both to exacerbate the divide between mental and manual labour and to make emotional and affective labour abstract and its qualitative dimensions unseen.

As identified above, Marxist political economy research that identifies a 'new materialism' fails to recognise that Marx dealt with the concept of the nature of the material to involve the body and people's impact on one other, in his thinking. Indeed, Marx was inspired by Spinoza, which is overlooked in Marxist new materialist research. In 1976, Ollman said that the 'nub of our difficulty in understanding Marxism, whose subject matter is not simply society, but society conceived of *relationally*' (1976: 14–15, emphasis added). Capital, labour, value, commodities, etc. are all relations, containing within themselves integral elements of what they are. Marxists tend to see features in the labour process as externally tied. But Marx was not unaware of the corporeal or nature. This does not mean he would be a 'new materialist' today. It does mean that there could be space for dialogue across an age old 'divide' between Marxists and poststructuralist researchers, reflected in the way both disciplines have begun discussions on 'new materialism'.

There are hints of ontology in Marx's work that do not overlook the corporeal or the interrelatedness of life beyond the social. In *Marx, The Body and Human Nature* (2015), John C. Fox argues (similar to earlier points made by Althusser) that like Spinoza and Hegel—and indeed, influenced by them—Marx rejected thinking about a being's nature in terms of substance. Marx also knew that all beings, including human beings, are interdependent. This is the basis for the relationship between humanity, objects and the material. Objects are not separate from, but are part of our nature as human beings. Fox cites Marx extensively from 'Excerpts from James Mill's Elements of Political Economy' to look at Marx's central theses on nature and the corporeal. Usually called 'Comments on James Mill', this less cited piece was written in 1844 and first published in Marx and Engels' *Gesamtausgabe*, published in 1932 and then translated and published by C. Dutt in the *Collected Works*. In his Paris Notebooks, Marx commented on classical economists, and his comments on James Mill are the most developed and coherent. He develops many of his other points in *Economic and Philosophical Manuscripts*. Marx writes that relations between material and humanity are needed to 'complete... existence and to realise essence' (Marx, 1975d: 267, cited in Fox, 2015: 132). Marx's use of 'essence' looks like it follows a tradition of argument first developed by Spinoza. Fox cites Marx saying 'man lives from nature, i.e. nature is his body, and he must maintain a continuing dialogue with it if he is not to die.

While it would be an exaggeration to say that Marx was not ontologically dualist, he did not neglect discussions of nature and the body and looked at the agential in the material (which is also seen in *Fragment on Machines*). These are the moments in Marx's work that allow for possibilities of cross-disciplinary dialogue that may lead to better discussions about emancipation and a better-informed critical political economy. Indeed, researchers have abandoned some of Marx's most important insights. The new materialist revival in Marxist critical political economy should recognise this. An ontology of corporeality and possibilities for transformation via social forces are found throughout Marx's work, making the possibilities for a Marxist new materialism primarily based in his work (rather than interpretations already mentioned) far more plausible with possibility for transversality of interpretation.

In *Economic and Philosophical Manuscripts* (EPM), written in 1844 and published posthumously, Marx alludes to tools as part of an extended inorganic body in a way that suggests he thought about relationships with objects as less externally, than internally, derived.

To say that man's physical and mental life is linked to nature simply means that nature is linked to itself'. Also in EPM Marx states that:

> As a natural, corporeal, sensuous objective being, [the human] is a suffering, conditioned and limited being... the objects of his drives exist outside him as objects independent of him; but these objects are objects of his need, essential objects, indispensable to the exercise and confirmation of this essential powers. To be sensuous, i.e. to be real, is to be an object of sense, a sensuous object, and thus to have sensuous objects outside oneself, objects of one's sense perception. To be sensuous is to suffer (to be subjected to the actions of another). Man as an objective sensuous being is therefore a suffering being, and because he feels his suffering, he is a passionate being. Passion is man's essential power vigorously striving to attain its object.
>
> (Marx, 1844/1959)

In *Comments on James Mill*, Marx states that: 'Instead of money, or paper, it is my own personal existence, my flesh and blood, my social virtue and importance, which constitutes the material, corporeal form of the spirit of money'. Fox cites Foster and Burkett to discuss external and internal relations with tools:

> ...in ancient Greek usage, the word 'organ' also means 'tool' and organs were initially viewed as 'grown on tools' of animals whereas tools were regarded as the artificial organs of human beings... characteristic of the natural dialectical worldview of the ancient Greeks was the recognition of a close relationship between tools as extensions of human being and the organs of animals because they were both part of the general process of adaptation to natural conditions.
>
> (Foster and Burkett, 2000: 408, cited in Fox, 2015: 135)

Marx's use of 'organic' and 'inorganic' are influenced by Hegel. The extended inorganic body is not an independent self-contained entity one comes across in the traditional debate concerning nature or substance. 'Instead,' Fox argues, 'it represents the depth and breadth of involvement explored by Spinoza and those worked within his legacy, a view of being as open and interdependent' (2015: 135). Indeed, Marx was heavily influenced by Spinoza which, again, the Marxist neo-materialists overlook. Further to this, recognition of where Althusser and the post-autonomists have intervened to identify Marx's recognition of the corporeal, as well recalling the debates between Marx and Feurbach (Marx, 1845/1938) would enhance Marxist neo-materialism. Not a Marxist neo-materialist as such, but within the post-autonomist camp, Negri, in *The Savage Anomaly* (1991), engages with Marx's dialectic cast in a Spinozian frame. Negri is right to spot possible sangam in contemporary discussions of praxis, revolution, and solidarity with these philosophers in mind (recognising that Marx probably did not call himself a philosopher).

The radical perspectives initiated by Marx and Spinoza should be re-investigated if only to ask, what *exactly* is it about our 'selves' that allows us to act to make our own histories, as Marx postulated? Fracchia asks us to look at the corporeal possibilities for and limitations to how involved we can be in making our own histories in conditions not of our own choosing (Fracchia, 2005: 55). He notes that Marx's understanding of use value and concrete labour are vital to the logic of capitalist exploitation and exchange value. To identify the relevance of Spinozian ideas in Marx's work, Fracchia investigates the confluence between absolute and relative surplus value. Workplace exploitation can be detected by identifying 'deformation of the body, the flip side of which is that the free cultivation of bodily attributes and capacities is essential to any historical materialist notion of freedom' (Ibid.: 41).

So while Marx was perhaps not a monist, he recognised relations between the material, living labour and objectified labour. Ontologically he does not exclude agency of machines, where 'living (active) machinery, which confronts his individual, insignificant doings as a mighty organism' (Marx, 1858/1993: 693). Automation, as I argue in Chapter 4, is not a blunt instrument, where one robot replaces one human. Instead, technologies perform more types of work and fulfil more aspects of work, a trend that can sometimes give more work to people rather than render more efficient labour processes. Machines are also given more authority, requiring transformed subjectivities of workers as discussed previously. Marx's *Fragment on Machines* was read by post-autonomists (Negri, 1991; Tomba and Bellofiore, 2013) who viewed it as a fresh reading of capital, power relations and subjectivity when faced with technology. During his lifetime Marx observed the ways in which early industrialisation turned 'living labour into a mere living accessory of this machinery, as the means of its action, also posits the absorption of the labour process in its material character as a mere moment of the realisation process of capital' (Marx, 1858/1993: 693). These augural comments continue with: '[machinic] knowledge appears as alien' and 'external' to the worker where the worker is 'superfluous' (brackets added) (1858/1993: 605). In this text, Marx identifies the machine in the labour process and describes its capacity for quantification and division and of abstracting labour, commenting that 'the worker's activity, reduced to a mere abstraction of activity, is determined and regulated on all sides by the movements of the machinery, and not the opposite' (1858/1993: 693). In this way, Marx identifies agency, and even authority, to the machinery, where 'objectified labour confronts living labour within the labour process itself as the power which rules it; a power which, as the appropriation of living labour, is the form of capital' (Ibid.). The means of labour, Marx wrote, is transformed, controlled *and* absorbed by machinery.

Where Is the Study of Affect in (Critical) Political Economy?

I have already claimed that mainstream political economy (including the discipline of international political economy) relies on a dualism of mind and body. In fact, most political economy in political science and International Relations (which is usually called 'international political economy' or 'global political economy') does not look at technology in the labour process or recognise workers' subjectivity and affectivities. Here, I present findings from an audit of key journals in international political economy to identify research that looks at work and labour. I list the articles' arguments and identify these works' ontological positioning; concluding that these articles do not consider the body nor ontological questions where research on the body, the material and the subjective begin. This de-ontological position leads to a paralysis in research. For these reasons, I recommend researchers who look at work and labour in *critical* political economy consider their ontological assumptions and prepare for a full analysis of quantified labour to recognise how its divisibility works to obscure emancipatory relations. Then, I look at Marxist feminist research in critical political economy where social reproduction is recognised, noting that this research encapsulates the issues at stake for quantified workers.

Audit of Key Political Economy Journals

In 2012, I looked for the study of work and employment in critical international political economy (Moore, 2012). In this article, I note that a range of researchers have researched 'flexible labour markets, work, unions, migration, production and poverty' (Amoore, 2002; Bieler, 2008; Cerny, 1999; Davies, 2006; Harrod, 1987; Lewis, 2009; O'Brien, 2000a,b; Phillips, 2009; Ryner, 2006, cited in Moore, 2012: 232); but I encourage further discussions between those who have developed, within the British school of international political economy a distinctive critical political economy and researchers in industrial relations, labour process theory, heterodox economics, comparative political economy and varieties of capitalism literatures.

Now, to explicitly carve out an emerging area in critical political economy, I set out, here, to ask where the study of the body and the corporeal is, in political economy and international political economy journals. So first, I outline articles on work and labour in two key journals in the area. Then, I look at the nascent area of political economy research which looks at corporeal, the body, the material, and work, and encourage a positive dialectic for discussions, where research in Marxist social reproduction meets new materialism research emerging from feminist research in other disciplines.[1]

In 1998, in the journal *New Political Economy* (NPE), Carnoy gives an account of how technologies are changing the world of work, emphasising the need for pedagogies and curriculum to correspond with the new technologies. These themes are rarely seen in international political economy journals, but reflect my research concerns regarding how the political economy of knowledge has infiltrated the education curriculum (Moore, 2010). However, Carnoy assumes that work and work expectations would rapidly change with the growing IT bubble. He hesitates when identifying the corporeal features of this transformation by stating that people will be expected to shift jobs several times during a working life, to move geographically and 'if necessary, to learn entirely new vocations' (1998: 124). However, the greater part of the analysis relies on an uncritical view of how education must change to prepare people for an exhilarating new world of work. The article emphasises cognitive skills that are needed, i.e., 'creativity, enterprise and scholarship' (Blunkett, 1998). It is one of many articles that rely on a Cartesian division.

Gardiner, in the same year and also in the journal NPE, published a piece that looks at the failure of the human capital thesis in economics to take reproductive labour into consideration. Gardiner cites Mill's recognition of the disproportionate share of women in housework, 'women are in the constant practice of passing quickly from one manual, and still more from one mental operation to another' (Mill, 1865: 29, cited in Gardiner, 1998: 4). Mill was happy to place teachers and doctors in the category of productive human capital but does not view women's affective labour in other spheres such as domestic or digital work in the same way. Thus, the author overlooks social reproduction and the corporeal dimensions of work. In *International Organization*, Caraway et al. (2012) set out to investigate whether workers' pressure groups have had an impact on IMF loan conditions. Interestingly, this piece reports that labour conditionalities have been present in only one-fourth of all IMF programmes since 1987.

Governments of countries with strong labour movements suffer fewer impositions affecting workers' interests than those with weak preexisting representation. Rather than examining specific interests and related pressures on government and IMF decision-making, this article demonstrates that 'countries with stronger labour movements will receive less intrusive, labour related loan conditions than those with weak labour movements' (Ibid.). The IMF technically only negotiates with governments and has no direct involvement with domestic interest groups, so the argument of this article, i.e. that citizen pressure groups have had an impact on IMF conditionality is debatable. Furthermore, the almost exclusive reliance on IMF-owned data for proof that interest groups have had an impact on final conditions demonstrates an absence of consultation with people experiencing reforms and the corporeal aspects of rising uncertainties in all post-austerity cases. Corporeal and material aspects of structural adjustment include the rise in precarity and a reduction of places to work (transferring investment in offices to home work for example) as seen in the computing industry context; forced living conditions such as the rise in young people continuing to live at home and the lack of home-owning channels; the rise in work-related illnesses, and the inability to put food on tables and clothes on bodies directly resulting from loss of wages. Ontologically, this article is committed to the cognitive and the rational and avoids any deeper investigation.

Political economy research that begins to fill in the absence of corporeality in understanding work in *New Political Economy* has been published by Barrientos (1996) and Onuki (2009), whose pieces look at, respectively, women working in Latin America and Filipino care workers in Japan. Mulholland and Stewart (2013) look at workers' struggles with lean logistics. Hudson highlights recognition of material transformation in production as value creating, which will contribute to the critical political economy debates (Hudson, 2012), but does not look at the corporeal aspects of materiality. Other research on work, labour and production in this same journal includes Breen (2012) and May (2002) and relies on policy-based methodologies and idea-based rationales. In *Review of International Political Economy,* research that begins to demonstrate an understanding of the limitations of cognitive or mental and text-based research includes Elias (2010) and Steans and Tepe (2010). However, other pieces in related fields in this and other journals include Nederveen Pieterse (2002), Lockea and Romis (2010), Larner (2002), Paczynska (2007), Kong (2006), Scheuerman (2001), and Murphy (2014); writing pieces which rely on text-based methodologies, policy and organisational analyses, effectively prolonging the absenting of bodies, the corporeal, or studies that reflect everyday struggle.

Research that can challenge the omission of the corporeal includes interventions from feminist IPE, research on unfree labour, autonomist ideas, the burgeoning literature on precarity and some aspects of neo-Gramscian research. Cameron et al. (2013) put the focus on the body and its relation to the state, a much needed comment on the oversight in most political research that has taken a turn toward the knowledge/power nexus. Too often, 'arguments ignore the physical materiality inherent to the constitution and daily reproduction of social relationships which require our body to be sold on the labour market in order to receive an income and thus survive; that is, the compulsion to be a commodity' (Bruff, 2013: 73). Raess (2006) asks us to look at "human corporeal organisation as a 'first fact' of historical materialism". Hudson (2012) challenges political economy researchers to look more closely at the material, or 'stuff that things are made of' (Bakker and Bridge, 2006, cited in Hudson, 2012) in analyses of production. What is missing from much political economy is research that looks at corporeal dimensions of everyday life and suffering in capitalism, and the experiences of unprotected and precarious workers whose lives are being put under intensified pressure directly because of new forms of technologically induced quantification. In conclusion, most political economy and international political economy research focusses on issues that are not about the corporeal or overlook those aspects. Much more needs to be done to pry political economy research from the allure of international organisations' policy documents and the assumptions of secondary literature. As it is now, the canon of work in this area is ontologically shallow. Researchers can learn from the insights from new materialism in feminist and Marxist circles, and it is necessary to do so, for a rich understanding of the quantified self at work.

Marxist Social Reproduction and Measuring Unseen Labour

I now turn to identify how research in the Marxist social reproduction arena provides a framework for me to look at the current stage of management efforts in the period of agility that I outlined in Chapter 2. Agile, as I have emphasised, accepts that constant transformation and change are part of our contemporary world of work. What agile advocates overlook is the labour of emotional and affective resilience necessary to withstand constant change. This form of work is usually not paid, and predominantly impacts women. As such, the unseen parts of work that allow workers to continue to work and to be cared for (or to care for themselves) are captured in a process of social reproduction of capitalist labour relations (Dowling, 2016; Gill and Bakker, 2003; Kofman, 2012; Weeks, 2011), work that reaches behind, below and above the seen behaviours at work. This involves attitudinal aspects of work, as well as workers' emotional expression and engagement with clients and co-workers to predict the possibility of bodily collapse. In the quantified workplace, management attempts to measure unseen labour through gathering physiological and psychological data. In the case of the company analysed in the next chapter, heartrate data (because heartrate is linked to stress) and weekday lifelogs that asked workers to rate their own subjective stress, productivity and wellbeing were collected.

Unseen labour happens at the physiological, psychological, affective and emotional levels. Unseen labour fuels social reproduction and maintains capitalist social relations, usually for free. Measuring affective labour helps capital to control labour by helping management identify how likely precarious workers are to collapse and become unable to work. Practices of affective measure seen in electronic performance tracking, surveillance and interface systems of the gig economy, and the threat of automation and algorithmic management, exacerbate, rather than resolve precarity. New techniques outlined below reflect an agile management system where affective and emotional labour involves the ability to withstand chaos and constant change. However, sites of social reproduction are used for 'novel control over bodies and labour power' but also encompass 'sites of resistance and refusal' (Staples, 2007: 121).

Measuring unseen labour is a form of control by means of the 'modulation of affect' by both recording and trying to control bodily capabilities through self-tracking devices, and thus 'varying the resistance of a body' (Bogard, 2010). These behaviours are not necessarily 'intentional' but, when seen in the aggregate, are used by management as though they are. This can be compared to the way that companies use data from consumers' product searches or purchasing patterns to push advertising toward them, as though one click gives evidence of continuous intentionality (Jarrett, 2014). For example, applying 'socio-metric solutions' (which involves a device worn around the neck) tracks and records workers' movements around offices, tone of voice and communication, and are used to identify patterns of movements and to assist management decisions regarding where to place furniture, best practices in communication or otherwise answer questions about efficiency. Management would like to observe and know about the labour involved in the processes of deciding, consciously or subconsciously, how to move one's arms, what tone of voice to use and where to go in the office. It is very easy to see how this will move into a discourse of what physical movements are required and most effective in offices, resonant of Taylor's depiction of the supposed correct movements for a pig-iron shoveller.

Pinning to the corporeal, affective labourers are not engaging in creative production using their own affective capacities; they are engaged in a type of affective repression in which required subordinate performances corrode their own psychosomatic and bodily wellbeing. Attempts to regulate and modulate affect are part of this process. Affective labour is, by definition, innumerable (Dowling, 2007; Hardt and Negri, 2000) and its outputs are potentially only seen as disembodied exhaust (Smith, 2016). Nonetheless, management pursues its capture with increasing intensity, not to give it value and perhaps, to start to pay for it, but because worker collapse, due to expectations of inevitable change endemic to agility, could also lead to mass resistance.

Work design techniques to measure *emotion* come about because lowered mood levels and stress can indicate evidence of burnout and imminent collapse that is symptomatic of periods of *change* expected from the new 'agile' world of work. The term affect is often used incorrectly in sociology as a fashionable euphemism for emotion or feeling (Ducey, 2007: 191). The attempt to capture *affect* occurs because comprehends that its full realisation could lead individuals to join forces and take full workplace control. New technologies offer the possibility to measure this otherwise unseen labour, including variable moods and subjectivities. Our research notes that these technologies come in similar packages as health and fitness, such as FitBits (measuring steps, sleep and heartrate); productivity tracking software like RescueTime (tracking individual screen time and judging productivity according to tailored categories); and daily lifelog emails asking participants about subjective stress, productivity and wellbeing. Other such projects include the Global Corporate Challenge and JawBone Up, which both offer a variety of tools and a dashboard that reveals data that is increasingly attractive to companies.

Theoretically, the capture of unseen labour power through self-tracking for corporate wellness programmes, leads to the transformation of concrete labour into abstract labour through commodification of unseen labour, giving the outputs of this labour a new prescription and label that eliminates any possibility for negativity: wellbeing. With this realisation, and

> ...even if the measurement of this new productive reality is impossible, because affect is not measurable, nonetheless in this very productive context, so rich in productive subjectivity, affect must be controlled.
>
> (Negri, 1999: 87)

Through attempts to capture unseen labour, management attempts to transform concrete to abstract labour and in doing so, recognises it as productive (see Jarrett, 2016). By highlighting the political and ideological moments of production, where the politics emerge from the possible use of data captured from unseen labour in the employment relationship; and where idealised health and wellbeing become an ideology; I address Burawoy's classic critique from 1984 where he notes labour process research overlooks these aspects in the labour process, and Massumi's critique of theories of affect that begin with stasis rather than process (2002).

Similarly, some Marxists argue that the 'deformation of the body, the flip side of which is that the free cultivation of bodily attributes and capacities is essential to any historical materialist notion of freedom' (Fracchia, 2005: 41). In Bergson, a similar counterpoint appears in the concept of intuition. This is a type of qualitative awareness of the field of becoming, which has its roots in the inner life, and orients to the creative becoming of life (Carr, 1912: 21). Intuition arises in holistic experiences, awareness of unique moments or beings, and in creative emotions such as joy, sympathy and love. Bergson portrays creative processes – including art and music – as occurring within the field of intuition, driven by the creative emotions (Bergson, 1997: 13–15, 175). The post-Marxist take on the affective turn typically emphasises affective labour, sometimes as part of a broader account of immaterial production (Hardt and Negri, 2000; Lazzarato, 1996; Virno, 2004). Affective labour is often seen as part of the process of human liberation through socialisation of production (e.g. Dowling, 2007; Hardt and Negri, 2000; Holmes, 2004; Virno, 2004). However, this view on affectivity risks reproducing the 'creative worker' discourse and the neglect of the body that it entails.

Without access to the qualitative, capitalism becomes a system of empty self and social reproduction, where data simply affirms the order it has already prefabricated. The system is circular and beset by a contradiction; it is functional, but lacks a functional goal, because it does not recognise the qualitative, or use-value, the unconscious, symbolic exchange. It is a functional system whereby everything functions to reproduce the system. Meaning and value, as subjective phenomena, are irretrievably lost, and distinct institutions become functionally equivalent. Paradoxically, it becomes a functionalism without functions (see Baudrillard, 1981: 77–8). This process reflects the saturation and implosion of capitalism, rather than its dynamism as an expanding system. Increasingly, this requires that the formerly inaccessible qualitative field be quantified so as to bring it in line with the economy. On a world scale, global cities, as command and control hubs for the world economy (Sassen, 1991: 3–4), arguably reproduce the Cartesian model by serving as the ruling brain and ego of the world system. A quasi-monopoly on processes of quantification and financialisation allows the continued dominant position of such sites. Quantification does not generate independent facts. The relationship between questions and answers within the system's quantitative reasoning is circular: the system receives answers which affirm it, because the questions are less a free choice than a 'test' or because they present false choices which lead back to the system (Baudrillard, 1987: 28–9).

Unseen Labour and Its Capture, the Quantified Self at Work

Emotional work is the other 'unseen labour' that is ripe for capture. Emotional labour is a moral obligation imposed by corporate power and it is usually expected of women. It can be both positive and negative; both emotional and affective labour are under the microscope of contemporary management initiatives. Negri (1999) posits that the use value of labour cannot be measured in contemporary conditions in the same way it was during previous eras, because labour no longer exists outside of capital as it did during feudalism. However, labour is also not directly 'inside' capital, nor is it a straightforward 'nonwaged reproduction of the labourer, added to labour's use value' (Clough, 2007: 25). Rather, in real subsumption, work happens constantly, all of the time, and is both nowhere and everywhere. Work is now all-of-life. Capital attempts to locate value in affect, transforming the potential for resistance into something productive for capital. Indeed, 'capital produces its own outside from inside the viscera of life, accumulating at the level of the preindividual bodily capacities and putting preindividual bodily capacities to work' (Clough, 2007: 25).

Hochschild (1983/2012) in *The Managed Heart* gave this type of work the name 'emotional labour' which is conducted at all stages of employment and for all purposes. Emotional labour is the self-management of emotion at work, whether it is suppressing anger or frustration with customers, or providing entertainment and attempts to produce joy in customers or co-workers. Hochschild outlined the emotional labour required in cabin crew and debt collection work (1983/2012) and Brook lists 'nurses, Disneyland workers, retail and childcare workers, schoolteachers, psychotherapists, holiday representatives, call-centre workers, bar staff, waiters and many others' (2009: 8) as requiring workers' emotional labour. Emotional labour involves the suppression of negative emotions brought about by instability and disruption endemic to the agile management model, where change is perceived as inevitable, and where the disruption and emotional anxiety should be supressed or re-invested. Quantified work is the panacea of the future, to identify how likely it is that workers will collapse or revolt. As identified, the measure of affective and emotional labour is a strategy to manage resistance.

Hochschild (1983/2012) in *The Managed Heart* looks at the way 'deep acting' affects the labour process and employment relationship. Displays of emotion confirm inequality, where deferential behaviour is seen as appropriate in 'servants and women' (1983/2012: 84). Hochschild talks about surface and deep acting as a 'resource', not like resources in therapy or art that are meant to facilitate self-discovery or fulfilment, but 'a resource to be used to make money' (1983/2012: 55). Emotional labour is the self-management of emotion at work, whether it is suppressing anger or frustration with customers, or providing entertainment and attempts to produce joy in customers or co-workers. Emotional labour is a moral obligation imposed by corporate power and is usually expected of women. It is one visible aspect of affective labour. Firth states that emotion 'usually refers to an individuated physical feeling (not mental or intellectual) that is passive (not active) and has a more-or-less irrational relationship to the world and outer life'. Firth contrasts this to affect, which is a 'necessary part of social and ecological assemblages, which passes through the unconscious field' (2016, 131). Dowling (2012: 111) looks at affective labour in service work, describing how waitresses at the high end of the restaurant market are subject to training manual requirements telling her to be

> ...concerned and dependable and maybe a little provocative. I am myself, the self I most want to be. I am committed to you and I will delight you. This is how we coproduce the product of my labour: your dining experience.

On a bodily level, affective labourers are not engaging in creative production using our own affective capacities; we are engaged in a type of affective repression in which required subordinate performances corrode our own psychosomatic and bodily wellbeing.

Management strategies of the contemporary agile management system discussed in the previous chapter are explicitly oriented around the capture and control of affect. As change and instability are both celebrated and imposed in agile systems, and workers' resultant stress made possible, if not likely, affect is measured not to improve wellbeing as the metaphorical packaging of workplace wellness initiatives portray, but because organisations rely on healthy workers to function. The production of subjectivity, emotions and responses to stressful situations (like workplace changes) are all features of affective and emotional labour, and the agile management of the quantified workplace relies on its capture.

If Bergson and Deleuze are right, then attempts to track all of life and work as seen in quantified affective and emotional labour are not an improved mapping of subjects and of life, but a subtler and more total regime of control, which extends Taylorist management into the field of the (formerly) qualitative. New technologies encourage people to identify with a representational, molar image of the self which emphasises self-branding and social performance, and fully neglects desire and becoming. Both Deleuze and Bergson reject dualism, because they see becoming (the qualitative) as ultimately underpinning being (the quantitative). In Bergson, the present self, which is a mind-body assemblage, is the point of intersection of the two fields of space and time. Space and time in contemporary workplaces are precarious and so-called agility systems capture this phenomenon. In an agile management system, the intention is to capture affective and emotional labour as they occur in conditions of precarity. When this process of capture is commodified, it becomes 'wellbeing'. In this labour process, concrete, personally valued labour, is made abstract.

Indeed, the output of physical, mental, emotional and affective labour is abstracted into measures of exchange value, and constant pressure is placed on the capitalist to 'keep up' with competitors by revising work procedures and checking that workers are as productive as those of competitors. Co-director for the Organization Design service line at McKinsey calls *agility* an almost ubiquitous situation, where 'enormous changes [are] coming from both inside and outside of the organization' and where 'you thrive on change and get stronger and it becomes a source of real competitive advantage' (Aghina, 2015). Work outputs need to be quantified by capital to assess a company's progress in achieving this aim, hence the need to monitor, control and measure work output and to invest in the latest technology to keep up with competitors in these times of endemic transformation.

Abstract labour is the root of estrangement of the product of labour from the individual and this process is all embracing within the dynamic of neoliberal capitalism. Abstracting unseen labour is the source of workers' alienation, whereby everything, including emotions and subjectivity, is commodified for the market place through quantification. Building on Marxist feminist research and feminist new materialism, the next sections look at the process of subjectification, or the ideal neoliberal moment where affective and emotional labour have been captured and commodified, and how precarious workers are expected to further align themselves to a new world of incessant changes.

Subjectification and Self-Precarisation: The Elimination of Refusal to Machinic Slavery?

Specifically, neoliberal capitalism 'must constitute itself subjectively.... develop the desires and habits necessary for it to perpetuate itself' (Read, 2010: 114). Neoliberalism remains a Cartesian subjectivity and system, abandoning rigid separations of Fordism and insisting on processual, systems-level thinking. It continues to subordinate such thinking to the project, as defined by a managerial self, effectively replacing truth with instrumentality as the main epistemic criterion. The managerial self, who manages both her/his subjectivity and the outer world, reproduces the Cartesian trope of the subordination of (risky) body to (rational) mind. Rolnik describes it as a process of each self, envisioned as an entrepreneur, 'managing all its relationships, choices, behaviours according to the logic of a costs/investment ratio and in line with the law of supply and demand' (2011: 47). She terms neoliberalism as a 'mirage of a smoothed-over, stable life under perfect control', a refusal of life as immanent difference-production (Rolnik, 2011: 28–9).

In the process of become precarious, 'everyone had to develop a relationship with the self, to control one's own body, one's own life by regulating and thus controlling oneself' (Lorey, 2011). Seeking one's inner self is a 'dominant feature of contemporary governmentality' (McRobbie, 2011: 127). (McRobbie, 2011: 127). Such discourse is heavily appropriated by authors such as Florida (2002) who celebrate the supposed transformative power of the knowledge-based economy despite its contradictions (Jessop, 2000). The upshot is a reified reality in which observable quantitative facts become fetishised effects of class power. Ajana reasons that the 'will to knowledge, is, indeed, never a neutral pursuit' (Ajana, 2017: 5). Quantification creates a gap between material relations and capitalist perceptions of these relations (De Angelis, 1996: 16, 20). This misperception is inherent to a neoliberal power relation because it serves as the basis for how people actually act (Ollman, 1971: 202). Quantification then operates as though it were observable, regular social laws, but the laws can only be observed as 'those which capital succeeds in imposing' (Cleaver, 1979: 66), reflecting Cartesian dualisms which are foundational in modern culture and which subordinate observed bodies to observing minds. Indeterminacy underpins such binaries and shows the difficulties in maintaining the primacy of the quantitative. This world is one where the qualitative, immaterial, affective and creative are increasingly central to production. The vivisection of the self into different component parts – observer and observed, public and private, worker on different projects and so on – is crucial to neoliberal production, even as it blurs all clear epistemic criteria for such separations, rendering them increasingly arbitrary effects of an ungrounded corporeal capitalist command.

Bergsonian duration is fundamentally immeasurable, because it is continuous and qualitative, and cannot be divided up into parts (Fujii, 2007; Guerlac, 2006: 166). What exists is never simply the given, or the observable or measurable, but also a field of qualitative forces which constantly produce difference and newness. Each of us has two selves, the external projection shown to others and the inner, deep self (Bergson, 1997: 173, 193–4); the former simply being the latter when oriented by attention to life. Scientific measuring processes can only ever see the superficial, external, 'spatial' self, not the deep inner self which exists in time (Guerlac, 2006: 76–7). It misses the moments when free agency and desire escape from determination. Life does not follow linear trajectories, but spreads out in different directions like a fan. From a purely instrumental point of view, this rarely matters because people can interact with objects without knowing their qualitative nature (2006: 160). Attentive stress pushes precarian and managerial subjects into the sensorimotor closure of 'attention to life'. But to transcend the field of survival, or to escape the repetition of habitual classifications, one needs to enter the field of the qualitative. The reduction of the whole of life to quantification is equivalent to locking-in existing categorical 'interests' and spatial schemas. If Bergson (and Deleuze) are right that there is no universality to inherent divisibility, then 'setting up differences of quantity between purely internal states' (Bergson, 1913/2001: 1) is a facet of particular projects of instrumentality, leading to the possibility that the quantification of work is not an improved mapping of subjects and of life, but a more subtle and more total regime of control.

While neoliberal precarity is a re-composition of capitalism, it repeats processes that were already present in Marx's critiques. As he (1990/1867) argued, fetishised quantification bears 'the unmistakable stamp of belonging to a social formation in which the process of production has mastery over man, instead of the opposite' (174–5). Since such relations are effects of a form of social life, they can be changed along with the form that grounds them (Cohen, 1978: 127). Quantification affects subjectification through the creation of a certain kind of possessive individual, partly by personalising social problems as questions of individual responsibility, prudence or morality (MacPherson, 1962; Skillen, 1978); an effect of a process of repression, through which the 'passions' are subordinated to the 'interests' (Hirschman, 1997).

Self-precarisation requires people to think they are part of a production process without recognising the exploitative elements of it. Burawoy described how workers take part in management systems that are designed to exploit them (1985). In contemporary digitalised work, the cult of perpetual busyness and headiness of creativity functions in a similar way, to obscure the inequalities inherent, requiring personification under what King calls a 'façade' (2010: 298). Quantification in digital labour now requires individual workers to relate to an externally defined totality of social labour, where direct connections among participants are inherently competitive; whether in the playful, gamified types of wellness activities at work seen in athletes' online communities organised through Strava or RunKeeper, discussed as labour because of the production of value inherent (Till, 2014), or the explicitly competitive work platforms used by Uber and Upwork where clients are sought in virtual shared spaces. The medium of quantitative exchange itself connects and regulates the distribution of labour (Marx, 1867/1990: 165), 'serving as a connecting link between people' (Rubin, 1928/1972: 10) that reduce possibilities for resistance that could be achieved by qualified, affective connections, class consciousness and resistance.

In addition to allowing horizontal and vertical economic integration without horizontal connections among workers, measuring unseen labour through quantification also allows workers to be pitted against one another as different quantities of labour sometimes through gamification techniques, even when their real activity is coordinated and cooperative. Without quantification, production could not be disguised as exchange, and surplus value could not be extracted. Although Marx (1867/1990) argues that the exchange value of commodities arises from real quantities of labour expended in their production, this labour is itself only comparable based on an illusory quantitative equivalence (1867/1990: 142, 150). So, when affective labour is reduced to the quality of being abstract human labour, masters of measure come across difficulties in looking at attributes to render it quantifiable. As De Angelis (1996: 13) argues, this process brackets out both differences among types of labour and the life experiences of workers. It also turns workers into objects (Meszaros, 1970: 144) since it renders our labour, even unseen labour, equivalent to numbers and data.

Machinic Enslavement and What Counts

The political economy of quantification leads to management that 'has always served to gain mastery over matter, to control [workers'] variations and movements...' and to submit workers 'to the spatiotemporal framework of the State' (Deleuze and Guattari 1987: 389). Capitalism relies on 'the determination of a state or standard' (1987: 291; c.f. 105), which determines *what counts*. Neoliberalism in its most advanced form becomes a 'society of control' (Deleuze, 1992), the latest phase of an axiomatic capitalist system (Deleuze and Guattari, 1987: 434, 453) which is inherently anti-creative (1987: 144) and which heavily relies on quantification. The 'rise of the robots' (Ford, 2016) may not be as terrifying as mainstream media has trumpeted, but machines are certainly not disappearing and are increasingly being used to measure and monitor work and activities seen to affect work (such as physical movement and levels of health) at levels that approach 'technological fascism' (Dancy, 2017). Dancy, who is very experienced in self-tracking and globally known as the 'mindful cyborg', noted that:

> Our relationship with machines in the future will be on an almost a nostalgic basis, teaching people how to be people if you look at that long 50-year loop: machines teaching us to be human. What will happen is that so much of our lives will become automated, the need to feel authentic will come from some data that will be collected and mimicked and fed back to us.

The machine/human assemblage will not, then, be power neutral but will ascribe further responsibilities to technology. Deleuze differentiates between the disciplinary dimension of Foucault's 'environments of enclosure' (1992: 3) whereby disciplinary enclosures exercise power through closed institutions like factories, prisons and schools. Each enclosure, or 'mold', contains its own set of rules and laws. Controls, on the other hand, are modulations, like a 'self-deforming cast that will continuously change from one moment to the other, or like a sieve whose mesh will transmute from point to point' or symptom-by-symptom (1992: 4), dividing up the mass which otherwise resists, through a 'numerical language... made of codes that mark access to information, or reject it' (1992: 5).

In *Du mode d'existence des objets techniques* Gilbert Simondon (1958/1980) calls for a transformation of our relationships to technics (see Combes, 2012; Read, 2016). Simondon looks at the regulation of the machine as alienating for most people, whereby only some are given the ability to regulate the machine. This philosopher is critical of the Fordist capitalist enterprise for egalitarian aspirations of technical becoming: the alienation of the worker results in a rupture between technical knowledge and its conditions of use. The rupture is intimately pronounced. Regulating the machine is often separated from using the machine, similar to the separation of manual from mental work in the Taylorist model, where workers are not permitted to regulate the machine: a rupture that inspired the entire free software movement. The engineer was given high status during the time of scientific management, but this has faded in subsequent periods. Nonetheless, humans are used to being 'tool bearers'. So what happens when machines become tool bearers and we find we cannot regulate them? In the preface to *Du mode d'existence des objets techniques* (Simondon 1958/1980), Hart notes that

> The contemporary interest in the body originated, not so much as a reaction against the centuries of rationalism, but as a result of the devastating effects of the shock caused by the advent of automatic machinery. As Marx was acutely aware, it was the replacement of the human hand by the machine tool, which caused the rupture. As long as man perceived himself as demiurge, as master whose hands remodelled nature, his self-image was secure. But when the machine or the individual technical object was available not merely as tool but standing in for him in execution as a separate individual, it was equivalence to the loss for man, in a single step, of a crucial part of his inhereitance.
>
> (Hart xvi, xvii, in Simondon 1958/1980)

Further, what happens when those machines 'regulate us'? Perhaps we pursue this regulation when we set out to self-track. When we are given no choice but to self-track, this relationship is more ambivalent.

Precarity is disguised as smooth spaces of time, but as numbering becomes subject we enter striated experiences as we quantify our 'selves'. Workers as self-controlling interiority are part of a work assemblage. Workers under a regime of self- and other-tracking enter into a collective assemblage of enunciation, incorporeal transformation attributed to bodies. Workers enter into a local assemblage as pulse, step and temperature are recorded by devices and inputted into software becoming a machinic assemblage where person becomes machine becomes person. So, the division between mind and body becomes a dualism that must begin to incorporate the machine and its authority through subjectivity. At the point that the 'autonomic self' discussed in Chapter 1 is measured as related to work and production, it becomes striated and made abstract: a physicosocial model of work, an invention of the State apparatus. The number has 'always served to gain mastery over matter, to control its variation and movements... to submit them to the spatiotemporal framework of the State' (Guattari, 1984: 20). Capitalism is a system of disjunction that constantly decomposes social relations and capitalist expansion requires axiomisation, or the subjection of qualitative processes of desire and becoming particular to quantitative systems of formal value.

Right after WWII, Norbert Wiener (1948/1965) claimed that cybernetics is 'automated slavery'. Baruch Gottlieb says that 'every civilization based on slavery has to contend with a perverse excess of material capacity which has no place in the servitude. What to do with the intelligence, imagination and dreams of the slave, or, even that of the resource cow?' (Gottlieb, 2016). Deleuze and Guattari developed a theory of machinic enslavement as an alternative to traditional, disciplinary social subjection (1987: 456–60). These are distinguished in that the former includes humans as constituent parts of machines or assemblages, whereas the latter constitutes them as a subject related to an outer object (1987: 457). To the extent that people provide feedback into the makeup of institutions, as in today's 'cybernetic and informational machines', they are enslaved rather than subjected (1987: 458). Machinic enslavement rests on perpetual participation and the administration of knowledge (Raunig, 2010: 28), including the capture of the imagination and dreams Gottlieb referred to, and captured in themes like lifelong learning and constant connectedness (2010: 112). This is a good description of quantified selves at work, which encourages people to identify with a representational, molar image of the self that emphasises self-branding and social performance, and neglects desire and becoming. Machinic enslavement can operate even where there is no visible hierarchy or subjection, as a particular kind of systemically inserted machine (Raunig, 2010: 16–17). In this system, 'control and self-control interweave as modes of subjectivation' (Raunig, 2010: 94). A type of 'extensive' machine, or social relation, allows an escape from 'identitary closing effects' and leads to a flight from stratification (Raunig, 2010: 34). Against the majority, which can be quantified and counted, Deleuze and Guattari counterpose a power of the 'nondenumerable' (i.e. what cannot be quantified), associated with flows and becomings (1987: 469).

As outlined, precarity generalises effects of insecurity that increase the drive to regulate and predict. Precarity manifests psychologically as generalized hopelessness (Berardi, 2009: 30), a 'chronic state of near collapse' (Invisible Committee, 2009: 31), overstimulation and 'attentive stress' (Berardi, 2009: 42), 'present shock' and time-space collapse (Foti, cited Neilson and Rossiter, 2005), that feels uncontrollable. Lorusso (2017) refers to precarity as a form of Derridean 'hauntology' and Fisher's *Ghost of My Life* (2014) because precarity is not 'fully part of the present' but rides on an 'anticipation shaping current behaviour', or the dream that present activities will lead to something better, a goal oriented vacuum of constant anxious strive or the failure of the present to become what we hoped. From an autonomist viewpoint, precarity is a systemic capture of the hopeful movements of exodus of the 1960s/1970s, when resistance often took the form of 'refusal of work', by the 'slacker' or 'dropout' (Shukaitis, 2006), with refusal to submit to Fordist work routines (Brophy and de Peuter, 2007: 180–1). Capitalism is said to have pursued this exodus into the field of life beyond work, and captured escaping flows by expanding labour into these spaces (Federici, 2008; Frassanito Network, 2005; Mitropoulos, 2006; Neilson and Rossiter, 2005), and appropriating radical ideas, introducing a wave of flexibilisation and selling it as liberation (Berardi, 2009) and blurring work-life boundaries in the process. In effect, capitalism followed the fleeing workers into the autonomous spaces of the qualitative, and, in order to bring the workers back into capitalism restructured these spaces along quantitative lines. Continuous appropriation manifests capitalism's continued capability to re-invent itself when faced with resistance (Berardi, 2009: 77).

In the early 2000s I talked to a range of precarious digital workers on their experiences of work at the Fab Lab centre in Manchester. The emerging picture is a picture of overwork and stress which contradicts dominant images of the freedoms of creative and digital labour:

> I have dealt with unreasonable expectations and impossible management cultures in full time work… I would like less stress and more freedom to work on what I want, as this is where the real "innovation" happens.
> I deal with constant overwork and funding problems.
> The main problems are the economic recession, people losing control over their lives.
> Play? At the moment it's all work.
> Near deadlines stress is a real problem, and whatever the ergonomics, sitting for 12+ hours a day is bad for your health and posture.
> We need realistic expectations. You can work 80 hours a week for a while, but you must remember that it won't do you good in the long term.

These quotes from digital workers reveal a set of persistent recurring problems, including unreasonable performance expectations, and pressure (through incentives and self-conception of capability and necessity). There is a growing acceptance that jobs require flexibility, volunteering, and the extraction of surplus value, which reflects an emerging form of self-perception keeping the precariat in the 'condition of animated suspension'

(Berlant, 2011: 256) also seen in the interview quotes above. Weber's 'Protestant ethic of capitalism' requires loyalty, hard work and thrift, and these codes of conduct should be part of people's predispositions. An ethical working life demonstrates the right to salvation, or predestination, according to the Calvinist and Lutheran churches. An ethical worker in these terms will appear very differently to the precarious worker, who, if the individual is a freelance artist for example, may appear to the outward eye as a lazy or disloyal subject. The champions of capital seek to rationalise the process of cultural production through expanded quantification. Alongside manufacturing and retail industries, in the creative and information industries, capitalism has taken over (Raunig et al., 2011: 2) or simulated and cloned (Rolnik, 2011) the dynamics of these struggles; quantification through digitalisation of labour is symptomatic of this process, as we will see in the following chapters.

Affective Subjectivities and Spaces of Resistance

Atzeni (2015) asks: 'Can precarity be seen as the new common ground, the new common condition around which different and newly emerging subjectivities can mobilise? Is precarity reconfiguring the organisational and political forms of working class representation?' There are many signs of resistance to the worst effects of digitalised labour emerging, from everyday forms of resistance to more formal trade union organising. Active resistance includes workers' hacking or appropriation of apps, sousveillance where people 'watch the watcher' using their own methods to gain access to information they do not normally have, culture jamming, using anonymity networks and personal devices at work, situational leveraging where people may 'steal' breaks and masking them as work, and feet dragging when asked to complete tasks that exceed agreed working hours. Cases have also emerged in which workers use self-tracking for resistance and self-protection. In one case, a project worker without a fixed contract used self-tracking to protect himself from unpaid overtime. He tracked time spent on projects to prove he was being underpaid and to ensure his employer's compliance with the European Working Time Directive. Ross talks about other forms of direct action in the context of exploitative digital labour, naming 'pervasive sabotage, chronic absenteeism and wildcat strikes' (2008: 35). From a labour process perspective, technology itself has not caused the conditions of precarity and the broken employment relationship. Rather, the use of data from technologies and the invisibilisation of power relations reflect age-old practices which are now intensified through more intimate tracking possibilities. Worker organising and resistance has begun to reveal the revived agency in labour power as a response to the latest incarnation of Ricardo's machine question.

For solidarity to emerge from the precariat, class consciousness in the Marxist sense is necessary. Some have claimed that class has fundamentally changed vis-à-vis concepts of labour. Virno wonders whether the multitude is too centrifugal to hold a class consciousness 'of its own' (Virno, 2004). Standing (2011) has asked whether a 'multi-class' configuration that identifies the precarity matters, since it is identifiable in other ways. Work ascribes worth to our species-being (Sayer, 2005) and people find dignity and self-worth within labour. Technology and social media has been a medium for social uprising and resistance (Gerbaudo, 2012) and digital activism's 'firebrand waves' have been escalating since the early 1990s (Karatzogianni, 2015). Fishwick argues that critical subjective connections in the labour process are crucial for resistance, where:

> ...contestation in and around the production process is central to the formation of the working class as a political subject. Not only does it create objective conditions of shared experience, it also allows for a collective subjective interpretation of these experiences that extends beyond the workplace and permits the articulation of coherent and salient political interests as a class.
>
> (2015: 215)

Ross writes about the case of precarious cultural workers and notes that precarious workers share pressures and insecurities. He notes that the expectations placed upon the precariat for self-management and agility, are a 'warmed over version of Social Darwinism' (2008: 36). It is easy to see how this operates in practice, as the value of social performances is *entirely reduced* to managerial metrics without remainder.

Lordon's *Willing Slaves of Capital* looks to the work of Spinoza and Marx to ask why people continue to serve capital and have not overcome it, given its abuses. Affect and its power to act can be triggered by the positive and the negative (which is often overlooked in the literature on affect). A 'last straw' can trigger the multitude, whence institutional power, in the Spinozan sense of 'pouvoir', can no longer contain people's 'sadness' and our inter-affections and enlisted conatus will drive us to revolt. Lordon shares Spinoza's point of 'indignation', where political affect is brought to bear. Joy, desire and passion (and unseen labour, as I argue) are classically appropriated by capital. Lordon asks whether the social reproduction of capitalism could be appropriated to reproduce subjectivities of resistance, where 'collective human life reproduces itself', he says, and 'the passions that work to keep individuals subordinate to institutional relations can also, at times, reconfigure themselves to work against those same relations' (Lordon, 2014: 138–9).

One can contrast an instrumental relationship, with the body used by the mind to pursue rational goals, with an expressive relationship, in which bodily or affective forces express themselves in the world, through the mind. Self- and other-tracking reproduce an instrumental relationship. They tend to unite body and mind under the sign of mind, as techniques of managerial (mental) control, what Rose (2001) terms the 'politics of life itself'. The difficulty, however, is that this politics does *not* speak to 'life itself', any more than Fordism or medievalism. What it speaks to is a particular *quantitative, spatial representation* of life. Emphasising empowerment, Hardt and Negri (2000) illustrate affect and immaterial labour in the post-Fordist climate as providing possibilities for resistance and formation of communities. The emphasis on affect in management strategies can be seen, on the other hand, to be tied up with labour control and social reproduction (Hartmann, 2002, cited in Carls, 2007: 46). As a tool of resistance, affect functions in this system as a structure which enables or disables our power to act (through the body). Affect is the 'power to act that is singular and at the same time universal' (Negri, 1999: 85). This prefigures and inspires the Deleuzian distinction between active and reactive forms of affect or force. Affective labour is the internal work that takes place before emotions are expressed and involves both the possibility for revolt and repression from it. It is linked to the biological aspects of work, whereby:

> Labour works directly on the affects; it produces subjectivity, it produces society, it produces life. Affective labour, in this sense, is ontological – it reveals living labour constituting a form of life...
>
> (Hardt, 1999: 99)

For Spinoza, affect was an intensely embodied concept which refers to the active ways in which bodies affect one another and co-produce social life. The full positive realisation of affect means that the 'power to act' is enacted and solidarity is immaterial, becoming also conscious and corporeal. Affect transcends what is immediately conscious. For this reason, affective resistance is a serious threat to management. Simply put, affective solidarity would lead to the most difficult form of resistance to stop, akin to invasive management techniques of technological control to infiltrate all aspects of life; affect already infiltrates all-of-life.

The concept of transindividuality is another possible route for emancipation. Simondon (1958/1980) describes technical objects as having an infinite number of possible uses when they are individualised but notes that their convergence is the point at which they are useful and become a system. He looks at the case of a 'made to measure' car, indicating that only non-essential parts are contingent and work 'against the essence of technical being, like a dead weight imposed from without' (18). Simondon defends the human as the organiser of the technical, stating that automation is never perfect nor complete and always contains a 'certain margin of indetermination' (4). He states that 'far from being the supervisor of a squad of slaves, man is the permanent organiser of technical objects which need him as much as musicians in an orchestra need a conductor' (4). In a similar way, people can recognise their individual existence without becoming atomised or hostile, instead, realise that our interrelations are what strengthen us and prevent us from abdicating and delegating our humanity to a robot (2).

Attentive stress and disposability are intensified by unrealistic expectations fostered by a quantified, machine-like image of human productivity, further intensified by permanent indebtedness leading to a sense of permanent inadequacy (Gill, 1995; Graeber, 2011). Tracking and monitoring technologies appear to provide objective data on human capabilities, but this claim elides their social context. They measure only users, creating an illusion that the precarian worker – constructed by the affective and social field of which these technologies are a part – is identical with humanity, the defining point of human bodily capabilities, and the point from which we should start – an outer limit of 'human nature' which restricts political and social possibility. While to some degree measuring emotion, feeling, and bodily responses, quantifying work with new technologies attempts to capture the field of affect *stricto sensu* – the social and psycho-structural underpinnings of affective responses. Such technologies only measure variance within the range defined by precarian affect, providing an illusory, pseudo-objective view of what might be possible outside this range. Worse still, the ideology of quantification of all of life and work perpetuates the image that the mind controls the body, and thus, from a Spinozian perspective, serves to contain the body's power within a mental frame largely constituted by neoliberal ideology and subjectivity (the managerial self, quantified productive performance, magical voluntarism, and so on). The anxious, depressed, precarian worker's body, flayed by the reactive affects of precarity, is capable of less and different things, than the empowered, conscientised, actively desiring worker (or work-refuser) – or perhaps even than the Fordist worker or the 19th-century worker, the peasant or the hunter-gatherer. Human possibilities are arbitrarily closed off by the reification of measurements which are, in circular fashion, measuring the very system they constitute. Butler's work on *Precarious Life* looks at the body as containing mortality, vulnerability and agency (2004: 26). While this text is not about resistance as such, Lorey notes that Butler's recognition of the shared 'vulnerability of life' (Lorey, 2010) is a call to leftist politics to orient our 'normative obligations of equality and universal rights' around our corporeality and vulnerability (Ibid.). Many argue that it is now time for the precariat to invent itself and identify a real alternative, an alternative that does not prey on insecurity but builds solidarity, a constituting of the political without the requirement for a single leader, without requiring a class identity in the orthodox sense.

Precarity is now used in academic and public discourse to mean the abandoned worker, the vulnerable, the person whose life is tied up with ongoing risk and stress. At the 'From Precarious Work to Decent Work' ILO 2011 Workers' Symposium on *Policies and Regulations to combat Precarious Employment*, trade unionists, ITUC, the Global Union Federations, workers' groups, and trade unionists met to discuss the symptoms of rising precarity noted by the Occupy Together movement, escalating unemployment and underemployment and the crisis of democracy and collapsing economies in the West. The documents produced from these meetings outline the problem, highlight strategies for viable responses including how to organise or better put, enable informal workers' organisation. The Labour arm of the ILO, ACTRAV, composed the *Symposium on Precarious Work* in 2012 to look for ways to mitigate the fact that 'people everywhere, it seems, are suffering from precarity as a result of economic and financial crisis, and weak Government policy responses to these' (ACTRAV, 2012: 1). Suggestions include:

> Combating precarious work requires a comprehensive policy response that includes economic, fiscal, and social policies geared towards full employment and income equality, a regulatory framework to reduce and ultimately eradicate precarious work, and greater efforts to empower workers by promoting the extension of collective bargaining and ensuring that all workers can access and exercise their right to associate, and to bargain collectively, freely, and without fear. Minimum wages globally, basic income security through a universal Social Protection Floor and policies to combat the erosion of the employment relationship are indispensable to limit precarious employment, indecent working and living conditions.
>
> (ACTRAV, 2012: 3)

At the international level, discussions on a new Labour Convention about violence against women and men in the world of work are current. Technology in workplaces may facilitate psychosocial violence. In 2016 I attended meetings at the ILO in Geneva as an invited adviser to the trade union delegation to discuss the possibility for discussions around this. Pav Akhtar, UNI Global Union's Director for Professionals and Managers, invited me as an expert on technology and work. I provided research from the Quantified Workplace company case study I outline later in this book, which was referenced in the resulting document that was published on International Women's Day in 2017, entitled 'Violence and harassment against women and men in the world of work: Trade union perspectives and action' (Pillinger, 2017). The document outlines a range of ways people have been collectively organising and working with trade unions, NGOs and IGOs to combat violence at work which includes possibilities made by technology. At the meetings in Geneva and in the published document, Akhtar and I argued that technology is a means for structural violence against workers alongside well known abuses which themselves have overlaps; for example domestic violence against home-workers involved in Mechanical Turk digital labour. New trade union strategies against these abuses are emerging in platform and digitalized labour arenas. Further research must look at how the dark side of precarity can be challenged and overcome at the personal and the institutional levels.

Conclusion

In this chapter, I have outlined the ways in which the affective and cor-poreal turns have influenced research in feminist and critical geography literature and new materialism, providing insights into the implications for the type of 'self' that self-tracking devices require under conditions of precarity. With a call to reinvestigate Spinoza's work to understand this emerging hegemonic struggle, I have attempted to motivate a shift in the ontology of most mainstream political economy research from one that relies on a dualism of body and mind to one that acknowledges work and social change relating to technological advancements as the site for struggle in contemporary capitalism.

To conclude, I ask, why are prominent observers such as Standing, Butler and Atzeni concerned with *precarity* and the perception of danger and threat that it is seen to pose? Have we begun to read this social movement turned all-of-life from the lens of the Protestant Ethic of capitalism, which provides the basis for the social factory or the socialised worker through encourag-ing work as linked with a wholesome identity? Indeed, 'work was his life', was once engraved on Protestant tombs (Peccoud, 2004: 35). Perhaps some level of acceptance of discomfort, at least in areas with some influence from Protestantism, with unstructured forms of work and working times, stems from the sentiment of the ethic of productivity as linked with prosperity. In any case, Standing and Butler largely overlook the origins of the concept of emancipation as derived from a particular view of the multitude that pre-carity can inspire put forward by Virno and Negri. These authors, and the growing urge to write more widely about precarity that I have documented in this chapter reflect a rising sensitivity to the discord between work as linked with dignity, and not simply decency. Decency may be quantifiable, whereas dignity is a human condition that is outside the realm of capitalist norms. Perhaps the basic levels of decent work can be found within quanti-fied, precarised work, but dignified labour cannot. Precarity has been read with both a hue of agency and emancipation; and contradictorily, under the weight of crude disempowerment and oppression. These contradictions are not addressed in the literature but appear as competing tropes. Along the terms of the autonomist and post-autonomist movements, precarity should be mobilised to challenge capitalist labour relations. Defeating early emancipatory hues of 'sharing' in the 'sharing economy', it is more likely that precarity prevents friendship, community building and trust, as people fight for limited 'gigs'. Precarity and related unstable work arrangements can tarnish solidarity building, advancing the erosion of human empathy across bodies and thus preventing solidarity building (Pedersen and Lewis, 2012), unfortunately preventing the chance for resistance through affective shared subjectivities and class consciousness.

This chapter indicates the ways in which quantified unseen labour is a process of making something that was concrete into something abstract, paradoxically reducing workers to numbers at an abstract level whilst removing responsibility and accountability from the remnants of observable management. Given the empirical and philosophical gap in the literature on these issues, I have looked for ways to theorise the most recent trend in quantification of workers' precarity, where the drive to measure and track both mental and physical labour has become increasingly trialled and applied in workplaces, both through wearable devices and algorithmic methods. Workers are now being told they must become and remain agile. This is a curious concept when aligned with material conditions of precarity in all levels of work, the impact of which is seen in the following chapter where I outline empirical scenarios where workers are digitally quantified.

I have noted in this chapter that there is a need for (critical) political economy researchers to take note of the affective and corporeal turns, and to look to a lineage of philosophers and activists who recognise the body as inseparable from the mind to make the fullest and best arguments in defence of *qualified* life. I advocate the investigation of Spinoza's and Marx's primary texts and of those approaches across disciplines that have moved away from Cartesian assumptions to identify their value for political economy interrogations. Molloy (2013) has broken ground with 'Spinoza, Carr, and the ethics of The Twenty Years' Crisis', demonstrating some interest in Spinoza outside philosophy, post-autonomist and feminist research where most of this research lies. But because it reflects limited interests and does not recognise contemporary precarious lives, mainstream research on work and labour in political economy that is solely based on policy reports published by intergovernmental organisations and governments lack depth and breadth. Contemporary research usually overlooks the corporeal dimensions of precarity increasingly captured by management rhetoric and advocacy of specific self-management techniques. Thus, we should give priority to empirical research that looks at how people experience capitalism and theoretically look at the impact of technologies on work and management practices. These explicit suggestions will help us to overcome Negri's claim that 'political economy has become de-ontological' (Negri, 1999: 87). These discussions provide the backdrop for the next chapter where I outline empirical cases that involve both attempts at worker control and workers' resistance to it.

Note

1 This section contains text that is adapted from this publication: Moore, P. (2015) 'Tracking Bodies, the Quantified Self and the Corporeal Turn', in Kees van der Pijl (ed.) *The International Political Economy of Production* (Cheltenham: Edward Elgar): 394–408.

Bibliography

ACTRAV (2012) 'From Precarious Work to Decent Work.' *Outcome Document to the Workers' Symposium on Policies and Regulations to Combat Precarious Employment* International Labour Organisation, Bureau for Workers' Activities (Switzerland: International Labour Organisation).

Adorno, T. (2005) *The Culture Industry: Selected Essays on Mass Culture* (London: Routledge).

AFL-CIO (2016) *Our Principles on the On-Demand Economy*. www.aflcio.org/ Issues/Jobs-and-Economy/Our-Principles-on-the-On-Demand-Economy (accessed 16/02/17).

Aghina, W. (2015) 'The Keys to Organisational Agility' interview transcript, McKinsey and Corporation. www.mckinsey.com/business-functions/organization/ our-insights/the-keys-to-organizational-agility (accessed 16/02/17).

Ajana, B. (2017) 'Digital Health and the Biopolitics of the Quantified Self' *Digital Health* 3: 1–18.

Anderson, B. (2011) 'Population and Affective Perception: Biopolitics and Anticipatory Action in US Counterinsurgency Doctrine' *Antipode* 43(2): 205–236.

Atzeni, M. (2015) Precarious Work and the Organization of Workers': The Futures We Want, 3rd ISA Forum on Sociology (10 – 14/07/16, Vienna Austria'. http:// futureswewant.net/maurizio-atzeni-precarious-work/ (accessed 16/02/17).

Balaram, B. (2016) 'Fair Share: Reclaiming Power in the Sharing Economy' Royal Society of Arts. www.thersa.org/discover/publications-and-articles/reports/ fair-share-reclaiming-power-in-the-sharing-economy (accessed 16/02/17).

Barrientos, S. (1996) 'Social Clauses and Women Workers in Latin America' *New Political Economy* 1(2): 274–278.

Barry, A. (2013) 'The Translation Zone: Between Actor-Network Theory and International Relations' *Millennium: Journal of International Studies* 41(3): 413–429.

Baudrillard, J. (1981) *Simulacra and Simulation* (Paris: Editions Galilee). http://fields. ace.ed.ac.uk/disruptivetechnologies/wp-content/uploads/2011/10/Baudrillard-Jean-Simulacra-And-Simulation2.pdf.

Baudrillard, J. (trans. Foss, P., Patton, P. and Johnston, J.) (1987) 'In the Shadow of the Silent Majorities... or the End of the Social and Other Essays' Semiotext(e), Inc. https://monoskop.org/images/c/c4/Baudrillard_Jean_In_the_Shadow_of_ the_Silent_Majorities_or_The_End_of_the_Social_and_Other_Essays.pdf

Beller, J. (1998) 'Capital/Cinema' Deleuze and Guattari' in Kaufman, E. and Heller, K. J. (eds) *New Mappings in Politics, Philosophy and Culture* (Minnesota: University of Minnesota Press): 76–95.

Bengtsson, E. and Ryner, M. (2015) 'The (International) Political Economy of Falling Wage Shares: Situating Working-Class Agency' *New Political Economy* 20(3): 406–430.

Berardi, F. (Bifo) (2009) *Precarious Rhapsody* (New York: Minor Composition).

Bergson, H. (trans. Pogson, FL) (1913/2001) *Time and Free Will, an Essay on the Immediate Data of Consciousness* (New York: Dover Publications, Inc.).

Bergson, H. (1997) *Essai Sur Les Donnees Immediates de La Conscience* (Paris: PUF).

Berlant, L. (2011) *Cruel Optimism* (Durham, NC: Duke University).

Blackman, L. (2008a) *The Body* (Oxford, New York: Berg Publishers).

Blackman, L. (2008b) 'Affect, Relationality and the Problem of Personality' *Theory, Culture & Society* 25(1): 27–51.

Blackman, L. (2011) 'Affect, Performance and Queer Subjectivities' *Cultural Studies* 25(2): 183–199.

Blackman, L. and Venn, C. (2010) 'Affect', special issue, *Body & Society* 16(1).

Blunkett, D. (1998) The Learning Age (Cm 3790) (The Stationery Office) Life-long Learning summary. www.lifelonglearning.co.uk/greenpaper/summary.pdf (accessed 12/02/17).

Bogard, W. (2010) 'Digital Resisto(e)rs' *Essays in Critical Digital Studies*: cds012. http://ctheory.net/ctheory_wp/digital-resistoers/.

Bourdieu, A. (1998) *Acts of Resistance: Against the Tyranny of the Market* (New York: The New Press).

Boyarin, D. (1995) *Carnal Israel: Reading Sex in Talmudic Culture* (Berkeley: University of California Press).

Braidotti, R. (2000) 'Teratologies' in Buchanan, I. and Colebrook, C. (eds), *Deleuze and Feminist Theory* (Edinburgh: Edinburgh University Press): 156–172.

Braidotti, R. (2002) *Metamorphoses: Towards a Materialist Theory of Becoming* (Cambridge and Malden, MA: Polity).

Braverman, H. (1974) *Labour and Monopoly Capital* (New York: Free Press).

Breen, K. (2012) 'Production and Productive Reason' *New Political Economy* 17(5): 611–632.

Brook, P. (2009) 'The Alienated Heart: Hochschild's Emotional Labour Thesis and the Anti-capitalist Politics of Alienation' *Capital and Class* 33(2): 7–31.

Brophy, E. and De Peuter, G. (2007) 'Immaterial Labor, Precarity and Recomposition' in McKercher, C. and Mosco, V. (eds) *Knowledge Workers in the Information Society* (Lanham, MD: Lexington).

Bruff, I. (2011) 'The Case for a Foundational Materialism: Going Beyond Historical Materialist IPE in Order to Strengthen It' *Journal of International Relations and Development* 14(3): 391–399.

Bruff, I. (2013) 'The Body in Capitalist Conditions of Existence: A Foundational Materialist Approach' in Cameron, A., Dickinson, J. and Smith, N. (eds.) *Body/State* (Farnham: Ashgate).

Brush, P. (1988) 'Metaphors of Inscription: Discipline, Plasticity and the Rhetoric of Choice' *Feminist Review* 58(1): 22–43.

Burawoy, M. (1985) *The Politics of Production: Factory Regimes Under Capitalism* (London: New Left).

Butler, J. (1993/2011) *Bodies That Matter: On the Discursive Limits of Sex* (New York: Routledge).

Butler, J. (2004) *Precarious Life: The Powers of Mourning and Violence* (London: Verso).

Cameron, A., Dickinson, J. and Smith, N. (eds) (2013) *Body/State* (Farnham: Ashgate).

Cammack, P. (2003), 'The Governance of Global Capitalism: A New Materialist Perspective' *Historical Materialism* 11(2): 37–59.

Caraway, T. L., Rickard, S. J. and Anner, M. S. (2012) 'International Negotiations and Domestic Politics: The Case of IMF Labor Market Conditionality' *International Organization* 66(Winter): 27–61.

Carls, K. (2007) 'Affective Labour in Milanese Large Scale Retailing: Labour Control and Employees' Coping Strategies' *ephemera* 7(1): 46–59.

Carnoy, M. (1998) 'The Changing World of Work in the Information Age' *New Political Economy* 3(1): 123–128.

Carr, H. W. (1912/1970) *Henri Bergson: The Philosophy of Change* (New York: Associated Faculty Press Inc).

Cederstrom, C. and Spicer, A. (2015) *The Wellness Syndrome* (Cambridge and Malden, MA: Polity).

Charnock, G. (2008), 'Competitiveness and Critique: The Value of a New Materialist Research Project' *Historical Materialism* 16(2): 117–141.

Cleaver, H. (1979) *Reading Capital Politically* (Brighton: Harvester).

Clough, P. T. (2007) 'Introduction' in Clough, P. T. with Halley, J. (eds.) *The Affective Turn: Theorising the Social* (Durham, NC and London: Duke University Press): 1–33.

Clough P. T. (2008) 'The Affective Turn: Political Economy, Biomedia and Bodies' *Theory, Culture & Society* 25(1): 1–22.

Clough, P. T. and Halley, J. (eds) (2007) *The Affective Turn: Theorising the Social* (Durham, NC and London: Duke University Press).

Cohen, G. A. (1978) *Karl Marx's Theory of History: A Defence* (Oxford: Oxford University Press).

Cohen, R. L., Hardy, K., Sanders, T. and Wolkowitz, C. (2013) 'The Body/Sex/Work Nexus: A Critical Perspective on Body Work and Sex Work' in Wolkowitz, C., Cohen, R. L., Sanders, T. and Hardy, K. (eds) *Body/Sex/Work: Intimate, Embodied and Sexualised Labour* (Bastingstoke: Palgrave Macmillan): 1–27.

Colman, F. (2008) 'Affective Vectors: Icons, Guattari, and Art' in O'Sullivan, S. and Zepke, S. (eds) *Producing the New: Deleuze, Guattari and Contemporary Art* (London: Continuum): 122–131.

Colman, F. (2014) 'Digital Feminicity: Predication and Measurement, Materialist Informatics and Images', *Artnodes* 14: 1–17.

Colman, F. and McCrea, C. (2005) 'The Digital Maypole' *Fibreculture Journal* FCJ-034 6 http://six.fibreculturejournal.org/fcj-034-gestures-towards-the-digital-maypole/ (accessed 11/03/17).

Combes, M. (trans. LaMarre, T.) (2012) *Gilbert Simondon and the Philosophy of the Transindividual* (Cambridge, MA: MIT Press).

Connolly, W. E. (2013) 'The New Materialism and the Fragility of Things' *Millennium: Journal of International Studies* 41(3): 399–412.

Coole, D. (2013) 'Agentic Capacities and Capacious Historical Materialism: Thinking with New Materialisms in the Political Sciences' *Millennium: Journal of International Studies* 41(3): 451–469.

Coole, D. and Frost, S. (eds) (2010) *New Materialisms: Ontology, Agency, and Politics* (Durham, NC: Duke University Press).

Coole, D. and Frost, S. (eds) (2010) *New Materialisms: Ontology, Agency, and Politics* (Durham, NC: Duke University Press).

Cooper, D. (2011) 'Theorising Nudist Equality: An Encounter between Political Fantasy and Public Appearance' *Antipode* 43(2): 326–357.

Cudworth, E. and Hobden, S. (2013) 'Of Parts and Wholes: International Relations beyond the Human' *Millennium: Journal of International Studies* 41(3): 430–450.

Dancy, C. (2017) in discussion with the author March 17th, 2017.

Davies, M. (2005) 'The Public Spheres of Unprotected Workers' *Global Society* 19(2): 131–154.

Davies, M. (2006) 'The Public Spheres of Unprotected Workers' *Poverty and the Production of World Politics: Unprotected Workers in the Global Political Economy* (Basingstoke: Palgrave): 89–112.

Davies, M. (2009) 'Works, Products, and the Division of Labour: Notes for a Cultural and Political Economic Critique' in Paterson, M. and Best, J. (eds) *Cultural Political Economy* (London: Routledge): 48–63.

Davies, M. and Ryner, M. (eds.) (2006) *Poverty and the Production of World Politics: Unprotected Workers in the Global Political Economy* (Basingstoke: Palgrave Macmillan).

Davies, W. (2016) *The Happiness Industry: How the Government and Big Business Sold Us Well-Being* (London: Verso Books).

De Angelis, M. (1996) 'Social Relations, Commodity-Fetishism, and Marx's Critique of Political Economy'. http://homepages.uel.ac.uk/M.DeAngelis/FETISH6.pdf (accessed 11/03/17).

De Landa, M. (1997) *Thousand Years of Nonlinear History* (New York: Swerve Editions).

De Landa, M. (2006) *A New Philosophy of Society: Assemblage Theory and Social Complexity* (London and New York: Continuum).

Deleuze, G. (1978) 'Spinoza's concept of Affect' *Cours Vincennes* (24/01/1978). www.webdeleuze.com/php/texte.php?cle=14&groupe=Spinoza&langue=2 (accessed 11/03/17).

Deleuze, G. (1988) *Spinoza: Practical Philosophy* (San Francisco, CA: City Lights Books).

Deleuze, G. (1992) *Postscript on the Societies of Control* (Cambridge: MIT Press).

Deleuze, G. and Guattari, F. (1987) *A Thousand Plateaus: Capitalism and Schizophrenia* (London: University of Minnesota Press).

Dowling, E. (2007) 'Producing the Dining Experience: Measure Subjectivity and the Affective Worker' *Ephemera* 7(1): 117–132.

Dowling, E. (2012) 'The Waitress: On Affect Method and (Re)presentation' *Cultural Studies <=> Critical Methodologies* 12(2): 109–117.

Ducey, A. (2007) 'More than a Job: Meaning, Affect, and Training Health Care Workers' in Clough, P. and Halley, J. (eds) *The Affective Turn: Theorizing the Social* (Durham, NC: Duke University Press): 187–208.

Dyer-Witheford, N. (2005) 'Cyber-Negri: General Intellect and Immaterial Labour' in Murphy, T. S. and Mustapha, A. K. *The Philosophy of Antonio Negri: Resistance in Practice* (London: Pluto): 136–162.

Elias, J. (2010) 'Making Migrant Domestic Work Visible: The Rights Based Approach to Migration and the "Challenges of Social Reproduction"' *Review of International Political Economy* 17(5): 840–859.

Federici, S. (2004) *Caliban and the Witch: Women, the Body and Primitive Accumulation* (London: Autonomedia).

Federici, S. (2008) 'Precarious Labour: A Feminist Viewpoint' *In the Middle of a Whirlwind, WordPress.* https://inthemiddleofthewhirlwind.wordpress.com/precarious-labor-a-feminist-viewpoint/ (accessed 15/02/17).

Firth, R. (2016) 'Somatic Pedagogies: Critiquing and Resisting the Affective Discourse of the Neoliberal State from an Embodied Anarchist Perspective' *ephemera* 16(4): 121–142.

Fischer, A. and Tepe, D. (2011) 'What's Critical about Critical Theory: Capturing the Social Totality das Gesellschaftliche Ganze' *Journal of International Relations and Development* 14(3): 366–375.

Fisher, M. (2014a) 'Good for Nothing' *London Occupied Times* 19/03/14. http://theoccupiedtimes.org/?p=12841 (accessed 16/02/17).

Fisher, M. (2014b) *Ghosts of My Life: Writings on Depression, Hauntology and Lost Futures* (London: Verso).

Fishwick, A. (2015) 'Paternalism, Taylorism, Socialism: The Battle for Production in the Chilean Textile Industry, 1930–1973', in van der Pijl, K. (ed.) *Handbook of the International Political Economy of Production* (Cheltenham and Northampton, MA: Edward Elgar): 211–228.

Florida, R. (2002) *The Rise of the Creative Class (and How It's Transforming Work, Leisure, Community and Everyday Life)* (New York: Basic Books).

Ford, M. (2016) *The Rise of the Robots: Technology and the Threat of Mass Unemployment* (London: Oneworld).

Fox, J. G. (2015) *Marx, the Body and Human Nature* (London and New York: Palgrave Macmillan).

Fracchia, J. (2005) 'Beyond the Human-Nature Debate: Human Corporeal Organisation as a 'First Fact' of Historical Materialism' *Historical Materialism* 13(1): 33–61.

Frassanito Network (2005) 'Precarious, Precarization, Precariat?' www.metamute. org/editorial/articles/precarious-precarisation-precariat (accessed 16/02/17).

Frey, C. B. and Osborne, M. A. (2013) 'The Future of Employment: How Susceptible Are Jobs to Computerisation?' *University of Oxford Working Paper* 17/09/13. www.oxfordmartin.ox.ac.uk/downloads/academic/future-of-employment.pdf (accessed 16/02/17).

Gantt, L. O. N. (1995) 'An Affront to Human Dignity: Electronic Mail Monitoring in the Private Sector Workplace' *Harvard Journal of Law and Technology* 8(2): 345–425.

Gardiner, J. (1998) 'Beyond Human Capital: Households in the Macroeconomy' *New Political Economy* 3(2): 209–221.

Gerbaudo, P. (2012) *Tweets and the Streets: Social Media and Contemporary Activism* (London: Pluto).

Gill, S. (1995) 'The Global Panopticon? The Neo-Liberal State, Economic Life and Democratic Surveillance' *Alternatives* 20(1): 1–49.

Gill, S. (1995) 'The Global Panopticon? The Neo-liberal State, Economic Life and Democratic Surveillance' *Alternatives: Global, Local, Political* 20(1): 1–49.

Gill, S. and Bakker, I. (eds.) (2003) *Power, Production and Social Reproduction: Human In/security in the Global Political Economy* (London: Palgrave Macmillan).

Gill, R. and Pratt, A. (2008) 'In the Social Factory? Immaterial Labour Precariousness and Cultural Work' *Theory Culture & Society* 25(7–8): 1–30.

Goddard, M. (2011) 'From the Multitudo to the Multitude: The Place of Spinoza in the Political Philosophy of Antonio Negri' in Lamarche, P., Rosenkrantz, M., and Sherman, D. (eds) *Reading Negri: Marxism in the Age of Empire* (Chicago, LaSalle, IL: Open Court, Carus Publishing): 171–192.

Goldstein, J. (2013) 'Terra Economica: Waste and the Production of Enclosed Nature' *Antipode* 45(2): 357–375.

Gottlieb, B. (2016) 'Knowledge 2: The Status of Truth' *Telekommunism* blog. http://telekommunisten.net/ (accessed 16/02/17).

Graeber, D. (2011) *Debt: The First 5000 Years* (New York: Melville House).

Gregg, M. (2010) 'On Friday Night Drinks: Workplace Affects in the Age of the Cubicle' in Gregg, M. and Seigworth, G. *The Affect Theory Reader* (Durham, NC and London: Duke University Press): 250–268.

Gregg, M. and Seigworth, G. (eds) (2010) *The Affect Theory Reader* (Durham, NC and London: Duke University Press).

Grosz, E. (1987) 'Notes Toward a Corporeal Feminism' *Australian Feminist Studies* 2(5): 1–16.

Guattari, F. (1984) *Molecular Revolution* (Harmondsworth: Penguin).

Guattari, F. and Negri, A. (1990) *Communists Like Us* (New York: Semiotext(e)).

Gunnarsson, L. (2013) 'The Naturalistic Turn in Feminist Theory: A Marxist-Realist Contribution' *Feminist Theory* 14(3): 3–19.

Hardt, M. (1999) 'Affective Labour' *Boundary 2* 26(2): 89–100.

Hardt, M. and Negri, A. (2000) *Empire* (Cambridge, MA: Harvard University Press).

Hardy, J. (2017) '(Re)onceptualising precarity: Structure, Institutions and Agency' *Employee Relations* 39(3): 263-273.

Harrod, J. (2006) 'The Global Poor and Global Politics: Neomaterialism and the Sources of Political Action' in Davies, M. and Ryner, M. (eds.) *Poverty and the Production of World Politics: Unprotected Workers in the Global Political Economy* (Basingstoke: Palgrave Macmillan): 38–61.

Hatfield, I. 'Self-employment in Europe' (IPPR 04/01/15). www.ippr.org/publications/self-employment-in-europe (accessed 16/02/17).

Hirschman, A. O. (1997) *The Passions and the Interests: Political Arguments for Capitalism before Its Triumph* (Princeton, NJ: Princeton University Press).

Hoschild, A. R. (1983) *The Managed Heart: Commercialisation of Human Feeling* (Berkeley and Los Angeles and London: University of California Press).

Hudson, R. (2012) 'Critical Political Economy and Material Transformation' *New Political Economy* 17(4): 373–397.

Huws, U. (2014) *Labour in the Global Digital Economy: The Cybertariat Comes of Age* (New York: Monthly Review Press).

Invisible Committee (2009) *The Coming Insurrection* (Cambridge, MA: MIT Semiotext).

Jarrett, K. (2014) 'A Database of Intention?' in Konig, R. and Rasch, M. (eds) *Society of the Query Reader: Reflections on Web Search* (Amsterdam: Institute of Network Cultures): 16–29.

Jarrett, K. (2015) 'Devaluing Binaries: Marxist Feminism and the Values of Consumer Labour' in Fuchs, C. and Fisher, E. (eds) *Reconsidering Value and Labour in the Digital Age* (Basingstoke: Palgrave Macmillan): 207–223.

Jarrett, K. (2016) *Feminism, Labour and Digital Media: The Digital Housewife* (New York and London: Routledge).

Jessop, R. D. (2000) 'The State and Contradictions of the Knowledge-Driven Economy' in Bryson, J. R., Daniels, P. W., Henry, N. D. and Pollard, J. (eds) *Knowledge, Space, Economy* (London: Routledge): 63–78.

Kalleberg, A. L. (2009) 'Precarious Work, Insecure Workers: Employment Relations in Transition' *American Sociology Review* 74(1): 1–22.

Kapur, J. (2007) '"New" Economy/Old Labour: Creativity, Flatness, and Other Neoliberal Myths' in McKercher, C. and Mosco, V. (eds) *Knowledge Workers in the Information Society* (Lanham, MD: Lexington): 163–176.

Karatzogianni, A. (2012) 'WikiLeaks Affects: Ideology, Conflict and the Revolutionary Virtual' in Karatzogianni, A. and Kuntsman, A. (eds) *Digital Cultures and the Politics of Emotion: Feelings, Affects and Technological Change* (Bastingstoke: Palgrave Macmillan): 52–73.

Karatzogianni, A. (2015) *Firebrand Waves of Digital Activism 1994–2014: The Rise and Spread of Hacktivism and Cyberconflict* (Basingstoke: Palgrave MacMillan).

Karatzogianni, A. and Kuntsman, A. (eds) *Digital Cultures and the Politics of Emotion: Feelings, Affects and Technological Change* (Bastingstoke: Palgrave Macmillan).

Katz, L.F. and Kruger, A. B. (2016) 'The Rise and Nature of Alternative Work Arrangements in the United States, 1995–2015' *National Bureau of Economic Research* NBER Working Paper No. 22667 issued September 2016. www.nber.org/papers/w22667.ack (accessed 16/02/17).

King, B. (2010) 'On the New Dignity of Labour' *ephemera* 10(3/4): 285–302.

Kirshenblatt-Gimblett, B. (2005) 'The Corporeal Turn' *The Jewish Quarterly Review* 95(3): 447–461.

Klair, A. (2017) 'Insecure Work Is Up by A Quarter Since 2011. Which Sectors Are Driving This? Touchstone Blog 07/02/17. http://touchstoneblog.org.uk/2017/02/insecure-work-quarter-since-2011-sectors-driving/ (accessed 16/02/17).

Kofman, E. (2012) 'Rethinking Care through Social Reproduction: Articulating Circuits of Migration' *Social Politics* 19(1): 142–162.

Kong, T. Y. (2006) 'Labour and Globalization: Locating the Northeast Asian Newly Industrializing Countries' *Review of International Political Economy* 13(1): 103–128.

Laclau, E. and Mouffe, C. (1985) *Hegemony and Socialist Strategy: Towards a Radical Democratic Politics* (London: Verso).

Larner, W. (2002) 'Globalization, Governmentality and Expertise: Creating a Call Centre Labour Force' *Review of International Political Economy* 9(4): 650–674.

Lazzarato, M. (1996) 'Immaterial Labour' in Hardt, M. and Virno, P. (eds) *Radical Thought in Italy: A Potential Politics* (Minnesota: University of Minnesota Press): 133–147.

Lockea, R. M. and Romis, M. (2010) 'The Promise and Perils of Private Voluntary Regulation: Labor Standards and Work Organization in Two Mexican Garment Factories' *Review of International Political Economy* 17(1): 45–74.

Longhurst, R. (2012) 'Becoming Smaller: Autobiographical Spaces of Weight Loss' *Antipode* 44(3): 871–888.

Lordon, F. (2014) *Willing Slaves of Capital: Spinoza and Marx on Desire* (London and New York: Verso).

Lorey, I. (2010) 'Becoming Common: Precarization as Political Constituting'. www.e-flux.com/journal/17/67385/becoming-common-precarization-as-political-constituting/ (accessed 16/02/17).

Lorey, I. (2011) 'Virtuosos of Freedom: On the Implosion of Political Virtuosity and Productive Labour' in Raunig, G., Ray, G., and Wiggenig, U. (eds) *Critique of Creativity: Precarity, Subjectivity and Resistance in the Creative Industries* (London: Mayfly): 79 - 90.

Lorusso, S. (2017) 'A Hauntology of Precarity' Institute of Network Cultures blog 21/02/17: http://networkcultures.org/entreprecariat/a-hauntology-of-precarity/#more-314 (accessed 16/02/17).

MacPherson, C. B. (1962) *The Political Theory of Possessive Individualism: Hobbes to Locke.* (Oxford: Clarendon Press).

Marx, K. (1844/1959) *Economic and Philosophical Manuscripts of 1844* (Moscow: Progress Publishers).

Marx, K. (1845/1938) *Theses on Feuerbach* in *The German Ideology* (Lawrence and Wishart).

Marx, K. (1858/1993) 'Fragment on Machines' in Marx, K., *Grundrisse: Foundations of the Critique of Political Economy*, translated and with a foreword by Martin Nicolau (London: Penguin Books).

Marx, K. (1867/1990) *Capital, Volume 1* (Harmondsworth: Penguin).

Massumi, B. (2002) *Parables for the Virtual Movement Affect, Sensation* (Durham, NC: Duke University Press).

May, C. (2002) 'The Political Economy of Proximity: Intellectual Property and the Global Division of Information Labour' *New Political Economy* 7(3): 317–342.

McCrudden, C. (2008) 'Human Dignity and Judicial Interpretation of Human Rights' *The European Journal of International Law* 19(4): 655–724. http://ejil.org/pdfs/19/4/1658.pdf (accessed 16/02/17).

McFadden, P. (2015) 'The Production of Politics in Front-Line Service Work: 'Body Work' in the Labour Process of the Call Centre Worker' *Global Society* 29(1): 89–106.

McRobbie, A. (2011) 'The Los Angelesation of London: Three Short Waves of Young People's Micro-Economies of Culture and Creativity in the UK', in Raunig, G., Ray, G., and Wiggenig, U. (eds) *Critique of Creativity: Precarity, Subjectivity and Resistance in the Creative Industries* (London: Mayfly): 119–132.

Meszaros, I (1970) *Marx's Theory of Alienation* (London: Merlin).

Mitropoulos, A. (2006) 'Precari-Us?' *Mute* 29: 88–92. www.metamute.org/editorial/articles/precari-us (accessed 12/08/15).

Mokre, M. (2011) 'GovernCreativity, or, Creative Industries Austrian Style' in Raunig, G., Ray, G. and Wuggenig, U. (eds) *Critique of Creativity: Precarity, Subjectivity and Resistance in the "Creative Industries"* (London: MayFly): 109–118.

Molloy, S. (2013) 'Spinoza, Carr and the Ethics of the Twenty Years' Crisis' *Review of International Studies* 39(2): 251–272.

Moore, P. (2010) *The International Political Economy of Work and Employability* (Basingstoke: Palgrave Macmillan).

Moore, P. (2012) 'Where Is the Study of Work in Critical International Political Economy?' *International Politics* 49(2): 215–237.

Moore, S. and Hayes, L. J. B. (2017 in press) 'The Electronic Monitoring of Care Work – The Redefinition of Paid Working Time' in Moore, P., Upchurch, M. and Whittaker, X. (eds) *Humans and Machines at Work: Monitoring, Surveillance and Automation in Contemporary Capitalism* (London: Palgrave Springer).

Moore, P. and Piwek, L. (2017) 'Quantified Change Management and the Affective Worker' (under second revision for journal Body & Society August 2017).

Mulholland, K. and Stewart, P. (2013) 'Workers in Food Distribution: Global Commodity Chains and Lean Logistics' *New Political Economy* 19(4): 534–558.

Murphy, H. (2014) 'The World Bank and Core Labour Standards: Between Flexibility and Regulation' *Review of International Political Economy* 21(2): 399–431.

Nederveen Pierterse, J. (2002) 'Globalization, Kitsch and Conflict: Technologies of Work, War and Politics' *Review of International Political Economy* 9(1): 1–36.

Negri, A. (1991) *The Savage Anomaly: The Power of Spinoza's Metaphysics and Politics* (Minneapolis: University of Minnesota Press).

Negri, A. (trans. Hardt, M.) (1999) 'Value and Affect' *Boundary 2* 26(2): 77–88.

Negri, A. (trans. Bove, A.) (2002) '*Approximations: Towards an Ontological Definition of the Multitude Multitudes*' Originally '*Pour Une Definition Ontologique de La Multitude*' *Multitudes* 9: 36–48.

Neilson, B. and Rossiter, N. (2005) 'From Precarity to Precariousness and Back Again: Labour, Life and Unstable Networks' *The Fibreculture Journal* FCJ-022 Issue5.http://five.fibreculturejournal.org/fcj-022-from-precarity-to-precariousness-and-back-again-labour-life-and-unstable-networks/ (accessed 15/02/17).

Nogueira, C. M. (2009) 'Double Workload: A Study of the Sexual Division of Labour among Women Telemarketing Operators in Brazil', *Work Organisation, Labour and Globalisation*, 3(1): 69–79.

Office of National Statistics (ONS) (2016) 'Part-timers Contribute to Strong Growth in Self-Employment' *ONS.gov* 13/07/16. www.ons.gov.uk/news/news/parttimerscontributetostronggrowthinselfemployment (accessed 16/02/17).

Office for National Statistics (ONS) (2017) *UK Labour Market: Feb 2017*. www.ons.gov.uk/employmentandlabourmarket/peopleinwork/employmentandemployeetypes/bulletins/uklabourmarket/feb2017#summary-of-latest-labour-market-statistics (accessed 02/02/2017).

Ollman, B. (1976) *Alienation: Marx's Conception of Man in Capitalist Society* (New York: Cambridge University Press).

Onuki, H. (2009) 'Care, Social (Re)production and Global Labour Migration: Japan's 'Special Gift' toward 'Innately Gifted' Filipino Workers' *New Political Economy* 14(4): 489–516.

Orzeck, R. (2007) 'What Does Not Kill You: Historical Materialism and the Body' *Environment and Planning D: Society and Space* 25(3): 496–514.

Paczynska, A. (2007) 'Confronting Change: Labor, State, and Privatization' *Review of International Political Economy* 14(2): 333–356.

Payne, P. G. and Wattchow, B. (2009) 'Phenomenological Deconstruction, Slow Pedagogy, and the Corporeal Turn in Wild Environmental/Outdoor Education' *Canadian Journal of Environmental Education* 14(1): 15–32.

Peccoud, D. (ed.) (2004) *Philosophical and Spiritual Perspectives on Decent Work* (Switzerland: International Labour Organisation).

Pedersen, V.B. and Lewis, S. (2012) 'Flexible Friends? Flexible Working Time Arrangements, Blurred Work-Life Boundaries and Friendship', *Work Employment Society*, 26(3): 464–480.

Peterson, V. S. (2005) 'How the (Meaning of) Gender Matters in Political Economy' *New Political Economy* 10(4): 499–521.

Pettman, J. J. (1997) 'Body Politics: International Sex Tourism' *Third World Quarterly* 18(1): 93–108.

Pillinger, J. (2017) *Violence and Harassment against Women and Men in the World of Work: Trade Union Perspectives and Action* report for International Labour Organisation (ILO) Bureau for Workers' Activities, ACTRAV. www.ilo.org/actrav/info/pubs/WCMS_546645/lang--en/index.htm.

Pink, D. (2011) *Drive: The Surprising Truth about What Motivates Us* (New York: Riverhead Books).

Plan International (2010) *Because I Am a Girl: The State of the World's Girls 2010: Digital and Urban Frontiers: Girls in a Changing Landscape* (Woking, UK: Plan International).

Precarias a la Deriva (2004) 'Adrift through the Circuits of Feminized Precarious Work' European Institute for Progressive Cultural Politics (EIPCP). http://eipcp.net/transversal/0704/precarias1/en (accessed 15/02/17).

Psychology Tools (2016) *Affect Regulation/Emotion Regulation*. http://psychology tools.com/technique-affect-regulation.html (accessed 15/02/17).

PWC (2016) 'Shared Benefits: How the Sharing Economy is Reshaping Business across Europe'. www.pwc.co.uk/issues/megatrends/collisions/sharingeconomy/ future-of-the-sharing-economy-in-europe-2016.html (accessed 15/02/17).

Raess, D. (2006) 'Globalization and Why the 'Time Is Ripe' for the Transformation of German Industrial Relations Human Corporeal Organisation as a 'First Fact' of Historical Materialism' *Historical Materialism* 13(1): 33–61.

Raise, K. (2004) 'Conflicting Values: Dialogue of cultures on Decent Work' in Peccoud, D. (ed) *Philosophical and Spiritual Perspectives on Decent Work* (Geneva, Switzerland: International Labour Organisation): 3–18.

Raunig, G. (trans. Derieg, A.) (2004) 'La Insecuridad Vencera: Anti-Precariousness Activism and Mayday Parades' European Institute for Progressive Cultural Politics (EIPCP). http://eipcp.net/transversal/0704/raunig/en (accessed 15/02/17).

Raunig, G. (2010) *A Thousand Machines* (Cambridge, MA: MIT Press).

Raunig, G., Ray, G. and Wuggenig, U. (2011) 'On the Strange Case of "Creativity" and It's Troubled Resurrection' in Raunig, G., Ray, G. and Wuggenig, U. (eds) *Critique of Creativity: Precarity, Subjectivity and Resistance in the "Creative Industries"* (London: MayFly): 1–6.

Read, J. (2003) *The Micro-Politics of Capital: Marx and the Prehistory of the Present* (NY: Suny Press).

Ricardo, D. (1821) *On the Principles of Political Economy and Taxation* (Cambridge: Cambridge University Press).

Roberts, A. (2015) 'Gender, Financial Deepening and the Production of Embodied Finance: Towards a Critical Feminist Analysis' *Global Society* 29(1): 107–127.

Rolnik, S. (trans. Holmes, B.) (2011) 'The Geopolitics of Pimping' in Raunig, G., Ray, G. and Wuggenig, U. (eds) *Critique of Creativity: Precarity, Subjectivity and Resistance in the "Creative Industries"* (London: MayFly): 23–40.

Rose, N. (2001) 'The Politics of Life Itself' *Theory, Culture and Society* 18(6): 1–30.

Ross, A. (2008) 'The New Geography of Work. Power to the Precarious?' *Theory, Culture and Society* 25(7-8): 31 – 49.

Rubin, I. I. (1928/1972), *Essays on Marx's Theory of Value,* Detroit: Black and Red. at www.marxists.org/archive/rubin/value/ch01.htm (accessed 16/02/17).

Sassen, S. (1991) *The Global City: New York, London, Tokyo* (Princeton: Princeton University Press).

Sayer, A. (2005) 'Class, Moral Worth and Recognition' *Sociology* 29(5): 957–963.

Scheuerman, W. E. (2001) 'False Humanitarianism?: US Advocacy of Transnational Labour Protections' *Review of International Political Economy* 8(3): 359–388.

Shukaitis, S. (2006) 'Whose Precarity Is It Anyway?' *Fifth Estate* 41(3). www. fifthestate.org/archive/374-winter-2007/whose-precarity-is-it-anyway/ (accessed 15/02/17).

Simondon, G. (trans. Mellamphy, N. with preface by Hart, J.) (1958/1980) *On the Mode of Existence of Technical Objects* (Ontario: University of Western Ontario).

Skillen, A. (1978) *Ruling Illusions: Philosophy and the Social Order* (Atlantic Highlands, NJ: Humanities Press).

Smail, D. (2009) *Power, Interest and Psychology: Elements of a Social Materialist Understanding of Distress* (Ross-on-Wye: PCCS Books).

Smith, G. J. D. (2016) 'Surveillance Data and Embodiment: On the Work of Being Watched' *Body & Society* 22(2): 108–139.

Smith, N. and Lee, D. (2015) 'Corporeal Capitalism: The Body in International Political Economy' *Global Society* 29(1): 64–69.

Somavia, J. (2008) 'ILO Director-General Somavia: People Vote for Decent Work' in Goris, G., Vandaele, J. (eds) *Mondiaal Nieuws*. www.mo.be/node/18207 (accessed 15/02/17).

Srnicek, N., Fotou, M. and Arghand, E. (2013) 'Introduction: Materialism and World Politics' *Millennium: Journal of International Studies* 41(3): 397.

Standing, G. (2005) 'Why Basic Income Is Needed for a Right to Work' *Rutgers Journal of Law and Urban Policy* 2(1): 91–102.

Standing, G. (2009) *Work after Globalization: Building Occupational Citizenship* (Cheltenham and Northampton: Edward Elgar).

Standing, G. (2011) *The Precariat: The New Dangerous Class* (London: Bloomsbury).

Staples, D. (2007) 'Women's Work and the Ambivalent Gift of Entropy' in Clough, P. T. and Halley, J. (eds) *The Affective Turn: Theorizing the Social* (Durham, NC and London: Duke University Press): 119–150.

Steans, J. and Tepe, D. (2010) 'Introduction – Social Reproduction in International Political Economy: Theoretical Insights and International, Transnational and Local Sitings' *Review of International Political Economy* 17(5): 807–815.

Striphas, T. (2015) 'Algorithmic Culture' *European Journal of Cultural Studies* 18(4–5): 395–412.

Tamborino, J. (2002) *The Corporeal Turn: Passion, Necessity, Politics* (Lanham, MD: Rowman & Littlefield).

Tari, M. and Vanni, I. (2005) 'On the Life and Deeds of San Precario, Patron Saint of Precarious Workers and Lives' *The Fibreculture Journal* FCJ-023 5. http://journal.fibreculture.org/issue5/vanni_tari.html (accessed 15/02/17).

Taylor, M. E. (2005) 'Opening the World Bank: Historical Materialism and Global Governance', *Historical Materialism*, 13(1): 153–170.

Taylor, P., Mulvey, G., Hyman, J. and Bain, P. (2002) 'Work Organisation, Control and the Experience of Work in Call Centres' *Work, Employment & Society* 16(1): 133–150.

Tepe-Belfrage, D. and Steans, J. (2016) 'The New Materialism: Re-claiming a Debate from a Feminist Perspective' *Capital & Class* 40(2): 305–326.

Terranova, T. (2000) 'Free Labor: Producing Culture for the Digital Economy' *Social Text* 18(2): 33–58.

Thrift, N. (2004) Intensities of Feeling: Towards a Spatial Politics of Affect. *Geografiska Annaler* 86B(1): 57–78.

Tipple, G. (2006) 'Employment and Work Conditions in Home-based Enterprises in Four Developing Countries: Do They Constitute 'Decent Work'?' *Work, Employment & Society* 20(3): 167–179.

Tomba, M. and Bellofiore, R. (2013) *The Fragment on Machines and the Grundrisse: The Workerist Reading in Question* (Brill Online: Historical Materialism Book Series).

Till, C. (2014) 'Exercise as Labour: Quantified Self and the Transformation of Exercise into Labour' *Societies* 4(3): 446–462.

Tronti, M. (1971) *Operai e capitale* (2nd edn) (Turin: Einaudi).

United Nations Division for the Advancement of Women (2005) *Gender Equality and Empowerment of Women through ICT*, Women 2000 and beyond (New York). www.un.org/womenwatch/daw/public/w2000-09.05-ict-e.pdf.

Van der Tuin, I. and Dolphijn, R. (2010) 'The Transversality of New Materialism' *Women: A Cultural Review* 21(2): 153– 171.

Van Veen, T.C. (2010) 'Technics, Precarity and Exodus in Rave Culture' *Dancecult* 1(2). https://dj.dancecult.net/index.php/dancecult/article/view/286/262It (accessed 15/02/17).

Virno, P. (2004) *The Grammar of the Multitude* (New York: Semiotext(e)). Available at: www.generation-online.org/c/fcmultitude3.htm (accessed 15/02/17).

Warr, P. (2007) *Work, Happiness, and Unhappiness* (New Jersey: Lawrence Erlbaum Associates, Inc.).

Weber, M. (1904/2001) *The Protestant Ethic and the Spirit of Capitalism* (London: Routledge).

Weeks, K. (2011) *The Problem with Work: Feminism Marxism Antiwork Politics and Postwork Imaginaries* (Durham, NC: Duke University Press).

Wiener, N. (1948/1965) *Cybernetics: Or the Control and Communication in the Animal and the Machine* (Cambridge: MIT Press).

Wetherell, M. (2015) 'Trends in the Turn to Affect: A Social Psychological Critique' *Body & Society* 21(2): 139–166.

White, M. A. (2008) 'Critical Compulsions: On the Affective Turn' *Review Essay* Topia 19: 181–188.

Wilkinson, R. and Pickett, K. (2009) *The Spirit Level: Why More Equal Societies Almost Always Do Better* (London: Allen Lane).

Witz, A. (2000) 'Whose Body Matters? Feminist Sociology and the Corporeal Turn in Sociology and Feminism' *Body and Society* 6(2): 1–24.

Wright, S. (2002) *Storming Heaven: Class Composition and Struggle in Italian Autonomist Marxism* (London and Virginia: Pluto).

4   Unseen Labour and All-of-Life Surveillance[1]

This chapter examines how the unstable matrix of the rise in exploitative work contracts, digitalised management interfaces and intensified tracking capacities negatively impact working conditions *and* provide an attempted means to capture and control all of life and work in conditions of *precarity*. New technologies offer the possibility to measure emotional and affective labour, including variable moods and subjectivities, reactions to situations, tone of voice, gestures and other movements that are seen to reflect people's emotional states and, as I argue, affect. The measurement tools for all-of-life in workplaces come in the same packages as health and fitness, as well as productivity tracking devices.

This chapter outlines how employers and clients capture and use data for what is called 'people analytics', reputation profiling, electronic performance management, platform work interface management and surveillance. I ask: given all of these areas for capture, why not capture emotional and affective labour? Wellness programmes have now begun to include information about workers' daily steps, stairs climbed and sleep and will soon be used to understand our states of 'well-being, mental health and financial wellness' (Kohll, 2016) as cited in Chapter 1. These are typical areas where unseen labour is captured in professional workplaces which are only somewhat less impacted by precarity. Digitalisation of unseen labour is different from the measure of work by older forms of technologies, as seen in scientific management, where there was some attention paid to fatigue (but not joy or distress). Unseen labour produces an 'immaterial' form of value creation (Lazzarato, 1996) through providing data that intends to reflect labour that was not considered possible for measure in the past. Measurement of productivity at work is now not limited to material outputs, but invades into subjectivities, affect and emotion (see Weeks, 1998).

The reasons that management are beginning to attempt to measure unseen labour could be due to the diminishing of traditional workplaces where managers could once physically see and speak to employees, a phenomenon evident in most industries; data accumulation can be a substitute for this lack of face-to-face contact. Or perhaps it is due to the awareness of sedentarism in workplaces which themselves occupy temporal and spatial dimensions as people began to use computers and other machines more frequently for work, perhaps impacting people's physical health and lowering productivity. In February 2015, the ONS announced that output per hour in the UK was 17 percentage points below the average for the rest of the major G7 advanced economies in 2013, which is the widest productivity gap since 1992. The Netherlands has also experienced a slowing in productivity growth (OECD, 2013). The Labour Force Survey in 2008/9 reported that 415,000 individuals in the UK were suffering from stress, anxiety or depression that people believed had been caused and worsened by current or previous work, second only in prevalence to musculoskeletal disorders (HSE, 2009, cited in Donaldson-Feilder and Podro, 2012: 6).

While unidirectional forms of productivity measure gathered by tracking techniques in factories and warehouses are well-known, non-industry corporations have begun to use technologies to gather data about workers in a way that not only measures productivity but is designed to increase motivation and productivity of more cognitive work. Here, I touch on the issue of new forms of surveillance that surround new methods of self- and other-tracking at work. Surveillance is no longer something that happens to 'other people'. It is all around us. We are expected to watch one another and watch ourselves. So, the first section of this chapter looks at the concept of surveillance and biopower and the workplaces where new technologies are now being deployed to monitor and control work as well as to provide services and work. This section leads into the delineation of why emotions and affective labour are the new terrain of capture for management along a continuum of management scrutiny. Introduced in Chapter 3 at the ontological level where research on affectivity challenges perceived divisions and hierarchies between the body and the mind, this chapter goes into a more specific characterization for how affect and emotional labour become areas of corporate colonization as seen in new workplace experiments. So, after looking at the concept of surveillance at work, I look at the ways that electronic performance monitoring, reputation management, people analytics and automation are effected and affect workers. I then outline the results from the research I carried out looking at one company's experiment which they called the Quantified Workplace, identifying how unseen labour was captured during a period of corporate change.

Surveillance at Work[2]

We live in a brave new world of the watched. Surveillance once was seen to be carried out only on suspected deviants or in wartime. Usually, someone knew who was watching and who was being watched or sought out. From witch hunts or suspicions of communist sensibilities to suspicion of infidelity; with the use of such vintage technologies as lie detectors, binoculars, Russian lomo cameras and invisible ink, reasons for surveillance were specific, individualized and understood. Advances in technology allow power to be enacted over bodies in a far more abstracted way than before. Foucault introduced the concept of biopower in *History of Sexuality (volume 1)*, asking:

> How could power exercise its highest prerogatives by putting people to death, when its main role was to ensure and multiply life, to put this life in order... the object of this biopoliticised power is the 'species' body, the body imbued with the mechanisms of life and servicing as the basis of the biological processes propagation, births and mortality, the level of health, life expectations and longevity.
>
> (Foucault, 1979/1976: 138–9)

Then, in a lecture at the Collège de France on 11 January 1978, Foucault defined biopower as a 'set of mechanisms through which the basic biological features of the human species became the object of a political strategy, of a general strategy of power' (Foucault, 1977–78/2009: 1). In his series of lectures in *Security, Territory, Population* Foucault examined how what is to be protected is defined and how it is made known and acted upon. Security becomes a fictitious force that expands to include more and more activities and events including production and thought processes, psychology and human behaviours. Foucault described biopower as a security that becomes centrifugal, a fictitious force that expands to include more and more activities and events, including production and thought processes, psychology and human behaviours, and biosensory tracking can be theorised along these lines. This is the 'new surveillance' Gary T. Marx (1988) began to talk about in the 1980s where watching can be carried out on anyone, anywhere and at any time, for no reason at all. The everyday, then, is particularly important for a discussion of quantification of selves and tracking. Self-quantification could be a way to recover from alienation in everyday life or a way to achieve authenticity and to resolve life's contradictions; or alternatively could lead to worsened alienation and create contradictions.

Inventions in sensory technologies in many cases have been adapted from older forms such as magnetic pendulums now used to track and record human steps and introduced new uses for such technologies as RFID, GPS and cameras. New sensors can recognise faces and detect body odour, and fingerprint timeclocks are now regularly used for enrollment at work. Analytics have advanced as it becomes possible to cross reference with the use of 'dashboards'. Cleaners' movement around lavatories and time spent cleaning each toilet and sink have been monitored in a manner resembling the monitoring of every second spent on each mechanical piece in scientific management. Factory workers, who now normally in the 'quality' sections of custom made cars as much previous work on the line has been taken over by robots, have no choice but to work within a specific timeframe because cars approach on a giant moving belt, where overhead flags designate the area within which a person may work and the moving belt forces the timeframe. Factory work is monitored by CCTV cameras and roaming managers. In one technological centre I visited, cameras are even set up to observe robots' work.

The innovation in new surveillance is that it can be selected based on context or 'geographical places and spaces, particular time periods, networks, systems and categories of person' (Marx, 2002: 10) rather than based on specific people whose identities are already known or suspected. Previously, we could differentiate between the observer and the observed fairly easily, and technologies facilitated rather than directed processes. The new surveillance is increasingly comprehensive and extensive, and includes individual and cross-referenced data, information that goes far beyond the traditional records kept by churches or schools. Information about individuals can now be generated by algorithmic processes for automated identification and generation of analytics, which remove a layer of human involvement. Digitalised surveillance introduces a 'step change in power, intensity and scope' (Graham and Wood, 2003). States' rationale for such intensified or 'close observation', a term that does not capture the extent of the practice (Marx, 2002: 12), range from the need to provide increased security against the threat of terrorism to the potential for research and development in a number of spheres from medical to urban design.

In the USA, the PATRIOT Act has been used to justify several activities that do not fall within its original remit of terrorist prevention. The NSA was permitted to carry out surveillance against drug dealers. The DEA was asked to lie about where it received data, as it was in fact passed on by the NSA. In the UK, surveillance techniques designed to prevent terrorism are being used against political protestors and to incriminate much lesser offenses such as violations of smoking bans and falsifying addresses (Schneier, 2015a: 105). Predictive policing techniques being developed in the USA and China give the state 'plenty of "precrime" and "thoughtcrime" data on its citizens to work with' (Adl, 2016). Bizarrely, our perceived knowledge of ourselves potentially could be less than the amount of knowledge that is held about ourselves by others, and even stranger, that data may be impossible for us to access. New technologies involve computer matching, profiling and data mining; work, computer and electronic location monitoring; DNA analysis; drug tests; brain scans for lie detection; various self-administered tests and thermal imaging, 'to reveal what is behind walls and enclosures' (Marx, 2005).

The data we produce simply by going online or using our 'smart' phones is very useful, as well as highly profitable for companies (Moore and Piwek, 2017). Schneier documents one reporter who set out to find out who was tracking his internet use and discovered that 150 companies did so within a 36-hour period (Schneier, 2015b). The ways companies do this is by installing tracking cookies onto browsers, usually without users knowing. Cookies work by remembering preferences, recording what an individual has bought as well as tracking how many people view a website. Many companies have been set up to collect online data that is seen to be useful for advertising, such as the Rubicon Project. Rubicon's Advertising Automation Cloud works by leveraging algorithms and analysing data points and selling that information. Other similar companies are AdSonar, Quantcast, Undertone and Traffic Marketplace. A particularly invasive one is Dictionary.com which installed around 200 cookies when users visited its site (Schnier, 2015b). Other techniques involve planting cameras and recorders in mannequins in stores to identify customers' habits (Heyes, 2014; Hornyak, 2012). This new world transforms the role of the customer in a process of reification, in which we are no longer customers, but we—or at least our daily activities—are products. Schneier likens the relationships we experience to those under feudalism, where companies are akin to feudal lords and we are the peasants (2015b).

While surveillance techniques in stores may surprise people and lead to such comments as 'it's a little creepy', because people still largely externalise market relations, a customer's response to hearing that there is a camera hidden in a mannequin might be as benign as: 'if you're an honest person and you're not up to anything in the store, I think it's fine' (Heyes, 2014). However, when surveillance is carried out in workplaces, people begin to respond somewhat differently. Surveillance in the workplace has a similar set of tensions regarding ethics of practice, but has taken different forms at differing levels of intensity, from clear cut cases of performance management during the period of scientific management to contemporary human analytics. Taylor and the Gilbreths and their disciples put intricate movements of bodies at the centre of the measure of performance; they observed people's homes for ideal family constructs as linked to work productivity; celebrated newly invented efficiency devices in kitchens; measured the extremes of people's capabilities through complex processes using the most up to date technologies at the time. The value and measure of work is still the beating heart of debates in political economy, but how much should employers be able to know about employees? Because the law has tended to focus on protections against discrimination, intense surveillance could impact hiring practices around pregnancy or gender identity. Historically, pervasive laws such as the Japanese Surveillance Law for Thought Offences of 1936 was used to fire people who were associated with the labour movement and Communist party (McCabe and Prete, 1995: 212). Will our thoughts soon be measured too?

Improved productivity and efficiency was the justification for scientific management, and accompanying surveillance was similarly justified, but it failed to capture qualified reasons why people may be more or less productive. Where should the line be drawn when these questions rise to the surface? Should your employer know about your health and wellbeing? Would knowledge about workers' health and wellbeing help employers identify better working practices and measure performance more accurately? At what point will it be used to surreptitiously discriminate and for appraisals? In some cases, predictive surveillance is perhaps necessary, such as in the case of construction sites where a worker's heart attack could lead to severe damage. In other industries, people may want to know why employers are beginning to experiment with motion and temperature sensors, such as the much-publicised incident at the Telegraph newspaper offices where the 'OccupEye' was placed under employees' desks. While the rationale for such devices was to control the use of lights to save electricity, the employer neglected to warn employees about the placement of these devices. It seemed an odd pursuit to try to track journalists' movements given their job description is to be out getting stories, but the wider implications caused significant reactions from employees. Journalists took the story to the public as a form of outcry. Some staff simply removed the batteries powering the units (Mance, 2016).

When Taylor and the Gilbreths wrote at the beginning of the century, manufacturing was the formula for accelerating an economy. With the rise of service industries in advanced countries in the 1950s, knowledge work started to replace factory work and work design gurus began to ask how knowledge work could be measured and valued. Peter Drucker, who advocated the integration of virtue as managerial vision and 'participative management' techniques, is the best known in this area. Knowledge workers working in service industries tended to have more insights into how to best do their jobs than their bosses, which could transform the entire concept of management as it had been known in the factory where mental and manual labour was intentionally separated. Drucker claimed that knowledge work should be guided rather than directed and the objectives of an organization should be jointly decided. Drucker's techniques contained four parts: 'centralised determination of corporate goals, decentralised definition of operational targets and task organization, measurements of performance against objectives and a system of rewards and punishments based on results' (Waring, 1991: 88–89). For this process to work, a corporation must have a 'strategy' which would comprise the 'compass bearing' of the 'corporate ship' preventing it from becoming the 'plaything of the weather'. Bringing 'values, beliefs and aspirations' into the workplace would inspire knowledge workers to work in tandem with the values of an organization which were set by management. Reminiscent of Weber's Protestant ethic, people should find an internal, tacit drive to align with an organisation's values with as much authenticity as could be mustered.

If management says that 'health and wellbeing' are the values of an organization, the best workers should internalize that value and begin to watch out for it, whether directing the gaze to themselves or to others in new and inventive techniques that fall along a continuum of surveillance. Employee health may never have been an entirely private domain, but employers are increasingly taking an interest in our health and wellbeing (Cederström and Spicer, 2015). Healthier workers may be happier and may indeed be more productive, but historically, workers largely had autonomy in how they went about staying fit for productivity.

Given the negative workplace experiences and challenges to the employment relationship that could result from intensified monitoring and surveillance of work, workers may not feel comfortable being involved in such initiatives. Companies do not usually explicitly require employees to use wellness tracking devices in professional settings, but as incorporation becomes normalised, employees risk feeling excluded from programmes if they choose to opt-out. An 'opt-out' from wellness initiatives risks being seen as someone who does not want to be well. Indeed, anyone living as anything but a 'happy person' may be in danger of becoming stigmatised. J. P. Gownder, an analyst at the research firm Forrester, predicts instances where people will actually experience feelings of being ostracized for not participating in corporate wellness programmes (Hamblen, 2015). The standardisation of wellness individualises lived experiences, and if people cannot achieve happiness, then they may feel inadequate. The disciplined, monitored employee in a neoliberal panopticon is seen to retain her autonomy, but the reality is that the process of perfecting the healthy self may never in fact, finish. Complete happiness and well-being may never be achieved. In the film 'Hector and The Search for Happiness', Hector, an unfulfilled psychiatrist, muses as part of his search for what makes people happy: 'many people only see happiness, only in their future'. It is increasingly seen as our fault if we as workers have not taken advantage of available wellness offerings. Employees who opt-out are seen as abnormal. In the film 'The Bothersome Man', Andreas becomes painfully aware that happiness is the only actuality he will be permitted to experience. Any attempt he makes to experience normal life where pain and imperfections occur leads to confused responses from associates and his partner. This is a dystopian world where perfect productivity, supreme health and impeccable aesthetics are idealised. Biometric surveillance facilitates a process of identity transformation under specific expectations (Ajana, 2013) and intensifies reputation regulation as employers continue to profile employees with the use of new technologies (Gandini, 2016; Pasquale, 2010). The next sections cover the application of digitalised quantification techniques, from electronic performance monitoring to wearable devices, and then look at the Quantified Workplace experiment where employees were asked to track several areas of work and life over the course of a year.

Electronic Performance Monitoring (EPM)

Electronic performance monitoring (EPM) involves email monitoring, phone tapping, tracking computer content and usage times, video monitoring and GPS tracking. The data produced from new technologies can be used as productivity indicators; indication of employees' location; email usage; website browsing; printer use; telephone use; even tone of voice and physical movement during conversation (see wearable technologies section). Perhaps the longest history of EPM is seen in call centre work

(Taylor et al., 2002) where various types of surveillance facilities lean on working practices. Emotion tracking is standard activity in Indian centres (Van Jaarsveld and Poster, 2013) and practices are increasingly normalised internationally.

In the early 1990s, a US Senator on the Labour and Human Resources Committee, in hearings on the Privacy for Consumers and Workers Bill (S. 516) warned that 'unrestrained surveillance of workers has turned many offices into electronic sweatshops... electronic monitoring should not be abused... Employees should not be forced to give up their freedom, dignity or sacrifice their health when they go to work' (Collins, 1991). Nonetheless, by 2010, an estimated 75 percent of American companies were shown to monitor employee communications and other at-work activities (Ball, 2010). The estimated change in the US market use of technology to monitor employees rose by 43 percent between 2007 and 2010 (Harpers Index, 2010 quoted in Schumacher, 2011: 138) and we are now in a period of what seems to be 'limitless worker surveillance' (Ajunwa et al., 2016).

Our facial images have been captured and stored by institutions for decades, from the library to the motor vehicle department. We are accustomed to some forms of identity cards and the terrible photo that only the immigration officer in an airport should ever see. Now, a machine collects facial images during every trip through the airport. While finger prints require more explicit consent and have normally only been collected if the hand belongs to someone under suspicion, our biometrics are now seemingly up for grabs. CCTV is nearly ubiquitous in some countries. Faces are becoming the new 'bar codes' for all kinds of things (Introna and Wood, 2004). Face + + Cognitive Services is one such facial recognition system being rolled out in China now. Face + + can detect and locate faces in images; compare faces; search and locate similar faces in a large collection; identify key points of face components it calls 'landmarks'; and analyse attributes including gender, emotion, head poses, and eye status (Face + +, 2017). In China, the platform has been used by the ride-sharing company Didi. The Face + + customer testimonial section on its website states that

> Didi is the largest ride-sharing company providing transportation services for over 300 million users across China, and the parent company of Uber China. With facial recognition service by Face++, Didi succeeded in building a safe and easy riding experience for both riders and drivers. Face Comparing offered great help in solving the problems of fraud and cheating.
>
> (Ibid.)

A smile will soon replace a fingerprint to unlock phones. Iris detection to unlock doors seems less and less like a far-fetched scene from a science fiction film.

In the workplace, likely areas for EPM with such functions are in work design decisions, such as the use of Sociometric Solutions for placing furniture in offices to facilitate optimal movement around offices. This 'solution' tracks movements around offices and people's tones of voice. Taking it to the next level, video cameras could de-anonymise such trackers. Virtual reality training could be an area for leadership and management training. VR is already used by the U.S. Army for training soldiers. The *Training Industry Magazine* reported in 2017 that VR management courses are available for managers in training to master effective skills using VR, where simulations for face-to-face coaching session with a problem worker help a budding leader develop responses to employees by playing back recorded sessions, which are also scored and ranked compared to colleagues and participants (Young et al., 2017). Social media can be used to 'predict personality type' from the Big Five traits of 'extraversion, agreeableness, openness, conscientiousness and neuroticism', and coaching sessions can help leaders to recognise their own personality types to improve use of social media. Information about employees' personality types can also be used to feed into coaching sessions and help people understand why people 'engage in specific behaviours that are revealed through other means' (Ibid.). This report indicates that social media analytics are not perfect, and there are ethical questions about acquiring data used to determine personalities without users' consent. The other possible trend is wearable devices that can record physiological data like heart rate which, the authors claim, can now give an 'objective assessment of our stress state' (Ibid.).

EPM can be used to micromanage employees and invade privacy, lower job satisfaction, increase stress and leads to low-trust, negative work relationships (Schumacher, 2011). Human dignity is at stake in the context of rising workplace surveillance and, as Rothstein pointed out, in relation to workplace monitoring:

> At work, human dignity is denied by treating the employee as a mere factor of production with fixed capacities and vulnerabilities determining her behaviour and ignoring both the worker's individuality in the face of statistical probabilities and the human potential to overcome or compensate for physical obstacles. The worker's dignity is denied when she is treated as a mechanism transparent to the view of others at a distance and therefore manipulable or disposable without the ability to confront the observer.
>
> (Rothstein, 2000: 383–84; also see Gantt, 1995)

Direct productivity monitoring enabled by software installed in work and personal computers reveals a new EPM technique. Examples include RescueTime, Toggl, ATracker and My Minutes which have been introduced in real estate design workplaces such as in the case of the Quantified Workplace study carried out by one company in the Netherlands, discussed below.

The constant onslaught of communications and information and expectations to personally manage work that was once done by another specialist in the company in timetabling and accountancy has led to 24/7 working lives (Bogost, 2013). The 'overwhelmed employee' checks her mobile devices up to 150 times a day and suffers from information overload, inability to find time to reflect and even just to think, leading to employee disengagement and undermining productivity (Hodson et al., 2014). People can now never really switch off, even while asleep or on holiday. These pressures are compounded in a new world of work where employees are 'always on', or even 'hyper-employed'.

The power of tracking work with EPM becomes even more attractive to employers with the possibility for the aggregation of 'big data'. Productivity can be monitored with increasing accuracy, offering detailed second-by-second frequency with the use of 'people analytics' that extrapolates from the data made available. People analytics is made possible by the reduced costs of data and information processing. It is of interest to business because it is seen to reduce costs in service-provider selection and/ or workplace re-organization and restructuring. It is the dominant selection method in the 'sharing economy' (discussed below). Implicit to the use of these technologies and the large amounts of data produced, as well as analysis from people analytics, is that the type of activity and the length of time spent on activities can be inherently linked to a qualitative judgment about a worker's performance; information that could be used in appraisals or hiring and firing decisions. Intimate performance dashboards provided by most EPM technologies incorporate contextual information obtained from tracking devices such as levels of physical activity, level of stress, or presence and absence scores. The data itself is seen as the indicator of value. However, as pointed out by Angrave et al. (2016: 7):

> ...the process of modelling and creating dashboards and traffic lights is not value neutral but depends on dominant paradigms and perspectives within accounting and operations management, which themselves reflect ideology, politics and power.

These practices are rapidly superseding other forms of management methods as data produced is seen to be a reliable indicator of productivity. New EPM is very different from traditional methods (Jeske and Santuzzi, 2015). Reliance on metrics from tracking devices potentially dehumanizes employees who are reduced to a collection of activity timestamps. The associated measures can result in biased performance evaluations; pressures for increased work or work intensification; reduction of autonomy (linked to privacy concerns) (Bhave, 2014; Haque, 2015); and perceived intensified control over individuals' work (Jeske and Santuzzi, 2015). These pressures lead to reduced commitment and lowered job satisfaction. EPM has the very real potential for uses of psychological bullying, and employees are concerned about the possibilities for workplace control based on what can be considered new surveillance methods (Ball and Margulis, 2011; Rosenblat et al., 2014).

In 2014, 36 percent of workers in a Gallup poll (Harter et al., 2014) said they checked work email outside of normal working hours and this number is not likely to drop. Employers are legally permitted to monitor workers' emails and internet browser history, with few restrictions. Facebook's terms of service are more binding than most governments', stating that 'you will not share your password... let anyone else access your account, or do anything that might jeopardize the security of your account'. There is little actual legal protection over these violations of privacy and employers have been increasingly known to ask potential employees for social media log-in information (Beesley, 2016). 'Workplace spying' (The Week, 2015) can, unsurprisingly, lead to anxiety and psycho-social discomfort, or what could even be called 'violence' (Akhtar and Moore, 2016). Research has shown that when employees perceive they have privacy it actually improves productivity: a feature of the 'transparency paradox' (Bernstein, 2012).

There are difficulties in adapting the concept of respect for private life into workplaces. The right to privacy is taken to cover professional or business activities and employees' communications, thus implying that employers may not, in principle, interfere in these areas. However, as Kilkelly (2001) states, such interference is acceptable in certain circumstances – notably 'in the interests of national security, public safety or the economic well-being of the country, for the prevention of disorder or crime, for the protection of health or morals'. This raises questions about the extent to which workers may be monitored and the relationship between their rights and employers' prerogative. Now I turn to look at questions of automation and a prescient question of machine management.

The Machinery Question Now: Will the Machine Manage Me?

David Ricardo introduced the 'machinery question' in 1821, referring to the 'influence of machinery on the interests of the different classes of society'. The 'machinery question', he indicated, centred on the 'opinion entertained by the labouring class, that the employment of machinery is frequently detrimental to their interests' (1821). Marx, in defense of the working class, indicated that

> like every other instrument for increasing the productivity of labour, machinery is intended to cheapen commodities and, by shortening the part of the working day in which the worker works for himself, to lengthen the other part, the part he gives to the capitalist.
>
> (1867/1990: 492)

Research on the capability of machinery to carry out human-like activities started in the 1950s when a researcher first coined the term 'artificial intelligence' in a report where the author wrote that progress can be made in getting machines to 'solve kinds of problems now reserved for humans' (McCarthy et al., 1955). The term artificial intelligence was abandoned after the 1950s as people discussed 'expert systems' and 'neural networks' (Ford, 2015), but resonates with simultaneous social concern that machines could actually steal paid work from humans. Ted F. Silvey, from the National Headquarters department of education staff of the Congress of Industrial Organizations (CIO) and American Federation of Labour (AFL), trade unionist noted that:

> Instruments substitute for man's mind, just as the rest of the machine takes the place of his muscles. Machines are acquiring the skill of human beings, but they must work faster and more accurately than anything of flesh and blood—and they never tire.
>
> (1957) (see Figure 4.1)

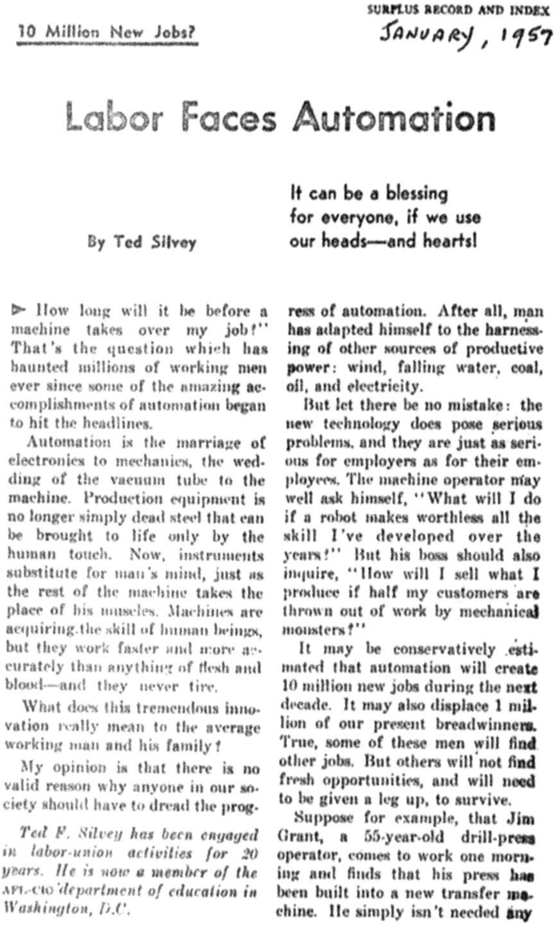

10 Million New Jobs?

SURPLUS RECORD AND INDEX
JANUARY, 1957

Labor Faces Automation

By Ted Silvey

It can be a blessing
for everyone, if we use
our heads—and hearts!

▷ How long will it be before a machine takes over my job?" That's the question which has haunted millions of working men ever since some of the amazing accomplishments of automation began to hit the headlines.

Automation is the marriage of electronics to mechanics, the wedding of the vacuum tube to the machine. Production equipment is no longer simply dead steel that can be brought to life only by the human touch. Now, instruments substitute for man's mind, just as the rest of the machine takes the place of his muscles. Machines are acquiring the skill of human beings, but they work faster and more accurately than anything of flesh and blood—and they never tire.

What does this tremendous innovation really mean to the average working man and his family?

My opinion is that there is no valid reason why anyone in our society should have to dread the prog-

Ted F. Silvey has been engaged in labor-union activities for 20 years. He is now a member of the AFL-CIO department of education in Washington, D.C.

ress of automation. After all, man has adapted himself to the harnessing of other sources of productive power: wind, falling water, coal, oil, and electricity.

But let there be no mistake: the new technology does pose serious problems, and they are just as serious for employers as for their employees. The machine operator may well ask himself, "What will I do if a robot makes worthless all the skill I've developed over the years!" But his boss should also inquire, "How will I sell what I produce if half my customers are thrown out of work by mechanical monsters?"

It may be conservatively estimated that automation will create 10 million new jobs during the next decade. It may also displace 1 million of our present breadwinners. True, some of these men will find other jobs. But others will not find fresh opportunities, and will need to be given a leg up, to survive.

Suppose for example, that Jim Grant, a 55-year-old drill-press operator, comes to work one morning and finds that his press has been built into a new transfer machine. He simply isn't needed any

Figure 4.1 Labor faces automation.

In this context, trade unions in the 1950s were concerned with man-ufacturing that the technologies involved in mass production worked to 'trivialize' man by its 'repetitive performance of bits. His craft skills, his creativeness, his human dignity, his uniqueness were, at best ignored and at worst, stomped on', causing the 'destruction of the workers' dignity as people' (Silvey, 1956: 3).

This same trade unionist also optimistically pointed out the possibilities that mechanization would reduce the work week and work year, 'both with full wage or salary income' (1958) and claimed that 'automation promises a time when a comparative handful of people will have to work in factories at the dull, repetitive tasks demanded by mass production' (1957: 30). Silvey's optimism as well as pragmatism is remarkable. He stated that

> in the long run, automation will make more jobs... but the challenge is to solve the problem in the short run, to give immediate aid to the worker whose fingers are caught in the door when it is slammed shut.
>
> (1957: 29)

The background for this was in the Depression. In 1933, the American Federation of Labour asked, in this trade union's publication *Monthly Survey of Business*: 'will the business machine run on its own power?' (see Figure 4.2). Written during the depression, the AFL referred to a slight decrease in unemployment after three years of steady increases, but were concerned, as was Silvey, that people were not able to buy the products they were producing. In 1958, Ted Silvey discussed the manufacture of a ball point pencil (what we now call a ball point pen) (see Figure 4.3). He stated in *Computers and Automation* that:

> The total number of ball point pencils manufactured in the United States in one year at current levels in business is 700 million. This vol-ume is produced by 24 companies. The number of workers needed for this fabulous production is insignificant. The number of people needed with money in their pockets to buy this output is highly significant – in fact gives full meaning to the point that with automation the *machines and instruments can do almost everything except buy what they make*!
>
> (Silvey, 1958, emphasis added)

In the 1970s Braverman (1974/1988) hinted at the origins of algorith-mic processes as a feature of the development of machinery, indicating that 'when the tool and/or the work are given a fixed motion path by the structure of the machine into that machinery in the modern sense begins to develop' (130). The machine's ability to run itself has become almost accepted in contemporary life, but what happens when humans begin to make decisions based on specific aspects of the machine's operations with little or no external interference?

MONTHLY SURVEY OF BUSINESS

of the

American Federation of Labor

No. 47

H)6501

May, 1933

WILL THE BUSINESS MACHINE RUN ON ITS OWN POWER

Administration measures have succeeded in priming the business machine. Fear of inflation has been the chief primer—people have been turning money into goods for fear their dollars would soon buy less. Both for family and business needs, people have been buying against future requirements, to take advantage of bargain prices while they last. This buying has quickened trade and industry, and business statistics would make cheerful reading, but for the fact that this gain is not based on increased buying power. However, the following records have helped to create an optimistic spirit among those who do not look below the surface: Freight carried on the railroads went above the 1932 level in the week of May 13, for the first time since depression; automobile sales are increasing and production has more than doubled since April first; steel production has also doubled—from 16 percent of capacity, April 1, to 38 percent, May 20; the Federal Reserve Board reports that industrial activity increased considerably during April and the first three weeks of May; the wholesale price index rose 4.8 percent and stock prices 53.8 percent in the same period. Most important of all, over 600,000 unemployed went back to work in April and jobs increased again in May (see graph).

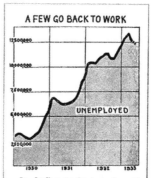

In April unemployment decreased from 13,359,000 to 12,730,000; 629,000 went back to work, or 4.8% of the unemployed. Trade union reports for May show another gain, not so large. This is the most significant of all business gains reported this spring; it is the largest since depression began. But unless employment gains more than this it will take nearly two years to get the unemployed back to work—and business cannot wait two years. (Source: A. F. of L. unemployment estimate, based on Government figures; projected to May by Trade Union reports.)

Cheerful as this news sounds, there is no evidence yet that it marks the start of recovery. Building and several other heavy industries still lag; the stimulus due to fear of inflation is petering out, deflation is still going on, the summer dull season is just ahead. Only one thing can keep business moving steadily forward on even keel—increased buying power. This means increased incomes for workers who are industry's largest group of customers. Workers' total income in April was only 43.9% of the 1929 average, a deficiency in buying power amounting to nearly $2,500,000,000 a month (see graph on page 2). Until workers' incomes are revived, business will have to be kept going by constant priming. What we need is to get the carburetor adjusted so there will be a steady flow of buying power. When workers' buying power does start definitely upward, it must increase faster than prices to keep business moving upward in balance.

Figure 4.2 Will the business machine run on its own power?

Today, the machinery question is 'back with a vengeance' (*Economist*, 2016: 3) because this question is infiltrating professional workplaces where all kinds of work increasingly can be automated. In 2012, the ImageNet Challenge set people to programme computers to recognize images. These 'challenges', or contests, co-ordinated by top researchers and corporations became a measure of success in the field, contributed to the rapid improvement in what is called 'deep learning', and the computer's ability to recognize images has now surpassed humans. This, and other experimentation, is bringing about the realization that tasks once considered the exclusive

Computers and Automation
magazine
issue of February,1958

A BALL-POINT PENCIL---IS A COMPUTER?

Ted F. Silvey
AFL-CIO National Headquarters Staff
Washington, D.C.

WHEN BALL POINT pencils originally were produced and marketed in the United States at the close of World War II, they sold for an individual price as high as the best quality fluid ink fountain pens — as much as $15.00 each.

As more small metal balls became available, and research developed a cheap non-smear paste ink, separate mass production of the few standard components made possible sale of the pencils at prices down to $1.00 each. Certain fancy styles still hold a price level of $1.60 to $1.95 on the retail market.

The development of fast automatic machinery specially designed for manufacture of ball point pencil components and their assembly reduced the manufacturer's cost still more, and the need to move the bigger production into the market brought big quantity buying for advertising purposes. Ball point pencils with imprinted company and product names began freely to be handed out at conventions and meetings, and as "lagniappe" with sales of other merchandise.

In December 1955 there began to appear on the U.S. market the "package deal" of multiple pencils, each one a different color. The specimen set herewith consists of a plastic case, four ball point pencils (black, red, blue, green) and a pocket clip hair comb.

The first plastic cases were solid color back and front. Some of them were slotted for school boys to wear at their waist by putting them on their belt (which is far superior to wearing toy gun six-shooters!). More recent cases have had a clear face front which gives a full window look-through.

The package deal sold for 98 cents retail. With single ball point pencils of comparable quality selling at $1.00 or more apiece, there was obviously a substantial price reduction.

This item of merchandise is not shoddy, but of good quality. The pencils are soundly constructed. The ink in the central tube is bright, of strong color, and there is enough of it to write without smearing for many hours. Refills are available at low cost, but with the pencils so cheap the refills are hardly worth bothering with. By the time the ink in the central tube is used up, the bright brass of the pencil tip would be tarnished in use, and the whole pencil reaching the moment to be discarded. (By unscrewing the pencil at the middle of the barrel, the simplicity of the components is easily seen.)

My inquiry of the buyer at the New York department store where these packages of pencils were on sale —

dumped into bin counters for customer self-service pickup to reduce selling cost — revealed they were NOT "loss leaders" to entice people into the store so they would be tempted also to buy a high-profit item.

The department store buyer said he was selling them at a profit, but he had been required to purchase 200,000 packages to get a low enough price to do so. My inquiry later of the manufacturer revealed the price to the department store was 60 cents, and that the manufacturers' actual cost was 52 cents. The manufacturer could make a profit with a mark-up of 8 cents, to allow the department store to have a mark-up of 38 cents to cover transportation, storage, handling, breakage and other loss, and profit.

During April and May, 1956, a still newer and faster machine for fabricating components and assembling the ball point pencils was put into use. Permission for me to see the machine when I was at the factory in New York City was refused since it is a close secret. The important point is that there is no limit except sales for the output of this machine. The manufacturer by June, 1956, is producing three million completed pencils a month. He stated he could easily turn out six million, or even 10 million a month, and asserted he would be able to go to ANY QUANTITY if he had the sales.

The total number of ball point pencils manufactured in the United States in one year at current levels of business is 700 million. This volume is produced by 24 companies. The number of workers needed for this fabulous production is insignificant. The number of people needed with money in their pocket to buy this output is highly significant — in fact gives full meaning to the point that with automation the machines and instruments can do almost everything except buy what they make!

Other consumer goods items also are being manufactured in tremendous volume. Factories with such marvelous production machinery cannot operate full time, else the quantity of goods would stack up unsold. Companies in this situation then begin to diversify their output, making various kinds of items. But not too far in the future there is the remedy of more income for workers and shorter working hours — traditional trade union answers to increased productivity from science and technology. Either the shorter work week (maybe 4 days instead of 5) or the shorter work year (11 and then 10 months instead of 12) — both with full wage or salary income — will be entirely feasible.

Figure 4.3 Ball point pen.

remit of humans are now at risk of automation, mechanization and digitalization. Frey and Osborne's much-cited report (2013) demonstrates that both repetitive and non-repetitive jobs are now susceptible. Tele-marketers, tax preparers, insurance underwriters and library technicians are at a high risk of automation, at 0.99 probability (1 = certain). Work in healthcare and social work (0.0035) and recreational therapy (0.0028) are also under threat. A great deal of legal casework research can now be done by computers using deep learning algorithms (Ford, 2015). Non-routine work such as driving and deciphering handwriting are now being done by machines (Frey and Osborne, 2013: 17).

In 2016, I visited a factory in the Netherlands where I was privileged to have the chance to ask unionised workers, who had witnessed changes in a car factory over several decades, what they thought about the arrival of robots into the plant. They talked to me at length about their experiences and judgements. They stated that for ergonomic reasons, robots actually provide a healthy work environment as they can do work that is dangerous or difficult for people. The cost of production can significantly be reduced and the time taken to produce units is reduced. Robots can help disabled people work better. Humans can learn to work better but robots only do what they are told. They can make people work better and feel challenged. Automation makes administration tasks easier. Robots do not complain, do not call in sick and do not make mistakes.

Workers in the car factory mentioned to me that there is no need for timing devices in their factory to make sure people are working quickly enough, because there is no choice. Targets are set and humans and robots must work together to meet them. However, if there is a problem on the line, people must compensate for the interruption by working faster, whether the reason for disruption is that something has gone wrong electronically, something has not been delivered, or any other reason. On an assembly line, a car appears every few seconds. People are required to keep up with robots and this is the primary incentive and method to time work.

Workers mentioned that robots, while efficient, cannot buy the things they make. They cannot correct mistakes if something goes wrong on the line, whereas a human would know how to quickly fix things. Robots, workers told me, have led to a significant loss of jobs and lower pay even though robots can never replace a human at a social level. For these reasons, the introduction of robots in workplaces should be accompanied with preparation and training for changes. The union head at the meeting I attended indicated that unions are concerned that companies are not preparing workers for the future, and automation is a clear part of factories' and other workplaces' futures. The question is whether companies will invest in people or whether they will only focus on short-term profit margins. When new systems are introduced, older workers suffer the most because in many cases, they are out of practice with learning. If elderly people cannot keep up, the chances are that companies will side-line them and not commit to lifelong learning.

Next, I look at another feature of changes that new technologies introduce to workplaces by looking at work in the 'gig economy'.

Gig Economy

The explicit threat of automation in factories has been updated by new patterns of labour selection in new work design models such as the 'sharing economy', facilitated by a new method of work selection and distribution called people analytics, which facilitate a process of identity management (Ajana, 2013) evident in new online platforms in the de-mand economy (AFL-CIO, 2016) where people buy and sell labour. The sharing economy or work in the 'human cloud' includes such platforms as Upwork, ODesk, Guru, Amazon Mechanical Turks, Uber, Deliveroo and Handy which are called 'online platforms' in the Digital Single Market European Commission terminology (discussed below). Huws (2015) and Cherry (2011) label this type of exchange and work as 'crowdsourcing' and Huws defines it as 'paid work organised through online labour exchanges' (2015: 1).

Crowdsourcing has facilitated companies' outsourcing of labour as well as introduced new platforms for freelance and self-employed work. As I pointed out in Chapter 1, self-employment is the only employment growth area in the United Kingdom. This trend is also rising internation-ally. The platform economy relies on self-employed contracts and as such, self-employed people have no access to regular employment benefits such as health care or maternity leave. Workers have very little legal protection and platforms are designed to reduce employer liability.

When gig economy platforms were first introduced, workers used them to top up incomes, and the work was mostly carried out in more ad-vanced countries. However, over time, workers with no other incomes in all regions have become heavily reliant on these spaces. Platforms such as Amazon's Mechanical Turks facilitated outsourcing of work to the global south, where the price paid for human labour has been lower and labour market regulation is localised and often limited (Bergvall-Kåreborn and Howcroft, 2014). But now, even professional tasks on these platforms are being 'broken down by their least common denominator...' and 'the way that tasks and human capital is being viewed and handled is... one that almost serves to dehumanise workers' (Cherry, 2011: 30). Companies have tended to follow minimum standards, particularly in the global south and often adopt unenforceable corporate social responsibility models which af-fect how outsourced labour occurs.

On the 'crowdwork' (Berg, 2016) platforms Mechanical Turks and Up-work, people place available job contracts online, and workers contact clients to pick up and sometimes bid for work. Work is often distributed in a piece meal fashion to various workers as part of outsourced labour. The work offered from such platforms ranges from graphic design to pro-gramming, but communication between the worker and client is usually very limited, leading to a distinct lack of transparency. This can raise eth-ical questions, because 'workers are unable to make judgments about the moral valence of their work' (Zittrain, 2008, cited in Bergvall-Kåreborn and Howcroft, 2014: 218). Further, intensified reputation self-management is standard practice in the online labour market, as freelancers seek work and as employers or clients actively profile employees with the use of new technologies (Bodie et al., 2016; Gandini, 2016; Pasquale, 2010). The chasing and utilising of social capital to enhance and further careers and to find work and employment is not itself new, but the type of reputations that workers form allows them to compete with other workers for work on these online platforms. Reputations are 'based on algorithmic-based third party elaboration that translated the opinions of others into reputation proxy' (Gandini et al., 2016). So reputations are acquired through algorithm, based on the number of tasks a worker took on and subsequent ratings by clients. For example, Uber drivers report that if they receive customer 'star' rankings below 5.6 or 4.5, they can be fired, despite some aspects of a journey like heavy traffic, 3G availability or treatment of the car by other passengers (like soiling from vomit and the like) which have nothing to do with a driver's performance. Drivers receive no help from the firm for related issues and often receive much less income than they were promised upon becoming drivers (Brownstone, 2015). Nonetheless, the paradox and fiction of algorithms is that they are 'absent' of 'human bias' (Frey and Osborne, 2013: 18). However, Bodie et al. (2016) point out that 'workers want to be treated as people, not ranked as fungible data sets or assessed as cost centres' (75).

I was privileged to be invited to speak at the Royal Society of Arts (RSA) in 2016 to share my research which was used to inform an RSA booklet on gig work. Mags Dewhurst, who is both an active member of Independent Workers Union of Great Britain and a same day medical pushbike courier for CitySprint UK Ltd. was also invited to speak. Mags, after the talks, agreed to carry out an email interview about some of the changes she has witnessed over the five years she has done this work. Magsindicated that there is a rise in technology such as the use of handheld computers (XDA/PDA like Palm Pilots) or apps-both in the courier industry and food delivery. These technologies have digitised what used to happen on paper and are used primarily for the collection of signatures to authorise pick up and collection of parcels. However, the related devices also allow companies to GPS track all couriers; all of their movements, as well live process of collection and delivery at every stage. Mags stated that:

> ...your every move and action are tracked in a digital audit trail. This is quite different from the days when couriers used to work off paper and rely solely on the use of the radio (walkie talkie) to receive jobs. Now everything is digital there is much less freedom and much higher amount of control, thus meaning we are much less 'independent', even though our contracts say we are totally free and independent.

I asked Mags, in her view, what is the biggest threat to workers' rights, in this context? She noted that bogus independent contractor/subcontractor contracts are prevalent in gig economy work. She indicated the rise of digitisation, automation and algorithmic management, stating that 'used in combination, they're toxic and are designed to strip millions of folks of basic rights'. I asked which rights are being stripped, in the context of her work? Mags indicated,

> All of them. The only bit of legislation that protects me would be the equality act, but that would only protect certain characteristics and would be hard to win anyway. Holiday pay, national minimum wage, sick pay, pensions, parental leave, redundancy, tax and in contributions... is removed via IC contracts.

I asked what kinds of organising Mags and colleagues have done, and she indicated that they have:

> Built a branch of the IWGB UNION. This is the mechanism we have found most effective for creating change it helped consolidate a fragmented community and gives people hope and strength in numbers through collective fights. So far we have won three major pay rises of 20–30% at London's big three courier companies; City Sprint, Ecourier and Absolutely Couriers. We also won at Gophr, a small app company, but they recently backed out of the agreement. We are also in the process of challenging our IC status in the courts at four of the big courier companies. We've also had limited success with the Deliveroo strike in August. Although we didn't manage to stop the new pay structure coming in, we helped the workers escalate their strike, created loads of positive publicity and helped to shine a big light on the gig economy and exposed the contradictions inherent in it-which are all present in the courier industry as well, obviously.

What more can be done to organise and reform work and what is stopping people from doing it? Mags indicated that the difficulty with unionising gig economy workers is that it is hard to get access to workers who are on the move constantly, where their work is scattered across large areas. Mags noted that 'if we can't get legislation to force companies to let unions in from the off, which is highly likely, then unions need to try harder'. She noted that a problem is that unions often have a very negative attitude that only serves to prevent action. Mags related that she often hears big unions complaining about anti trade union legislation, lack of participation and blames the government for why they are not winning. In her mind,

> ...this is the wrong attitude and is a recipe for inaction and is defeatist. If this is the attitude, of course nothing will happen and of course

you won't convince anyone to take action. What was great about the Deliveroo strike was that it was autonomous: the drivers did it by themselves; we merely assisted once it got going. It exposed the failings of government, business, and the unions!! Now slowly, the big guys are waking up and gearing up but I doubt much will happen. As ever we will rely on workers to have the courage themselves to take action and force change and that is where the real power lies.

Delivery drivers have been tracked for decades and the introduction of satellite technologies has allowed this practice to become ever more finite. One UPS driver told Harper's that the employer uses new metrics as a 'mental whip', noting that 'people get intimidated and work faster' (The Week, 2015).

The profiling of human behaviour through all these techniques and resultant big data (which in the employment sense is data that has been accumulated over time with links made between various types of data to give aggregate profile information, including scores and ratings) allows management to make judgments about who people are as well as to predict future behaviour. Computer generated data is expected to be reliable, neutral and help with forecasting (Amoore, 2013; Cheney-Lippold, 2011). The assumed neutrality and utility of data for these purposes is what is at stake in workplace power relations, whether the workplace is one of a freelance worker or a full-time employee. Workers are increasingly easily selected and discarded; replaced and disposable in this 'profane' referencing system (Gandini et al., 2016). Reputation in the online labour market has become incredibly important for work that happens in digital spaces, called 'virtual work' (Holts, 2013; Huws, 2013, 2014) and 'digital labour' (Fuchs, 2014). Online platform work is largely reliant on the 'big data' workers produce about themselves. It is largely unregulated, leading it to resemble a neo-Darwinist arena of uncertainty where discrimination is fully experienced offline but generated online: where social relations of work are masked and anonymised (Bergvall-Kåreborn and Howcroft, 2014: 218). Accountability is heavily skewed towards workers, which is exacerbated when casualised work is on the rise. Virtual work has already been proven to perpetuate precarity and pressures people to overwork (Huws, 2014; Moore and Robinson, 2016). People actively cultivate online reputations to attract further work, seen as an unpaid necessity, contributing to the conditions of precarity outlined in Chapter 3. Problems that arise, such as the obstruction of newcomers and difficulties in entrance points, becomes a closed loop of client/worker relationships. The logic of algorithmic reputation acquisition further penalises non-standard workers and leads to unequal life chances. Irregular career patterns can also result from time out of work for reproductive domestic labour, maternity leave, physical illness and mental health issues.

In mid-2016 the European Commission (EC) discussed implementing a Digital Single Market and presented a 'targeted approach to online platforms' (EC, 2016a). Online platforms cover 'a wide range of activities including... collaborative economy platforms' (EC, 2016b). The emphasis, however, is on services and free markets while there is no mention at all of workers' protections. The targeted approach is to be guided by (EC, 2016a):

- a level-playing field for comparable digital services
- responsible behaviour of online platforms to protect core values
- transparency and fairness for maintaining user trust and safeguarding innovation
- open and non-discriminatory markets in a data-driven economy

Research by the CIPD in March 2017 called *To Gig or not to Gig?: Stories from the Modern Economy, Survey Report* showed that 4 percent of UK working adults aged 18–70, or around 1.3 million people, work in the gig work context. The report states that six in ten gig workers surveyed would like the government to regulate it further and to guarantee basic employment rights, but many also thought that people in the gig economy 'make a decision to sacrifice job security and workers' benefits in exchange for greater flexibility' (2017: 48). Contradictory to the supposed liberations in a 'sharing' economy, many gig workers are unhappy with the levels of control exerted over them, despite the inherent insecurity of their contracts with businesses. Less than four in ten, or 38 percent, of gig workers reported they feel like they are their own bosses (2017: 21). Transport workers with their own vehicles, such as Uber drivers, are most likely to feel autonomous or in control 'like their own boss' (Ibid.). Delivery drivers are least likely to feel they are independent and have control over work, where 31 percent agreed they feel like their own boss and 47 percent saying the opposite (Ibid.). Fifty-seven percent of workers surveyed believe firms are exploiting the fact that there is very little regulation over this area of work and uses their labour to grow quickly. Often, workers take the work to boost their incomes, but since the median income is from £6 to £7.70 an hour (2017: 14), 60 percent of workers said they do not earn enough.

One case study in this CIPD report describes someone called 'Mary' who has been in the gig economy since 2013 after redundancy from her post as a legal secretary in London, when her job was outsourced overseas. Mary sold her home and moved to Southend-on-Sea where she takes on agency work and also finds jobs through an online service called PeoplePerHour:

[Mary states that:] 'You make a hidden bid saying how much you would charge to do the job, which only the client who has posted the job can see. The trouble is, anyone in the world can bid for the jobs, so you are competing with people who live in India who can afford to charge less to do the work.' Mary usually charges between £7.20 and £8.00 an hour depending on the type of work. A typical job will earn Mary about £40, of which £3.75 would be taken as an administrative charge by the site.

Mary stated that she cannot get enough work through these channels. She would like to retrain, but is not eligible for Jobseeker's Allowance and so has no support or spare money to do so. Mary notes that the work will suit some people better than others (CIPD, 2017: 5).

Overall, the Report recommends that the government should:

- Consult on the demarcation between 'employee', 'worker' and 'self-employed' and how they map on to employment rights, tax and benefits
- Run a high-profile 'know-your-rights' campaign with organisations such as CIPD, Acas, Citizens Advice Bureau and others
- Give sufficient resources to the Gangmasters and Labour Abuse Authority (GLAA) to monitor and enforce compliance
- Increase resources available to Acas so it can proactively work with organisations to improve their working practices
- Support the development of guidance on atypical working, setting out principles of good work and responsible employment
- Increase public investment in lifelong learning to reverse the recent decline in investment in adult skills
- Develop an effective all-age careers service

One example of the lack of worker protection is seen in the platform Upwork's website which provides a link to a section called 'Am I Safe Working Here?'. The 'I', however, refers to safety for clients rather than workers. Upwork provides a Work Diary which is a billable time system recording all work completed. The Diary takes a screenshot of a freelancer's screen every ten minutes to verify work and counts keystrokes during work sessions. Upwork Messages also provides an online messenger system allowing real-time discussion if desired. Upwork ensures clients their 'right to ownership of intellectual property' and will provide dispute assistance (Upwork, 2016).

Amazon's Mechanical Turks' Participation Agreement limits its role in the transactions between 'requesters' and 'providers', putting the emphasis on both to ensure legality of transactions and appropriate taxing. This Agreement indicates clearly to Providers that:

> you will not be entitled to any of the benefits that a Requester or Amazon Mechanical Turk may make available to its employees, such

as vacation pay, sick leave, insurance programs, including group health insurance or retirement benefits; you are not eligible to recover worker's compensation benefits in the event of injury.

(AMT, 2014)

These platforms allow the exchange of labour but do not provide basic necessities, demonstrating precarity. The next section discusses further how technology is being used in workplaces to capture unseen labour.

Monitoring and Tracking with Wearables

Wearable devices, as discussed in Chapter 1 and throughout this book, can be used to record levels and type of physical activity, heart rate variability as well as emotional and mood variances and stress levels. In this context, the emergence of workplace wearable devices and self-tracking technologies is seen in health and wellness initiatives in advanced countries to be cutting edge methods which improve employees' health and well-being and improve aggregate firm productivity (Nield, 2014; Wilson, 2013). Despite the increasing levels of interest in adopting wearables in workplaces, recent ADP UK (2015) research shows that more than half (52 percent) of employees have expressed concern with the amount of personal data that employers can access via the wearable technology used in workplaces. Workers feel that devices may be used as tools to 'spy' on them (The Week, 2015). These attitudes towards privacy vary across countries, with 60 percent of German employees expressing reservations but only 36 percent of Dutch employees feeling this way. UK workers are the most hesitant to use wearables with as few as one in five (20 percent) feeling comfortable with this possibility (ADP UK, 2015).

Warehouse and Factory Settings

The use of wearable tracking technologies for productivity originates in the factory and in warehouse work. Newly intimate forms of the technology are also being introduced. One warehouse operative, Ingrid (not her real name), who has worked in one warehouse in Britain for eleven years, provided information about a new wearable device that was rolled out in her workplace in February 2016. All warehouse work floor operatives were unexpectedly required to use a hand-worn scanner. The researchers asked what the workers were told the devices would be used for. Ingrid indicated that management told workers that the devices would provide management with information about any mistakes made and who in the warehouse had made them, meaning they can be provided with help to not make a similar mistake again. In practice, however, Ingrid indicated that the technology has been used not only to track individual mistakes but also to track individual productivity and time spent working and on breaks. Workers were told that management would hold individual consultations on the basis of the data, but this had not happened. Instead, after a certain amount of time following the devices' implementation, workers were told that people would be fired within days, and it was revealed that data from devices were part of the decision-making process for dismissal choices. Ingrid was not clear how the data was interpreted however, as seen in her response here:

> Recently they sacked 2 or 3 people, and they decided this based upon who did the least work. Maybe it was in May, when things get a bit quieter at work. They sacked 3 people: one of them was lazy, so I understand why. But the other 2 were very good. A week before the sackings, the management said 'everyone be careful, because we are going to fire someone from the temporary staff'. So everybody sped up.

Ingrid indicated concern that the data accumulation was being rigged. In one case she and co-workers suspected that specific people were given easier tasks during a period of amplified monitoring. While warehouse operatives are permitted to join trade unions, Ingrid indicated that she is not part of a trade union and that she is not aware of any membership in her workplace. In any case, no consultation was held with relevant trade unions nor with workers before the technology was integrated. Ingrid stated:

> We're aware that the tracking might be used to put pressure on us to work faster, and it might be used to sack people. But lots of us feel that we don't care anymore. Because physically we just can't do any more.

One night shift, Ingrid and a colleague went into the manager's office (the door was unlocked, she told me). They noticed spreadsheets on the desk and had a look. Ingrid saw lots of data about herself and her colleagues. While this was not surprising in itself, what was surprising was to realise that the data they had been told was the reason for terminating some workers was not actually reflected in the data in the diagrammes they had analogue hacked. While professional workers have access to their personal data when it is integrated into wellness programmes, the workers in the warehouse were not only not able to view data, but were also being lied to about its reading. As Ben Bradley says in the novel *I am Pilgrim*: 'computers don't lie, but liars can compute' (Hayes, 2013).

Amazon and Tesco warehouses monitor every minute zero-hour contracted workers spend on the performance console using arm-mounted terminals. The 'wearable terminal' is in effect a streamlined replacement for the clipboard, allowing workers to scan barcodes on packages from a small scanner worn on the finger. Information from barcodes, or location information, is listed on the upper section of the terminal that is strapped to the forearm. Devices operate on a local Wi-Fi network and can further adopt Bluetooth for synching with other devices. Adam Littler, undercover reporter, took a position through an employment agency as a 'picker' in the Amazon warehouse in Swansea. The wearable device he was given told him what to collect and gave him a requisite number of seconds within which to find the product, tracking his picker rate with a warning that he could be disciplined, and beeping if mistakes were made. For eleven hours shift workers

> are machines, we are robots, we plug our scanner in, we're holding it, but we might as well be plugging it into ourselves... literally work to the bone and there doesn't seem to be any reward or any let-up... the pressure's unbelievable.
>
> (Bennett, 2013)

Another employee stated that the conditions were like a 'slave camp' (Ibid.). Working conditions have become so intolerable that Amazon is offering unhappy employees up to 5,000 USD if they would like to leave their jobs (Cockburn, 2014). Indeed, employee health and safety usually is secondary to lean logistics and speed of work in depot work (Mulholland and Stewart, 2013).

In a similar experiment, Tesco tracked productivity as part of a nine million dollar investment into similar wearables adopted in 300 locations across the UK. At a distribution centre in Ireland, warehouse workers gather products from eighty-seven aisles of three-story shelves wearing armbands that track goods, with the incentive to free up time previously spent writing on a clipboard. The band allocates jobs to the wearer, forecasts a completion time, and quantifies movements among the area's 9.6 miles of shelving and 111 loading bays. A 2.8-in. display gives analytical feedback, verifying the order, or otherwise 'nudging a worker whose order is short' (2013). Tesco requires warehouse staff to wear armbands that track productivity. Employees receive a score of 100 if tasks are completed on time, and 200 if activities are finished in half the time required, raising questions about employee health and safety. A worker reported 'the guys who made the scores were sweating buckets and throwing stuff all over the place' (Rawlinson, 2013). Warehouse workers are at risk of being penalised if they do not record toilet breaks on devices (2013). The investment was specifically oriented around efficiency and lean production, and led to reducing the need for full time employees by 18 percent (Wilson, 2013).

The use of new wearable devices that allow location tracking and speed of warehouse work has led to rationalisation of workforces such as in the case of the retailer Tesco described above. Employee tracking in Amazon warehouses has resulted in reports of heightened stress and physical burnout.

Professional Settings

In professional settings, while sensory tracking devices are often provided for wellness initiatives they often have similar implications for activity management. Olivetti Research's Active Badge and successors such as the Sociometric Badge and Wearable Sensor Badge, can trigger automatic doors, transmit wearer identities and forward telephone calls. Some can also record workers' movements, speech, proximity and interactions, and analyse voice patterns and non-verbal cues to deduce mood and interpersonal influence (Lindsay, 2015; Mohan et al., 2009: 45). In early 2016, employee presence recorders were attached to desks in Britain's *The Daily Telegraph* newspaper offices without employee consent, which was badly received by the employees. The OccupEye devices were removed after journalists widely publicized the issue (Mance, 2016). In another example, an employee was told by her US employer to keep the GPS tracking device on her phone switched on even when she was not working. The employee was fired for disabling it during non-working hours. The employee sued her employer for economic and non-economic damages (Kravets, 2015). The potential for displacing management accountability for workers' stress levels and the support for decision-making on redundancy on the basis of data is very real in these contexts.

The main forms to track seen (physical data) and unseen (emotional and affective) labour involve armbands, GPS and indoor location tracking devices and the use of Radio Frequency Identification. In the 1990s Hitachi introduced the Business Microscope which is a nameplate type sensor worn on the collars of employees (a 'lanyard'). Inbuilt sensor technology measures and later analyses inter company communication and activities. Each sensor recognizes those of others and tracks body and behaviour rhythm data, and 'face time' to determine how well employees are talking to one another through things such as hand gestures and energy levels in voices. Data is then loaded to a server and analysed to identify the most productive communication styles across employees. In 2006, Citywatcher. com was the first to use Radio Frequency Identification (RFID) chips in humans. These chips were previously used to track animals. Citywatcher. com embedded tracker chips into two of its employees' arms in Cincinnati. These devices were first called 'digital angels'. In 2013, The Citizen Evolutionary Process Organism (C3PO) started an initiative whereby employees at the company Citizen in Portland, Oregon, which designs mobile technologies, upload information to a central database about their daily lives including exactly what they eat, any exercise completed, hours slept, and the like. The experiment is designed to identify whether healthier employees are also 'happier and more productive' (Finley, 2013), and the 'ultimate aim is to explicitly show employees how they can improve their work through better personal habits' (Ibid.). Darpa is researching ways to track soldiers' health. IBM has a tool to identify unhappy employees. A spinoff of this is the emergence of consultancies, such as the company Limeaid, that are designed to help companies identify the best use of technologies to enhance productivity.

As incorporation of in-work self-and other-tracking becomes normalized, professional employees risk feeling excluded from programmes if they choose to opt out, where both stigmatisation and financial penalty may incur for those employees (Hamblen, 2015; Rosenblat et al., 2014). Beyond the 'wellness syndrome' (Cederström and Spicer, 2015) and employee stigmatization, we have to ask questions about whether 'opting in' or 'out' is ever possible in any employment relationship. In the Quantified Workplace experiment I outline below, the Personal Data Protection Agency in the country in question put forward a series of queries to the local data analyst working on the company's study. The Agency asked, in a quite incisive manner: 'Is the relationship between an employee and employer ever actually consensual?'. Employers have significant leeway to gather information about employees, but new technologies available for human resource management have unprecedented possibilities for what employers can know about workers, inviting questions about the ethical implications, regulation, privacy, data protection, work intensification and data-based decision-making. Productivity data is an area of obvious direct interest to an employer and has different legal protection, but many devices can now track many other aspects of workers' everyday lives; increasingly, all of life is included in considerations for workers. For all of these reasons, the constant-on nature of work, the rise of algorithmic distribution and selection of work and threat of automation, and the use of wearable tracking devices have become significant concerns.

The Quantified Workplace[3]

From 2015 to 2016, one group of professional workers in an office in the Netherlands carried out an experiment they called the 'Quantified Workplace' project (hereafter labelled as QWP). Up to fifty employees were given the option to obtain a FitBit Charge HR Activity Tracker. Thirty employees enrolled. The company contracted one data analyst, Joost Plattel, who set up individualised dashboards and RescueTime for participants. Volunteers for the project received workday lifelog emails asking them to rate their subjective productivity, wellbeing and stress.

Importantly, the project occurred during a period of change management as one multinational company absorbed a smaller company that consisted of a tight knit group of real estate and work design consultants. The smaller company suggested and led the project. The manager running the project informed me that it was part of a move toward a more agile and mobile workplace. The project manager indicated that her/his intentions were to help workers adapt to an agile working environment, where change was to be expected and red tape reduced, and to see to what extent employees' self-awareness, stress, wellbeing and 'wellbilling' (the amount of revenue an employee generates for the company), was impacted during the period of transition (interview 5th October 2015). The company was interested in comparing subjectively and objectively measured productivity, as linked to health and activity tracking and 'billability'. I was not given access to the data gathered by the company on whether improved activity led to higher productivity and billability. But the project fit with the company's moves toward working anywhere (which was encouraged at the time that the project merger was put in place), increases in teamwork, and efficiency. Furthermore, the merger was a significant *change* for all who had worked in the smaller company, and all participants in the QWP had been employed in the smaller company. So, their experience of change, and thus agility in line with the company's new agile principles, was measured by the processes put into place by the QWP. As I the note below, unseen labour is identified as a feature in individuals' self-management of workplace changes. The areas of unseen labour I identify are the subjective measures outlined below, as workers were expected to manage any emotional or affective impacts as the company went through the merger and acquisition process.

Study Design and Methodology[4]

At the project launch event, consultants and the local data analyst spoke about how self-quantification can lead to improved wellbeing and self-awareness (requiring what we identify as unseen labour). 'Her', a film about a relationship between a man and his artificial intelligence lover, was shown. All consultants spoke about their hopes for the project, indicating that sensory tracking and other data collection in the workplaces is a budding management trend. The company's goal was to identify best practices for this type of endeavour.

Our agreed role on the QWP was to conduct independent academic research over one year. We were granted permission to conduct two surveys and conduct interviews with project participants and gained limited access to quantified and self-report data, provided participants consented. Some employees participated in different stages of the study and some agreed to share company-collected data with researchers. Some participants took part in interviews but did not agree to provide tracker data. Some provided data but did not participate in surveys. The summary of participation levels with demographic information is shown in Table 4.1.

Table 4.1 Summary of the Participation and Data Sharing Levels in Each Part of the Study

ID	Gender	Job Title	Age	Survey 1	Interview 1	Interview 2	Survey 2	FitBit	Self-Report	Rescue Time
1	Male	Consultant	41–45	1	1	1	0	1	1	0
2	Male	Project Manager	46–50	1	1	1	0	1	1	1
3	Female	Consultant	26–30	1	1	0	0	0	0	0
4	Female	Real estate agent	51–55	1	1	0	0	1	1	0
5	Female	Senior Consultant	36–40	1	1	1	1	1	0	0
6	Male	Director	51–55	1	1	1	1	1	1	0
7	Male	Account manager	41–45	1	1	1	0	1	1	1
8	Male	Senior Consultant	36–40	1	1	1	0	1	1	0
9	Male	Senior Consultant	36–40	1	1	1	0	1	0	0
10	Male	Consultant	26–30	1	1	1	0	0	1	0
11	Male	Interior Architect	36–40	1	1	1	0	1	1	0
12	Female	Senior Consultant	36–40	1	1	1	0	1	0	0
13	Male	Senior Consultant	41–45	1	1	1	0	0	0	0
14	Female	Director	41–45	1	0	1	0	1	0	0
15	Female	Consultant	26–30	1	0	1	0	0	0	0
16	Female	Senior Consultant	51–55	1	0	0	0	0	0	0
17	Female	Director	36–40	1	0	0	0	0	0	0
18	Female	Secretary	26–30	1	0	0	0	0	0	0
19	Male	Consultant	26–30	1	0	0	0	0	0	0
20	Male	Project Manager	36–40	1	0	0	0	0	0	0
21	Male	Senior Consultant	46–50	1	0	0	0	0	0	0
22	Male	Consultant	36–40	0	1	1	0	0	0	0
23	Female	Junior Consultant	21–25	0	1	1	1	1	1	0
24	Male	NA	NA	0	1	1	1	1	1	1
25	Male	NA	NA	0	1	1	0	1	1	1
26	Female	NA	NA	0	1	1	0	0	0	0
27	Female	Consultant	NA	0	0	1	1	1	1	0
28	Male	NA	NA	0	0	1	0	1	1	0
29	Female	Senior Consultant	NA	0	0	0	1	0	0	0
30	Male	NA	NA	0	0	0	0	1	1	0

Table by Lukasz Piwek

0 = didn't participate or didn't share data, 1 = did participate or did share data. Table also includes: age range, gender and job position held by participants.

NA = no data.

A mixed-method observational study design was used with opting-in employees, and two streams of data collection contributed to the analysis. The introduction surveys were conducted in Month 1 and a final debriefing online survey, which was roughly based on the interview questions, was conducted in Month 12. Semi-structured interviews were conducted in Months 3 and 8 (Figure 4.4). The other source of information was data collected by the company from participants including: (1) daily step count and average heart rate from FitBits devices (heart rate to be linked to stress); (2) average daily time spent on productive and distractive computer-based activities recorded by RescueTime; (3) data from daily self-reports provided by employees who rated their levels of subjective stress, well-being and productivity in response to weekday emails run by the company's contracted data analyst.

All relevant consent forms were signed by participants. Interestingly, and as already mentioned above, some tensions emerged in the process of data collection and dissemination resulting from a series of questions posed by the Autoriteit Persoonsgegevens (the Institute for the Protection of Personal Data), to the local data analyst (not researchers) about how data was collected, where data was stored, and the very possibility for authentic employee consent, given the sensitive nature of information collected.

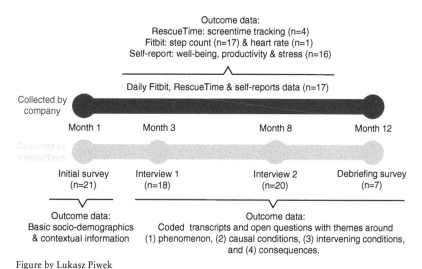

Figure by Lukasz Piwek

Figure 4.4 Timeline of QWP.

Measures from Initial and Final Online Survey

In the first month of the project, we sent an online survey to participants with a series of questions adapted from the grounded theory method I selected for analysis; the survey incorporated both open-ended and closed-ended questions, with mixed-type response scales and was split into two parts: (1) general socio-demographic questions, and (2) general information about participants' use of tracking technology, their general self-ratings of health, productivity, views on data privacy, as well as personal goals set for participation in the QSW study. The survey was constructed and distributed using the Qualtrics Research Suite and took approximately fifteen minutes to complete. A total of twenty-five participants agreed to participate in a survey and twenty-one fully completed it. Participants were presented with brief instructions on the purpose of the study, approximate time needed and confirmation that data was secured under the Data Protection Act 1998. Participants were asked to confirm they understood the instructions and consented to participation.

In the final month of the project a final survey was distributed, asking about final impressions, conclusions and ideas about QWP. Due to low participation in the final online survey (*n* = 6; see Table 4.1) and many incomplete responses amongst those who participated, quantitative data was excluded. However, written responses illuminate some reasons for resistance (see 'changed attitudes' section).

Interview Data Collection

A total of thirty-eight interviews were conducted at two intervals. I interviewed eighteen employees in the first set and twenty in the second. Interviews lasted for thirty to sixty minutes and I carried these out at the offices of the smaller company which was in the process of being absorbed into the larger one. All interviews were recorded on a digital audio recorder and professionally transcribed from audio files into a standard text format. Using an inductive grounded theory method, interviews were structured according to the following categories: metadata, phenomenon, causal conditions, intervening conditions and consequences. The summary of questions is shown in Appendix 1. The quantitative comparison of percentages of how frequently participants referred to themes during interview series 1 and 2 is shown in Appendix 2. From transcripts, computer assisted qualitative data analysis was conducted using *NVivo* software for the first set of interviews, by coding responses into a range of contextually specific categories. A compatible software tool was used to do the same with the second set.

While remaining sensitive to the data, I sought to identify employee emotions and behaviour changes in the areas of self-management, subjective productivity and self-awareness. Our qualitative approach allowed me to identify valuable data on participants' responses to the project revealing responses and, interestingly, a level of resistance to the project.

Measures from Trackers and Self-Reports

The company's data analyst collected, managed, distributed and stored daily data. Participants had personal data dashboards where they could view graphical summaries of daily data. At the end of the project, researchers received data from FitBits (step count [n = 17] and RescueTime showing levels of productivity [low, medium, high] which were calculated by screen time for specific computer-based activities such as browsing, writing and checking social networks [n = 4]. Researchers also received self-report data (n = 16) from email lifelogs: well-being (1–10 likert scale), productivity (1–5 likert scale) and stress (1–5 likert scale). Four out of eight participants (50%) who used RescueTime, and seventeen out of thirty-five participants (48%) using Fitbits agreed to share their data with researchers.

Surveys Results: Contextual Information about Participants

Twenty-one employees completed the initial survey distributed in Month 1 of the project (twelve male, nine female), with the job titles Consultant (29%), Senior Consultant (21%), Director (12%), Project Manager (12%) and other (26%; Appendix 3c). Over 67% rated their health as 'very good' or 'good' (Appendix 3a). Most participants rated subjective levels of productivity as being 'good' or 'very good' (86%; Appendix 3b). Overall, participants reported a range of definitions for subjective 'productivity' (Appendix 3e) with leading concepts being 'quality work' (19%), 'reaching goal' (17%), 'time management' (12%) and 'billability' (12%). Participants reported feeling most productive in the office (52%), home (24%) or on the road (10%; Appendix 3d). They reported a broad range of goals associated with QWP with the leading ones being: 'insight into work/life behaviour' (19%), 'increased productivity' (19%), 'exploratory data collection' (11%), 'increased physical activity' (8%) and 'tackling stress' (8%; Appendix 3f).

Fieldwork Results: Research Question I

Both research questions were inductive, conducted through semi-structured interviews. Our first research question was: 'How did employees respond to the project?'. To pursue the question, researchers asked about perceptions and judgements of the project; difficulties in using technology; and involvement with the project. We looked at coded interview responses from eighteen participants in Month 3, and twenty participants in Month 8 (Figure 4.1). Both interview results and withdrawal rates demonstrate evidence of passive and active resistance.

The first interviews revealed twenty-five responses indicating that employees had good first impressions:

> There is a kinda excitement, ok we will try, see what will happen…
>
> It's good to just experience yourself, like, ok, what will it mean to… to wear it?
>
> I think it's helpful. It gives the extra dimension to have sounding board to do with how you're living your life. If you're being healthy or doing sports so yeah so it's a little help.

Several responses indicated that employees also had critical and unsure reactions or felt the technology did not meet their expectations (at all/yet). Forty-one responses demonstrate overall critical or unsure impressions. Overtly negative responses include:

> I don't find it really interesting to be honest.
> I don't really see the purpose of it.
> I am quite critical.

In the final interviews the number of unsure and critical responses dropped to eighteen, but responses demonstrating difficulties in using the technology itself increased from 13 to 24.

Most of the responses regarding difficulties from the first interviews had to do with reading results, not knowing whether devices were working accurately, not understanding the technology or not knowing whether one is using the technology accurately. One employee explained:

> I don't really see the connection between the things I do on the computer and my heart rate.

Reasons for resistance are reflected here, showing employees' unease with the project, problems with and mistrust in the technology, privacy concerns, and mistrust in perceived reliability and legitimacy of the project.

Exit

Nine responses indicated FitBit abandonment either for a period, or altogether in the first two months. Figure 4.2 shows employees differed in their frequency of FitBit use – some used it for almost the entire project, while others engaged with it for less than one month/ occasionally. FitBit use decreased significantly throughout the project, reflected by the monthly total average step count recorded from all employees (Figure 4.5). There was a 30 percent drop in average steps recorded within the first three months, a 50 percent drop within six, and a 75 percent drop by the end (Figure 4.5). Overall, there was a considerable rate of abandonment from the project, with a 75 per cent rate of self-reported halt to using technologies continuously from the project.

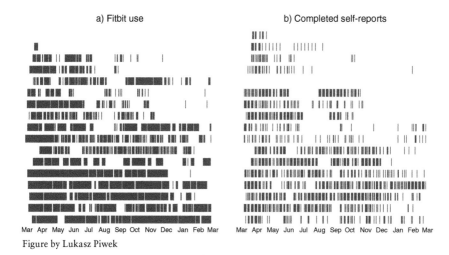

Figure by Lukasz Piwek

Figure 4.5 Frequency of (a) using FitBits and (b) completing self-reports. Bars indicate the use/completion use in specific time period, while gaps indicate the lack of use/completion.

Responses in the first interviews demonstrated scepticism about the validity of the FitBit's readings and wishes for more device intelligence:

> A big question for me and for a few others as well, is uh, how reliable the FitBit is.
> …this thing [FitBit] might be more intelligent than just recording my data.

One respondent in the second interviews indicated frustration:

> I don't get any answers, I just fill in my things, but I don't get an answer if it's good or not, I just want to know if I were good and just start working.

Privacy Concerns

One comment in the first interviews indicated employees originally thought there would be more 'complaints about privacy'. However, in the first interviews, three comments indicated concern about what personal data management were viewing, increasing to twenty-one comments in the final interviews. The biggest change in the data on employee experience from interviews is the increase in participants' sensitivity to privacy

Most participants were already cautious about corporate privacy practices, but had not thought about these in the workplace context. In the first survey, 66 percent agreed that 'consumers have lost all control over how personal information is collected and used by companies'; 62 percent disagreed that 'most businesses handle the personal information they collect about consumers in a proper and confidential way'; 43 percent disagreed that 'existing laws and organizational practices provide a reasonable level of protection for consumer privacy today'.

Other Resistance Related Statements

Responses to the question 'How/have your thoughts about the Quantified Workplace project changed?' indicate:

> I still [have] and even [have] more doubt the project. And I don't wear the Fitbit very often. And when I will wear it, it is for myself and to see how active I am.
> After monitoring my workplace behaviour over a couple of months I found out that it didn't change a lot.
> It confirmed my thoughts, which I had in the beginning. It is better to change your behaviour based on your feelings rather than a device.
> I learned not very much from it.

Results demonstrate both passive (interview statements) and active resistance (withdrawal) to the QWP.

The second research question was, 'What forms of unseen labour, as linked to agility, emerged during this period?'. The unseen labour that became evident through discussions was (a) self-management, measured by 'autonomy', 'goals' and 'mood management'; (b) subjective productivity; (c) self-awareness. As I will now show, the highest rates of increase in self-reported experiences reflecting unseen labour were in feelings of autonomy, desire for coaching and support, and concern for privacy. Goal-setting was not popular but some participants found it was helpful. While there were signs of people's increased sense of subjective productivity and self-awareness in the first interviews, final data demonstrates that these aspects, on aggregate, did not improve.

Unseen Labour I: Self-Management

Autonomy

In the first set of interviews, two responses demonstrate 'increased autonomy'. Most participants indicated they felt they already had autonomy in their workplace. By Month 8, nine responses showed perceived improvements in autonomy.

Goals

Both interviews and surveys asked whether participants had set goals and whether the project aided meeting goals. The initial survey demonstrates an aggregate of thirteen goals across participants (Appendix 3f). Only a few weeks after surveys were completed, five responses indicated employees felt their goals *were* being met. Several did not recall their goals. Seventeen responses in the final interview revealed that participants felt participation in the QWP helped them meet goals.

Mood Management

The second measure of self-management (necessary for agile working) is 'mood management'. In the first interviews, twenty responses indicated improved moods. In the final set, the number was seventeen. First responses included results of impacts on stimulated moods:

> It is a stimulation to make sure I make enough steps in a day.
> It stimulates me to go exercise when I am tired after a long day at work.
> It's a trigger for me to wake up a little bit earlier and relax in the morning.

Final responses included:

> Yes, it did and on the dashboard you can see how your mood says you was and how stressed you were but also how productive, so I think that's very interesting and yes, it motivates me, just like I said, to feeling that I was productive.
>
> The whole experiment is quite something, if I tell people about this, I really think, very cool that we're doing this and yeah, hopefully we're getting somewhere with it, so… it makes me motivated about having my part in the experiment and it should be a good part and motivated to help and motivated [around] what we're doing with this project, more about, okay, now I want to see, yeah, what it is really bringing for me.

Unseen Labour II: Subjective productivity

Fourteen interview responses indicated participants felt their subjective productivity was improving in the first months:

> I feel that I have everything under control.
> Sometimes I can feel productive even when I have a day off.
> Creativity is not measured in time or in space, it depends on the input you are getting but then again you have got to be creative, so you come up with your own input but it's not during office hours, so creativity can also be part of I think measuring productivity because you come up with new ideas when you're talking to people or you are sharing ideas.

Sixteen responses indicated improvement by Month 8:

> I learned about my feeling of productivity, so productivity has nothing to do with invoices we can send to our clients and before I was thinking, okay, productivity is like just hours I'm working for my clients, but

sometimes I feel very productive, just the internal things, so therefore it helps, the way I think about productivity.

I'm more aware of the productivity, I think that's it. It's not that I directly improve my productivity, but I'm more aware of at what moments I'm productive, yeah, but that's the next step, to base some actions on that.

Participants provided daily self-reports on levels of subjective productivity, stress and well-being. The frequency of completing self-reports was sparse and irregular for some (Figure 4.1). However, average total ratings were relatively stable (Appendix 4) showing participants experienced medium-to-high subjective productivity (70%: 3 or higher, 5-point scale), low-to-medium stress (83%: 3 or lower, 5-point scale) and high well-being ratings (78%: 7 or higher, 10-point scale). Final percentages actually show that there was, overall, a slight decrease in feelings of subjective productivity.

Self-Awareness

Overall data from interview responses however demonstrates a slight reduction in employees' self-reported sense of 'self-awareness'. The first interview results included responses claiming increased self-awareness resulting from the QWP, including:

I'm sure it makes you aware of things you do.
I see when I'm frustrated my heartbeat is higher.
[Participation in the QWP makes me] more conscious of activity, heart-rates and wellbeing.

The second interviews revealed improved self-awareness statements. One stated:

I think awareness is even more key than total change of behaviour, but that you are more aware of your body and what's the problems for it and that you address that and start to organise your agenda around it, so that's already a first stage in behavioural change.

While workers adapted to agility in many cases, the majority resisted the QWP both with passive, verbal conjectures, and by explicit exit from the project, revealing tensions in incorporating all-of-life measures in the labour process.

Agile models expect employees to self-manage the impact of constant machinic change and are reliant on subjectification of workers to thrive. The use of data-driven technology is seen to neutralise the effects of performance management and eliminate bias. But quantification of unseen work assumes that all actors under scrutiny start at an equal level of competences. No other factors were taken into account in carrying out the experiment, i.e. for workers' outside-of-work responsibilities or hobbies. One interviewee responded that the gamification aspect to the project grew boring quickly. While some people opted to appear anonymous in the shared dashboard, the respondent told me it was obvious who was who after a while. They quickly realized that some of the participants were already quite active athletes. Otherwise, any existing skills, working time capacity and/or access to social capital were ignored. Though it did not happen in the QWP, assumptions of equal access and equal participation capabilities can easily result in unequal judgements and appraisals or be seen as inducing extra stress, leading to work intensification. Further research must identify these risks.

As Marx stated in Das Kapital:

> Capitalist production... under its aspect of a continuous connected process, of a process of reproduction, produces not only commodities, not only surplus value, but it also produces and reproduces the capitalist relation; on the one side the capitalist, on the other the wage-labourer.
>
> (Vol. 1, Ch. 3: *Simple Reproduction*)

New sensory and tracking technologies reveal the possibilities for profit in unseen labour. Power relations in capitalist reproduction reflect the industrialising world Marx experienced, but now more than ever before machines are the symbols for accelerating the labour process and dragging workers with them. Workers' responses outlined above and their explicit disengagement with the QWP demonstrate awareness of the tensions surrounding new control mechanisms; ongoing struggles in the contemporary labour process where 'agile' is a key meme; and the urgency of review of all-of-life management strategies. Our study of the QWP demonstrates nascent affective resistance to a brave new world of all-of-life work, where monitoring and tracking of unseen labour may become ubiquitous. Future research must look at the risks this poses for workers and at forms of resistance that emerge against modulation and control methods in the quantified workplace.

Conclusion

Von Osten describes Taylorism as the 'rationalisation of body-machine-management relations' (2011: 135), a process taken further in quantified workplace initiatives that bleed into surveillance efforts in inventive ways in the context of agile management systems. The core technique of Taylorism was the external regulation of working bodies through cost accounting, time-motion measurement, and record-keeping. As I have outlined earlier in this chapter and in Chapter 2, the process was opposed by trade unions at the time it was introduced, despite it being hailed by managers as a 'path to prosperity, efficiency and social betterment' (Stone, 2004: 35). Unions were concerned that the standardisation and efficiency tests being conducted across Europe would lead to work intensification and speed up as well as automation. Taylorism, discussed in Chapter 2, undermined the tacit, qualitative knowledge that empowers workers, instead concentrating knowledge work within the planning division. The division of the work process into precise tasks removed skill, and tacit knowledge, from the work process itself.

Contemporary workplace uses of tracking devices outlined in this chapter are subtly different in that the worker may actually be able to see the data that is being accumulated about themselves, at least in the professional settings described here. What is preventing workers from being able to use the data captured to defend themselves? FitBit data has already been used in a courtroom to prove an injury kept someone out of work by comparing someone's data to general population data about average movements (Olson, 2014). What is stopping workers from making other cases to their employers, such as lack of sleep because of work stress? As we see in the following chapter, one employer has already started to use sleep data to make accommodating adjustments to work schedules. It takes a very ethical employer to think in these terms.

There are a very few codes of conduct for rolling out projects such as the one carried out in the Netherlands. Trade unions are starting to take notice of the impact of new technologies in workplaces. Above, I outline the recommendations made by the CIPD for gig economy regulation. In Chapter 1, I looked at the core principles put forward by the ICO in 2011, the 'Data Protection: The Employment Practices Code'. The Director of UNI Global Union Professionals and Managers, Pav Akhtar, outlined what UNI and its affiliates have done to mitigate the worst impacts of technological pressures on workers, and provided a list of principles in our article for the ILO ACTRAV's *International Journal of Labour Research*. While the recommendations are not as applicable for gig economy workers as more generally for surveillance at work, they have resonance for many of the new practices we have outlined (Akhtar and Moore, 2016):

1   *Openness*: Workers are entitled to know what forms of digital surveillance are being used and for what purpose. Hidden digital surveillance or the use of the information it produces can destroy trust in the workplace.
2   *Consent*: If workers are to be the subject of a particular form of monitoring, they should have specifically agreed to it, either through a clause in a contract or a separate agreement.
3   *Consultation*: New forms of digital surveillance should not be introduced without meeting standards of procedural fairness. Informing or consulting with unions and/or workers is the most appropriate means of ensuring that digital surveillance policies are workable and fair.
4   *Private spaces*: Workers should not be in fear of, or subject to, constant digital surveillance. All workers should be guaranteed areas, means of

communication and periods during the day in which they can be sure that they will not be monitored.

5   *Proportionality*: In accordance with the principles of the European Convention on Human Rights, a fair balance should be struck between the purpose of digital surveillance and the protection of workers' privacy, dignity and autonomy. This implies that surveillance should meet a legitimate aim, be necessary to meet that aim, and be the least harmful means for workers to meet that aim.

Workers hold some level of autonomy over the work conducted in some digitalized work contexts, which supposedly allows for unending flexibility for workers who are assumed to have identical life situations and no mitigating circumstances under the conditions of self-employment. Whereas traditional Taylorism targets external performance within enclosed factories, quantifying work with the technological efforts I have discussed here allows for the intensification of control of microsocial and the inner processes of unseen labour in open-ended working environments. Measure is currently intensifying in what we have called 'arthouses to warehouses' (Moore and Robinson, 2016). Manual workers, service workers and knowledge workers face a common adversary: the colonising technologies of the era of Industrie 4.0. Many types of labour have been calculated for millennia. The areas not yet fully colonised but which are now being scrutinised are the less immediately definable areas of labour that historically have been predominantly carried by women (which I conjecture in Chapter 3). Drucker (1992) put forward the perspective that knowledge workers' work cannot, by definition, be measured by traditional Taylorist devices. But quantifying workers of all trades and work of all calibres are part of managerial efforts to control and extract value from creative as well as physical labour in more precise, quantified ways.

In the short term, tracking work may lead to a rise in jobs—as seen in the UK in 2016–2017—raise productivity and, as employers hope, workers' wellbeing; however, like Taylorism, it raises new demands on workers, on both the seen and unseen attributes of labour. As I have outlined, it intensifies workloads by promoting hyper-employment, where the introduction of self-service administration systems has fewer workers who are doing more and leads to rationalisation of staff as seen in the warehouse examples above, all the while displacing accountability from management to individual workers. As seen, workers have not passively embraced all the experimentation in work design for precarious agility, but are beginning to exit prescribed projects and carry out everyday forms of resistance as seen above. The next chapter further crystallises the experiences of self-trackers with a series of first hand interviews I have conducted since 2014. The insights from these discussions are invaluable for understanding both where we are going with the quantified self at work, and what we may be able to do about it.

Notes

1 Parts of this chapter are adapted from my contributions to Moore, P. and Robinson, Andrew (2015 DOI, 2016 print) 'The Quantified Self: What Counts in the Neoliberal Workplace' *New Media & Society* 18(1), 2774–2792.
2 This and the following three sections contain adapted text from my contributions to the publication Akhtar, P. and Moore, P. (2016) 'The psycho-social impacts of technological change in contemporary workplaces and trade union responses', *International Journal of Labour Research* (journal of International Labour Organisation ACTRAV) issue edited by Anna Biondi and Vera Guseva 8(1–2): 102–131.
3 I gained funding from the British Academy/Leverhulme small grant award 2015–2017 to carry out this research. In writing the proposal, I invited two Co-Investigators to work on the project with me. Lukasz Piwek of Bath University agreed to do visualisations and work on generating statistics for the project and Ian Roper acted as an adviser to management literature I was not familiar with and helped with a write up of the history of work design which I have outlined in Chapter 2 of this book.
4 I would like to thank and acknowledge Dr. Lukasz Piwek of Bath University, one of my Co-Investigators on the project, for working on the survey and interview questions with me, for working with Joost Plattel (the company's local data analyst) to gain relevant data, for providing some statistical data from the data and the survey, coding the second set of interviews with me and for providing comments and suggestions for this section. Dr. George Michaelides of Birkbeck University also provided recommendations for methodological choices and procedure.

References

Adl, C. (2016) 'China Building Orwellian Technology to Predict "Thought Crime"' *YourNewsWire.com* 09/03/16. http://yournewswire.com/china-building-orwellian-technology-to-predict-thought-crime/ (accessed 02/02/2017).

ADP UK (2015) 'Putting Wearables to Work – New Technology Could Revolutionise the Workplace' *Personnel Today, Technology* 14/07/15. www.personneltoday.com/pr/2015/07/putting-wearables-to-work-new-technology-could-revolutionise-the-workplace/ (accessed 02/02/2017).

Ajana, B. (2013) *Governing Through Biometrics: The Biopolitics of Identity* (Basingstoke: Palgrave Macmillan).

Ajunwa, I., Crawford, K. and Schultz, J. (2016) 'Limitless Worker Surveillance' *California Law Review* (1053) 13/03/16. http://ssrn.com/abstract=2746211 (accessed 16/02/17).

Akhtar, P. and Moore, P. (2016) 'The Psycho-Social Impacts of Technological Change in Contemporary Workplaces and Trade Union Responses' in *Psycho-Social Risks, Stress and Violence in the World of Work* Special Issue (eds) Anna Biondi and Vera Guseva. *International Journal of Labour Research* 8(1-2): 102–131.

Amoore, L. (2013) *The Politics of Possibility: Risk and Security Beyond Probability* (Durham, NC: Duke University Press).

AMT (2014) 'Amazon Mechanical Turk Participation Agreement' *MTurk.com* 02/12/14. www.mturk.com/mturk/conditionsofuse (accessed 16/02/17).

Angrave, D., Charlwood, A., Kirkpatrick, I., Lawrence, M. and Stuart, M. (2016) 'HR and Analytics: Why HR Is Set to Fail the Big Data Challenge' *Human Resource Management Journal* 26(1): 1–11.

Ball, K. (2010) 'Workplace Surveillance: An Overview' *Labour History* 51(1): 87–106.

Ball, K. S. and Margulis, S. T. (2011) 'Electronic Monitoring and Surveillance in Call Centres: A Framework for Investigation' *New Technology, Work and Employment* 26(2): 113–126.

Beesley, C. (2016) 'Email, Phone and Social Media Monitoring in Your Workplace: Know Your Rights as an Employer' *US Small Business Administration (SBA)*. www.sba.gov/blogs/email-phone-and-social-media-monitoring-workplace-know-your-rights-employer (accessed 20/02/2017).

Bennett, A. (2013) 'Amazon Warehouse Staff in Slave Camp Conditions, Workers Say' *The Huffington Post* 25/11/13. www.huffingtonpost.co.uk/2013/11/25/amazon-staff-investigation_n_4335894.html (accessed 16/02/17).

Berg, J. (2016) 'Income Security in the On-Demand Economy: Findings and Policy Lessons from a Survey of Crowdworkers' *Conditions of Work and Employment Series* No. 74 (Geneva: ILO).

Bergvall-Kåreborn, B. and Howcroft, D. (2014) 'Amazon Mechanical Turk and the Commodification of Labour' *New Technology, Work and Employment* 29(3): 213–223.

Bernstein, E. (2012) 'The Transparency Paradox: A Role for Privacy in Organizational Learning and Operational Control' *Administrative Science Quarterly* 57(2): 181–216.

Bhave, D. P. (2014) 'The Invisible Eye? Electronic Performance Monitoring and Employee Job Performance' *Personnel Psychology* 67(3): 605–635.

Bodie, M. T., Cherry, M. A., McCormick, M. L. and Tang, J. (2016) 'The Law and Policy of People Analytics' Saint Louis University Legal Studies Research Paper, No. 2016/6, forthcoming in *University of Colorado Law Review*. http://ssrn.com/abstract=2769980 (accessed 20/02/17).

Bogost, I. (2013) 'Hyper-Employment, or the Exhausting Work of the Technology User' *The Atlantic* 08/11/13. www.theatlantic.com/technology/archive/2013/11/hyperemployment-or-the-exhausting-work-of-the-technology-user/281149/ (accessed 16/02/17).

Braverman, H. (1974/1998) *Labour and Monopoly Capital: The Degredation of Work in the Twentieth Century* (New York: Monthly Review Press).

Brownstone, S. (2015) 'Can Seattle Launch a Movement for a New Kind of Workers' Union?' *The Stranger* 11/11/15. www.thestranger.com/news/feature/2015/11/11/23134098/can-seattle-launch-a-movement-for-a-new-kind-of-workers-union (accessed 16/02/2017).

Cederström, C. and Spicer, A. (2015) *The Wellness Syndrome* (Cambridge and Malden, MA: Polity).

Chartered Institute for Personnel Development (CIPD) (2014) 'Getting Smart about Agile Working' *CIPD* 10/11/14. www.cipd.co.uk/knowledge/strategy/change/agile-working-report (accessed 20/02/17).

Chartered Institute for Personnel Development (CIPD) (2017) 'To Gig or Not to Gig? Stories from the Modern Economy' *CIPD* 03/2017. www.cipd.co.uk/knowledge/work/trends/gig-economy-report (accessed 21/03/17).

Cheney-Lippold, J. (2011) 'A New Algorithmic Identity: Soft Biopolitics and the Modulation of Control' *Theory, Culture & Society* 28(6): 164–181.

Cherry, M. (2011) 'A Taxonomy of Virtual Work' *Georgia Law Review* 45(4): 954–1009.

Cockburn, H. (2014) 'Amazon Offers Staff up to $5000 to Quit' *London Loves Business* 16/04/14. www.londonlovesbusiness.com/business-news/tech/amazon-offers-staff-up-to-5000-to-quit/7926.article (accessed 16/02/17).

Collins, C. (1991) 'Bill Would Require Notices When Bosses Snoop on Employees' *LA Times*, 11 March. http://articles.latimes.com/1991-11-03/business/fi-1400_1_employee-performance.

Donaldson-Feilder, E. and Podro, S. (2012) 'The Future of Health and Wellbeing in the Workplace' *ACAS Future of Workplace Relations Discussion Paper Series* (London: Advisory, Conciliation and Arbitration Service).

Drucker, P. F. (1992) *Managing for the Future* (London: Routledge).

Ducey, A. (2007) 'More Than a Job: Meaning Affect and Training Health Care Workers' in Clough, P. with Halley, J. (eds) *The Affective Turn: Theorising the Social* (Durham, NC: Duke University Press): 187–208.

Economist (2016) *Artificial Intelligence: The Return of the Machinery Question*, Special Report, 25 June.

European Commission (2016a) 'European Commission Updates EU Audio-visual Rules and Presents Targeted Approach to Online Platforms' *European Commission* 25/05/16. http://europa.eu/rapid/press-release_IP-16-1873_en.htm (accessed 16/02/17).

European Commission (2016b) 'Digital Single Market – Commission Updates EU Audiovisual Rules and Presents Targeted Approach to Online Platforms' *European Commission* 25/05/17. http://europa.eu/rapid/press-release_MEMO-16-1895_en.htm (accessed 16/02/17).

Face + + (2017) *Face Cognitive Services*. Homepage. www.faceplusplus.com/ (accessed 20/02/2017).

Finley, K. (2013) 'What If Your Boss Tracked Your Sleep, Diet, and Exercise?' *Wired* 04/17/13 www.wired.com/2013/04/quantified-work-citizen/ (accessed 16/02/17).

Ford, M. (2015) *Rise of the Robots: Technology and the Threat of a Jobless Future* (New York: Basic Books).

Foucault, M. (trans. Burchell, G.) (ed. Davidson, A. I.) (1977–78/2009) *Security, Territory, Population: Lectures at the College De France, 1977–78* (Basingstoke: Palgrave).

Foucault, M. (1979/1976) *The History of Sexuality Volume 1: An Introduction* (London: Allen Lane).

Frey, C. B. and Osborne, M. A. (2013) *The Future of Employment: How Susceptible Are Jobs to Computerisation?* Oxford Martin School Working Paper (Oxford). www.oxfordmartin.ox.ac.uk/downloads/academic/future-of-employment.pdf (accessed 20/02/2017).

Fuchs, C. (2014) *Digital Labour and Karl Marx* (New York: Routledge).

Gandini, A. (2016) *The Reputation Economy: Understanding Knowledge Work in Digital Society* (London: Palgrave Pivot).

Gandini, A., Pais, I. and Beraldo, D. (2016) 'Reputation and Trust on Online Labour Markets: The Reputation Economy of Lance' *Work Organisation, Labour and Globalisation* 10(1): 27–43.

Gantt, L. O. N. (1995) 'An Affront to Human Dignity: Electronic Mail Monitoring in the Private Sector Workplace' *Harvard Journal of Law and Technology* 8(2): 345–425.

Graham, S. and Wood, D. (2003) 'Digitizing Surveillance: Categorization, Space and Inequality' *Critical Social Policy* 20(2): 227–248.

Hamblen, M. (2015) 'Programs are Used to Weed out Workers Who Raise Premiums, One Attorney Says' *Computer World* 19/06/2015. www.computerworld.com/article/2937721/wearables/wearables-for-workplace-wellness-face-federal-scrutiny.html (accessed 20/02/17).

Haque, U. (2015) 'The Asshole Factory' *Bad Words* 21/04/15. https://medium.com/bad-words/the-asshole-factory-71ff808d887c#.az6gg7gds (accessed 16/02/17).

Harter, J., Agrawal, S. and Sorenson, S. (2014) 'Most U.S. Workers See Upside to Staying Connected to Work' *Gallup/ Economy* 30/04/14. www.gallup.com/poll/168794/workers-upside-staying-connected-work.aspx.

Hayes, T. (2013) *I Am Pilgrim* (London: Tranworld Publishers).

Heyes, J. D. (2014) 'Retailers Track Shoppers with Hidden Cameras in Eyes of Mannequins' *Natural News* 02/01/14. www.naturalnews.com/043370_hidden_cameras_retail_stores_consumer_tracking.html (accessed 20/02/17).

Hodson, T., Schwartz, J., van Berkel, A. and Winstrom Ottem, I. (2014) 'The Overwhelmed Employee: Simplify the Work Environment' *Global Human Capital Trends 2014: Engaging the 21st-century workforce* (Westlake, TX: Deloitte University Press): 97–104.

Holts, K. (2013) 'Towards a Taxonomy of Virtual Work' *Work Organisation, Labour and Globalisation* 7(1): 31–50.

Hornyak, T. (2012) 'No Dummy: This Mannequin is Spying on You' *CNet* 21/11/12. www.cnet.com/news/no-dummy-this-mannequin-is-spying-on-you/ (accessed 20/02/17).

Huws, U. (2013) 'Working Online, Living Offline: Labour in the Internet Age' *Work Organisation, Labour and Globalisation* 7(1): 1–11.

Huws, U. (2014) *Labour in the Global Digital Economy: The Cybertariat Comes of Age* (New York: Monthly Review Press).

Huws, U. (2015) 'A Review on the Future of Work: Online Labour Exchanges, or "crowdsourcing": Implications for Occupational Safety and Health' European Agency for Safety and Health at Work Discussion Paper (Bilbao, EU-OSHA). https://osha.europa.eu/en/tools-and-publications/publications/future-work-crowdsourcing/view (accessed 20/02/17).

Introna, L. D. and Wood, D. (2004) 'Picturing Algorithmic Surveillance: The Politics of Facial Recognition Systems' *Surveillance & Society* 2(2/3): 177–198.

Jeske, D. and Santuzzi, A. M. (2015) 'Monitoring What and How: Psychological Implications of Electronic Performance Monitoring' *New Technology, Work and Employment* 30(1): 62–78.

Kilkelly, U. (2001) *The Right to Respect for Private and Family Life. A Guide to the Implementation of Article 8 of the European Convention on Human Rights*, Council of Europe, Human Rights Handbook, No. 1.

Kohll, A. (2016) '8 Things You Need to Know about Employee Wellness Programs' *Forbes* 21/04/16. www.forbes.com/sites/alankohll/2016/04/21/8-things-you-need-to-know-about-employee-wellness-programs/#1ec78c4d610c (accessed 20/02/17).

Kravets, D. (2015) 'Worker Fired for Disabling GPS App That Tracked her 24 Hours a Day [Updated]' *Ars Technica* 11/05/15. http://arstechnica.com/tech-policy/2015/05/worker-fired-for-disabling-gps-app-that-tracked-her-24-hours-a-day/ (accessed 16/02/17).

Lazzarato, M. (1996) 'Immaterial Labour' *Generation.* www.generation-online.org/c/fcimmateriallabour3.htm (accessed 20/02/17).

Lindsay, G. (2015) 'We Spent Two Weeks Wearing Employee Trackers: Here's What We Learned' *Fact Coexist* 22/09/15. www.fastcoexist.com/3051324/we-spent-two-weeks-wearing-employee-trackers-heres-what-we-learned (accessed 16/02/17).

Mance, H. (2016) 'Telegraph Installs Then Removes Motion Trackers from Staff Desks' *Financial Times* 11/01/16. www.ft.com/cms/s/0/48537dce-b88c-11e5-bf7e-8a339b6f2164.html#axzz46TaWA1UK (accessed 20/02/17).

Marx, G. T. (1988) *Undercover: Police Surveillance in America* (Berkeley: University of California Press).

Marx, K. (1990/1867) *Capital, Volume 1* (Harmondsworth: Penguin).

Marx, G. T. (2002) 'What's New about the "New Surveillance"? Classifying for Change and Continuity' *Surveillance & Society* 1(1): 9–29.

Marx, G. T. (2005) 'Surveillance and Society Encyclopedia of Social Theory' *MIT.* http://web.mit.edu/gtmarx/www/surandsoc.html (accessed 20/02/17).

McCabe, H. and Prete, J. (1995) 'US-Japan Comparative Labour Laws: The Question of Ethics' in Natale, S. M. and Rothschild, B. M. (eds) *Values, Work, Education: The Meanings of Work* (Amsterdam: Rodopi): 203–222.

McCarthy, J., Minsky, M. L., Rochester, N. and Shannon, C. E. (1955) 'A Proposal for the Dartmouth Summer Research Project on Artificial Intelligence' *Stanford. edu* 31/08/55. www-formal.stanford.edu/jmc/history/dartmouth/dartmouth.html (accessed 16/02/17).

Moore, P. and Piwek, L. (2017) 'Regulating Wellbeing in the Brave New Quantified Workplace', Employee Relations 39(3): 308–316.

Moore, P. and Robinson, A. (2016) 'The Quantified Self: What Counts in the Neoliberal Workplace' *New Media & Society* 18(1): 2774–2792.

Mulholland, K. and Stewart, P. (2013) 'Workers in Food Distribution: Global Commodity Chains and Lean Logistics' *New Political Economy* 19(4): 534–558.

Nield, D. (2014) 'In Corporate Wellness Programme, Wearables Take a Step Forward' *Fortune* 15/04/14. http://fortune.com/2014/04/15/in-corporate-wellness-programs-wearables-take-a-step-forward/ (accessed 20/02/17).

Office of National Statistics (ONS) 'UK Labour Productivity Q3 (2013)' *ONS. GOV* 01/04/13. www.ons.gov.uk/ons/rel/productivity/labour-productivity/q3-2013/index.html (accessed 20/02/17).

Pasquale, F. (2010) 'Reputation Regulation: Disclosure and the Challenge of Clandestinely Commensurating Computing' in Levmore, S. and Nussbaum, M. C. (eds) *The Offensive Internet: Speech, Privacy, and Reputation* (Cambridge, MA: Harvard University Press): 107–123.

Rawlinson, K. (2013) 'Tesco Accused of Using Electronic Armbands to Monitor its Staff' *The Independent* 13/02/13. www.independent.co.uk/news/business/news/tesco-accused-of-using-electronic-armbands-to-monitor-its-staff-8493952.html (accessed 16/02/17).

Ricardo, D. (1821) *On the Principles of Political Economy and Taxation* (Cambridge: Cambridge University Press).

Rosenblat, A., Kneese, T. and Boyd, D. (2014) *Workplace Surveillance*, Data & Society Working Paper, Future of Work Project, Open Society Foundations (New York: Data & Society Research Institute).

Rothstein, L. E. (2000) 'Privacy or Dignity? Electronic Monitoring in the Workplace' *New York Law School Journal of International and Comparative Law* 19: 379.

Schneier, B. (2015a) *Data and Goliath: The Hidden Battles to Collect Your Data and Control Your World* (New York: W. W. Norton and Company).

Schneier, B. (2015b) 'How We Sold Our Souls – And More – To the Internet Giants' *Guardian* 17/05/2015. www.theguardian.com/technology/2015/may/17/sold-our-souls-and-more-to-internet-giants-privacy-surveillance-bruce-schneier (accessed 02/02/2017).

Schumacher, S. (2011) 'What Employees Should Know about Electronic Performance Monitoring' *ESSAI* 8(38): 138–144. http://dc.cod.edu/cgi/viewcontent.cgi?article=1332&context=essai (accessed 02/02/2017).

Silvey, T. F. (1956) 'Impact of Technological Change Upon Jobs and Labour Relations' *Panel Presentation at AFL-CIO National Headquarters* (Washington, DC) 8–9 May.

Silvey, T. F. (1957) 'Labour Faces Automation: It Can Be a Blessing for Everyone, If We Use Our Heads and Hearts!' *Surplus Record and Index Issue*, January 28–30.

Silvey, T. F. (1958) 'A Ball-Point Pencil: Is a Computer?' *Computers and Automation* [Magazine] Issue February: no page.

Stone, K. V. W. (2004) *From Widgets to Digits: Employment Regulation for the Changing Workplace* (New York: Cambridge University Press).

Taylor, P., Mulvey, G., Hyman, J. and Bain, P. (2002) 'Work Organisation, Control and the Experience of Work in Call Centres' *Work, Employment & Society* 16(1): 133–150.

Upwork (2016) 'Get the Job Done Right'. www.upwork.com/i/howitworks/client/ (accessed 16/02/17).

Van Jaarsveld, D. and Poster, W. R. (2013) 'Emotional Labour Over the Phone' in Grandey, A. A., Diefendorff, J. M. and Rupp, D. E. (eds) *Emotional Labour in the 21st Century: Diverse Perspectives on Emotion Regulation at Work* (New York: Routledge): 153–174.

Waring, S. P. (1991) *Taylorism Transformed: Scientific Management Theory since 1945* (Chapel Hill: The University of North Carolina Press).

The Week (2015) 'The Rise of Workplace Spying' *The Week* 05/07/15. http://theweek.com/articles/564263/rise-workplace-spying (accessed 16/02/17).

Weeks, K. (1998) *Constituting Feminist Subjects* (Ithaca, NY: Cornell University Press).

Wilson, H. J. (2013) 'Wearables in the Workplace' *Harvard Business Review*, September. http://hbr.org/2013/09/wearables-in-the-workplace/ar/1 (accessed 16/02/17).

Young, S. F., Braddy, P. W. and Fleenor, J. W. (2017) 'The Impact of New Technology on the Leadership Development Industry' *Training Industry Magazine*. www.trainingindustry.com/ezine/current-issue/the-impact-of-new-technology-on-the-leadership-development-industry.aspx (accessed 16/02/17).

5   Meet Some Self-Trackers

The first transcript is from an interview with Chris Dancy, who has been called the 'most connected man' on the planet and is now called the 'mindful cyborg'. His insights into contemporary digitalised life are significant, not least because of his personal experiences with extreme self-tracking. As mentioned in Chapter 1, Mr. Dancy has anywhere from 300 to 700 sensors running at any given time. I first came across Chris in 2013 when his name caught my eye as someone who had embraced self-quantification for empowerment and self-improvement. While on one hand Chris proselytised self-tracking, he was also one of the only people I could find who publicly warned about the dark side of the trends he was observing in data gathering and technological surveillance. Chris discusses his observations of the normalisation of self-tracking over time, and in the interview, warns of the possibilities of 'technological fascism'. He is also keenly aware of the corporeal aspects of tracking workers and discussed his bio-tracking methods of his own employees from an ethical position.

The next interview presented is with Bethany Soule, the co-founder of Beeminder, a self-tracking productivity 'commitment tool' that she says is 'goal tracking with teeth'. One week, Bethany used Beeminder herself to see whether she could meet the standard set by Nick Winter who carried out one 'Maniac Week'. The transcripts include Dr. Soule's own quest for a 'Maniac Week', where she set out to track the minutae of her week in order to be as productive as humanly possible. Using Pomodoro and a camera, Bethany attempted to shut out all of life in order to exclusively work as a coder. She indicates that she learned a lot about the ergonomics and intensity of work simply by watching the video of her accelerated week of work. In terms of the tracking software Beeminder, the use of financial reward incentives for tracking pursuits stands out as different from other productivity programmes. The psychological and social aspects of work and productivity are crystallised in Bethany's unique experiment.

Next, I provide a detailed interview with Robin Barooah, who is also an avid self-tracker as well as meditator. He runs the programme Sublime.org which allows people to use meditation tools that remind people to sit and time sessions elegantly as well as encourage 'mindful browsing'. Mr Barooah's insights are valuable because more than the other three interviewees, he talked about how he has used tracking techniques for self-awareness at a deeply affective level. He has tracked his emotions and compared them to other's, and used tracking to deal with depression and bad habits.

Finally, I present transcripts from a man who tracks every move he makes to identify productivity, whose talk I saw at a Quantified Self Meet-up in London. Ian (as I will call him due to his request to remain anonymous) told me that he believes the data he keeps about his activities is a true rendition of himself. He used an analogue spreadsheet to track all his activities in specific categories that he created, with a primary goal of increased productivity. Ian saw great value in having an archive about every second of his life, telling me that he can know himself better than anyone else in the world. I asked Ian whether his experiences have modified his behaviour or his values and he gave me some curious, introspective replies.

Interview with Chris Dancy

PM: Thank you so much for interviewing with me. First, I would be really interested to hear about the book you are writing.

CD: 'I am you, tomorrow' is a story, a life story, a mash up of the 'happiness project' combined with 'Tidy' by Marie Condo, a collection of stories about me, kind of wiring up and things I learned about myself and I guess, tips and tricks.

I feel very passionately right now, I believe strongly about the rise of this kind of connected consciousness that's happening, the spirituality aspects of how machines are democratising our relationship with existence itself and how that changes human evolution. Once we lose concepts regarding time, time is really the big thing on everyone's mind right now, whether it's feelings of mortality or the ephemeral nature of it, I think that can be traced to people's relationship with technology.

PM: Tell me a bit about yourself, your life, your work, your drive?

CD: The benefit of looking at this project, I look at it with more patience... I had spent so many years with computers at a myopic level, customising a tool bar, I felt in some strange way that there was a level of control I could exact over my life if I could turn my own life into an interface. What that experience was, so the interface really became anything I could touch that was digital, because interfaces are information collectors. The experience was something that I didn't really understand because the feedback loop using certain tools because of their inherent systems of collection, forced me to lie in those systems.

So, I'm not sure what came first, desire to quantify or desire to control, but since then I have done experimentation not to control but to measure, but then found that the results are the same. I end up with a more profound sense, uneasiness, in a body in a world where I don't matter.

PM: How do you think the Quantified Self movement started? What was it responding to?

CD: Some of the earliest meetings that I read about before they really got moving in 2008–2009, reminded me that there's something inherently unique about Silicon Valley. I trace it back to the diversity movement of 60s and 70s. Silicon Valley was a kind of bastion of safety, first in corporate diversity and inclusion with software companies in that area. This says a lot about how people's brains evolved. I don't know if we would have had such a technical revolution if it wasn't for radical need to corral people who were looking for safe places. Look at the gay movement in SF, some of my earliest peers worked for Adobe and Microsoft Word and all those great places, so with that as a stage, by the time you get to the 90s and network based computing and some of the earliest projects were very inclusive and included disparate communities within a larger community, and then that takes you to the Quantified Self movement. People who innately understood likeminded individuals was a route to accessing their own beliefs and desires. People at a point in their lives and careers where they conquered everything, post bubble, post exit, post inclusion, post diversity and then the talks we are still having today, some would say those problems are solved. People were and are on a technological spirit quest, for lack of anything else. I have listened to interviews with Gary (Wolf) and other folks about its nature and objective about that reality, we could say we need a God.

PM: You are called the 'mindful cyborg'. What do you mean by this? Did you have a personal rationale for tracking yourself? What was it?

CD: This term came from when I got tired of being called the 'world's most connected man'. Spending more time in contemplative practice is important to me and has been since 2014. That being said, everyone I encounter who has some technical leanings end up measuring something. As soon as they measure, they want to hack everything.

Hard to find words that resonate with what people relate to. All I did with the moniker with mindful cyborg is to cut to the chase, two things that people can connect with. Concepts of mindfulness, contemplation, Buddhism overused. No good word for a technology person who wants to be all of these things.

PM: What do you typically track today? Has it become 'second nature'?

CD: In 2017, I no longer need sensors, I realise I am a sensor. So often I'll measure something and just for shits and giggles I'll jot down what I think it will be, how far I have got etc. and it's weird how accurate I am at telling temperature or light variance or a range of other things. I see information everywhere, not just info but scarily accurate info. So as far as, do I still measure stuff, 10 years in, I still measure simple things: sleep, food, activity, meditation time, but there is no need to, I know these things innately. The strangest thing I have experienced is that I now know this about other people. I recently had an interview with Irish radio and I told everyone what their sleep etc. was. It became really obvious just by looking at the wear on people. I still measure a few things but I hate the concept of 'measuring' and I feel like I can do it innately, but I often tell people who want me to come wired up, because you wouldn't hire someone to be a clown at a party who is dressed in business attire.

It's become so mainstream now, my partner is 25 and he had been tracking steps and location and had never even heard the word tracking. Apple's Health Kit has changed all that.

PM: Has anything changed in the way people work today? Why?

CD: I spent two years in population health company and I see this increasing trend not only of normalisation but the ... health care providers gather data at a population level, even expect to track you, everything from the garishness of biometric screening to checking in with health coach once a week. Take the case of Humana giving out apple watches to 10,000 people. It almost seems like technological fascism, I don't understand why this is not examined at a greater/deeper level other healthcare is needed. Convenience trumps privacy.

It's easy for me to say that if it's convenient they'll just do it, HSA spend or toward deductibles. But where there is resistance to tracking, or becomes mainstream, you see automation. Some of earliest tracking were overnight trackers. Within a few years this will happen in driving and trucking and the same thing will happen in all access of work.

I have just got a Tesla, it tracks everything, so it allows me not to pay attention! In fact, that is the ultimate holy grail, we want the benefits of knowing everything without paying attention to anything, that is diametrically opposed to what we could call 'life'. Knowing is hurting, life is not knowing and everything just 'works'. That is literally, death: that is when there is nothing left for us to do.

PM: What is your perspective about work and labour and machines, from tracking and monitoring to automation?

CD: We need to look realistically at the role of machines in human life in 2017 and next 10 years, to answer the question about work and automation. If we were honest with ourselves, machines are teaching us to act like machines. We are not teaching machines to act human.

Our relationship with machines in the future will be on an almost a nostalgic basis, teaching people how to be people if you look at that long 50-year loop: machines teaching us to be human. What will happen is that so much of our lives will become automated, the need to feel authentic will come from some data that will be collected and mimicked and fed back to us.

If I just look 2008–2017, most people I interact with have become functioning iPhones. They speak in tweets, photograph in filters, our speech has evolved to emojis. When you meet someone who veers off that path, it's disconcerting. If I want help in a busy store I stand perfectly still and even if I'm last in line, the clerk will say can I help you? Something about humans suddenly locking up like a browser like a browser or iPhone, gets attention! Now is a good time to talk about how much can we 'give' machines if ultimately, they have to teach us.

PM: Has our relationship with 'management' and/or machines changed as a result of machines at work?

CD: I'd be out of my league to answer that question, I haven't worked with humans where I had a manager in almost 20 years, so historically I would be taking a stab in the dark.

I do manage some biological metrics with my own team. We are all measured and that data is available to us all. If someone is not sleeping, sleep is usually what I manage, I will purposefully divert work from them, until I notice those trends are going back to normal.

If I see employees' bedtimes are varying, I will make subtle changes in the background. I never talk to employees about this, I just change things where I can to improve the situation.

I see organisations that use the Jawbones weaponising employees' lack of sleep and promoting them as 'better humans'. You see it a lot in 'dev' culture, where people slept for two hours and are 'jacked up' on caffeine. I think it's the least human thing you can do, create a brag-worthy cultures.

This kind of culture excludes people who have other responsibilities such as family or people who don't have access to supplements or certain foods, it's a bad spiral on all sorts of levels. You're rewarded for being a single health nut. The message is, don't get married, don't know too many people, don't participate in political discussions online. We have homogenised the entire workforce, just add Vitamin D and sell people as milk. We put pictures of missing people on milk cartons, maybe people are the milk and the cartons...

PM: Do your employees 'opt in' to their data being viewed?

CD: The strangest thing is it that they all want to do it. They say, if they could be more like me their lives would be better. But learning about yourself isn't always as great as you might think. It's a slippery road.

We have this moniker we follow, everything has to follow: TASK which means, Trust, Aware, Safe, and Kind. We can't talk about data, tech, or each other unless it fits into this or brings out a sense of these things in that order.

PM: What is the future of technology and work? Privacy... surveillance... 'gig economy'...

CD: I can't see past the gig economy unless we get into something like Jaron Lanier who wrote about 'Who owns the future?'. I still think we are less than 20 years away from buying and selling out data from some kind of marketplace, the future of work is what you will give me and I will give you about myself. It makes me think of the Justin Timberlake movie (*In Time*) where everyone is swapping time and touch wrists to keep alive.

Work in the future? Well, privacy is work. The only thing left in the future is the ability to understand and dictate your information, that will be done for you. The concept of an app where Uber drivers make a selection not only based on 'where' I was, but also 'how' I was, so a driver in the opposite space. So, if I'm in a bad mood, someone will treat me differently.

This is all relating to intimate data exchange. I saw this early on with Uber. They were testing the Spotify integration at some point. The driver would then automatically play what they were playing on Spotify. I asked an Uber driver about that experience and they told me, 'it's interesting to hear everyone's music. What I miss, though, is knowing more about that person'. So, the human desire to know interesting details, not in a dark way, just connect/sharing what we jam to in that passive API way, that's what will be integrated.

Everything is customised now. There is a McDonalds app you can use to call ahead to get a Big Mac and they won't charge you or make it until you're a certain distance away. But will they stop adding mayo if you haven't walked enough?

Health convenience is going to get staggering.

Our ability to 'opt out'? Well, it will seem 'odd to opt out'. I don't think there are any digital Amish yet. But those people who say, 'I've had enough, I'm not partaking', I know people who are purposefully living a 1998 lifestyle, because they have enough money.

It costs a lot not to have internet access. I wonder whether in the future whether people will be able to afford not living with the internet. So, if a phone was only a phone, without wifi connected, you would be on the streets within a week.

Disconnected people will live amongst us in the future. But we now do everything without technology. The most garishly rich in the 1970s had farms and horses. You had estates and everything is done by hand, tailor to maid.

There was a guy in 2013 who lived without internet for a year. He said it took so long to find a pizza, without connectivity and only phone calls on your phone, you would probably be on the street within a couple of weeks.

Not being connected will constitute a new disability.

PM: What are the risks of machines and monitoring and work and what should be done to mitigate them?

CD: Nothing we can really do now, that horse has left the building. To mitigate, we need a complete overhaul of how we code and implement technology. I said in my TED Talk that we stop solving our human problems with technology, and start solving our technology problems with our humanity. Our humanity comes from a sense of perspective and a sense of awe. I think if we could create technology or code implement in a way that had a sense of awe and perspective but as we leave the world of screen time and we wear the technology and live inside the technology, we will be faced with the problem of our technological journey, so what life can be after the interface, wanting to become an interface, at this point in our generation, it's anti-choice, as an interface there's no choice. It's 'just in time' but there's no choice. If I ask Alexa to play music she'll only play Amazon prime. If I ask her to play Madonna she will only play Madonna I have listened to or is in my own folders.

Interview with Bethany Soule

PM: So I saw your talk earlier [here at Quantified Self Expo 2015] about your Maniac Week. I am intrigued to know: what made you want to do self-track intensively for as long as you did?

BS: You know, I have a, if you like, there's often, I mean, basically there's often like a ton of demands on my time for my personal life and in my work life and finding some balance is hard and being able to just focus in on one thing for a whole week and get to, you know, kind of check out of the family life for a while and just get things done was…

PM: Kind of a solution.

BS: Yeah, it was really, yeah, I was really intrigued by that idea of like, you know, can I be more efficient, you know, is there a limit to efficiency and I didn't answer to that part, you know, I'm not really sure what method to, you know, measure my, the efficiency of my code or my coding or something, but it felt enjoyable, [laughs], you know and it was, overall I would call it relaxing. I didn't, you know, I mentioned that I got this idea from Nick Winters, who managed to do a 120 hour work week. I did not get anywhere near 120 hours, I was like 87 as my productive time, but that's double, you know, my usual work week.

PM: 120, where do those hours come from?

BS: He actually packed his sleeping in there, so that he did seven days but only slept six times, so he kept, he like, you know, worked for 14 hours and then slept for, you know, six and a half or something and then another, however that worked, you know, so he was playing with his sleep, whereas I was like, this is vacation from all my other responsibilities, I'm going to sleep when I'm tired and wake up when I'm not, so yeah, I did seven days and I slept seven times.

PM: I think I could not give up sleep, there's one thing I refuse to do and it's to give up sleep.

BS: Yeah, turns out that I've noticed lately that that is one of my, like, I really need to work out my sleep schedule and making sure that I get enough, 'cause it really affects my mood and my ability to function.

PM: Was there a specific trigger that made you want to do this?

BS: So, first remember this is actually, you know, I'd had the idea kicking around my head for quite a while after reading Nick's blog and thinking, like, that sounds like a really fun thing to do, sort of a workathon, and then it was just opportunity arising because there was a family reunion in Canada and my husband was planning to go and take the kids, and you know, I worked out that I could kind of back out of that and have this opportunity to like have the personal life just completely shut off, send them out of the country, so...

PM: It was the opportunity, so I actually don't know what you do, do you mind telling me, so what is the work that you...?

BS: I'm a computer programmer, so technically I'm the CTO of Beeminder, there are actually only two of us full time employees working on it, we're a very small group and Danny, my co-founder, does some of the programming too but he kind of operates more as CEO, you know, in name and tries to shield me from more of the logistical and marketing side of stuff and then I write a lot of code, fixing bugs, making features, making the website run, making graphs for people and collecting data and stuff.

PM: Cool, what made you, what occurred to you, did you invent Beeminder?

BS: Yeah, we sort of, that grew out of a lot of personal experimentation, trying to find ways to be more productive and you know, like squash procrastination, so like in grad school, you know, the great thing about school is it gives you all these deadlines and you have to take them seriously and then in all the rest of your life, sort of when we were originally working on this, kept talking about realifying deadlines, like realified deadlines and how can I set myself arbitrary deadlines and you know, but actually take them seriously.

PM: Realified deadlines? I like that, yeah.

BS: Right, yeah, grad school, your professor gives you, you know, this paper by this time or going to have...

PM: Oh, of course, yeah.

BS: Like you get that done because it's external. That was actually a huge blow to me in my undergrad, with the first time I like had a personal crisis, a bunch of stuff in my personal life just like kind of fell apart and the very first time I ever turned a paper in late in my entire life was like, I was, you know, in my like junior year of college...

PM: Mitigating circumstances.

BS: You know and things were legitimately, like, horrible in my personal life and I went to the professor and I was just like, this is the worst thing that's ever happened to me, you know, but I can't get the paper done and was, okay, that fine and it's like, oh, ok. After that I don't know if I ever turned any other papers in on time until, like, the final year of college. [Laughter.]

PM: What would you say the role of technology itself is, say, in behaviour change? Like as a mediator...

BS: Yeah, is technology actually, I mean, you could accomplish some of these kinds of things without technology. We started doing these kinds of things with, like, taping a $20 bill to the bathroom mirror and then see if, you know, just kind of one on one personally, or selling a contract to your friends and say, you know, like, I'm going to try to get this, this and this done and if I don't do these things then I'm going to pay you money, that kind of thing. So, that's all social, I guess, of course, you wouldn't have to have technology to do that, but then when you start, like, for something, like I start selling a contract to my friends, then they want to know what I'm doing, they want to like, want to be able to check in and verify that I'm actually, that I am actually meeting whatever contracted goals I made, you know, what I said I'm doing. So then, you know, you start to see a role for technology to come in there in terms of just kind of visualisation and sort of, so also some accountability, I guess,

PM: Okay, so accountability is a part of it...

BS: Making that data available, but then, I don't know.

PM: I'm just curious about that, so I guess technology is a neutralising feature? You mentioned friends, that's interesting, so it's kind of, because you're already friends, so there's already like the trust dimension and I'm curious whether technology provides a sort of neutraliser, objective judge, do you know what I mean, it's like, oh well, and also about what we're saying about numbers, numbers don't lie? Some people might see the technology more as an intervention though?

BS: Yeah, with technology you want, kind of no friction, you don't actually want to activate the technology, that's the ideal, is to have it, like, just want it running in the background but you don't want to actively be interacting with it.

PM: That's just me, I mean, I guess every person is different, so...

BS: Well, there are ways in which sometimes the, you can use the technology to bring you back also, like if the interrupt is well placed, it can be useful. Just reminded me, so I track my time stochastically, I have a little programmer on my computer that at random intervals throughout the day pops up and asks what are you doing right now and then I have like this little taxonomy of tags, I've been doing this for eight plus years, where, you know, I write down, like, I have a tag for different kinds of projects I'm working on, so working on Beeminder and like I'll usually tag, for programming I'll tag for language I'm programming in and various, you know, whatever activity I'm doing, so the list of different kinds of tags for categorising time and then, so this, sometimes it act actually as a reminder that brings me back to focus, so like if I'm distracted on, you know, I'm looking at baby photos on Facebook and then tag time pings, I go, oh, you know, what are you doing right now, oh crap, I'm looking at photos on Facebook and that's, like, it can serve as a reminder to send me back to what I should actually be doing.

PM: So that's a neutral kind of, yeah, that's really interesting, so what would you say, how, in terms of Beeminder and probably from your experiences, knowing how users use it and things like that, how do you think it works best?

BS: The ideal scenario is if you have some sort of, you know, technology that you're using there, something like RescueTime, which is running on your computer in the background, you don't have to think about it at all and then you can send data from RescueTime to Beeminder and then we send you, we tell you if you're not doing, if you're, you know, doing too much watching videos on the internet or if you're like not spending enough time, you know, then we'll send you reminders and alert you that you're falling behind whatever, you know, goal you set for yourself, so that I think is kind of like the perfect scenario because you're just doing what it is that you're doing anyway and then Beeminder kicks in and it applies pressure when you're not doing enough of what you're meant to be doing. [Laughs]. It's all very, not enough specific pronouns in that.

PM: That makes sense and as a user, what would you recommend for people when they start the process, I mean, if you were going to recommend, or they were about to use Beeminder, what would you recommend?

BS: I think that the most successful case is like when people set up some kind of, you know, set up a goal from something that they're already using that we integrate with and then from there they tend to kind of, you know, they'll see success there, it's like [inaudible 0:13:51] lingo, you know, like a (turning ? 0:13:53) website that's really popular and then they can set up a, they might set up a Beeminder goal that's going to keep them making sure that they keep practising every day. Then, you know, as they see some value from this thing that they're kind of already doing and that we can sort of passively get this information about them having, you know, so it's just causing a behaviour change, then they see it as valuable and start adding, you know, other goals that they might have into Beeminder.

PM: So just to go back a little bit, what we were talking about, so you did the experiment, did you do this work in a way to help, like, so what were your reasons for doing it, I mean, one was obviously to get some projects done, to get some work done, was there another personal reason to do it?

BS: Curiosity and just, you know, opportunity and I like trying new things and experimenting, like does it work? I can try it out, I don't have to like it, maybe it'll be great, so...

PM: And do you think that your experience, so is there something that you would say you could think of in terms of a new world of work or new ways of working that could be to do something, can you take something away from that or...?

BS: Well, I know completely that I started using Pomodoros a lot more after this first Maniac Week experiment, 'cause I was kind of, I was like, what if I can't stay focussed, you know, like I'm supposed to be taking screenshots and I had this anxiety that maybe I wouldn't, even like the social pressure of I promise to publish this time lapse after the fact, like what if that's not enough and then it's just a bunch of pictures of me looking at things on the internet or, you know, whatever, so I set a steep road on Beeminder also to keep doing Pomodoros, so I had to do a whole bunch of Pomodoros every day and I discovered that that was really effective for me at kind of pushing me into like continue work, you know, like to get the work like flowing frictionlessly and so I have continued that since maniac week, that has like been the concrete thing that has changed in my work habits is that I do Pomodoros every day.

PM: Okay and there's no time that you stopped using the Pomodoros for a period or maybe...?

BS: On the weekend, yeah.

PM: So yeah, so that's something that you took away from the experience and kind of learned for your own work...

BS: Yeah.

PM: Would you say you learned anything new about your body in that experience of the Maniac Week?

BS: I was surprised at how uncomfortable sitting is, my posture is not great and I have not yet gotten myself a standing workstation that I can work with, like, that sounds like a really good idea, to be able to like switch positions more, 'cause I'm definitely, I'm clearly not doing myself any favours, sitting in front of a, you know, the way that I sit and have a computer, so just like physically, ergonomics, I should work on that and I haven't taken any steps, but that was something that I was very keenly aware of, how uncomfortable my sitting was. I also, a funny thing that I noticed, like, looking at the time lapse videos of myself, I noticed myself doing this a lot and like this, like actually literally like this while I was reading code and I kind of thought I, you know, I noticed myself doing that in the images and I was like, am I posing for the pictures or something, like what in the world is that and then, like, so I paid attention to myself for a while after then, you know, I really and genuinely do this when I'm, like, confused by something in my code, I'm like sitting there thinking about it, I do that, it's too bad I can't grow a beard, I guess. [Laughs]. The other thing that I noticed that was really, that I was just, I mean, a funny little thing that I noticed was that I prefer listening to music while I work, you know, at some point I was like in an empty office with headphones on listening to music and I was like, I can totally like put the music on the speakers and listen to it and it seemed more distracting when I was like in the ambient noise, instead of when it's playing directly into my ears, which was very, just strange.

PM: Oh right, okay, yeah and did you learn, or did you take sort of breaks to go walking and things like that, or is that something you already knew that you wanted to do or...?

BS: I definitely, yeah, I went for walks, did, you know, thinking walks, even, yeah, and I went to the gym.

PM: Can you explain how you spent your Maniac Week?

BS: Well I worked for 87 hours, where I was like focussed on tasks at my computer and yeah, so I actually basically just set up shop in my office, it was empty, there was nobody else there and I worked and you know, stuck with the computer when I was distracted, I, you know, walked out of the office probably at least once a day to like go get Doritos or something, but I pretty much worked, eat, sleep.

PM: So your impression of that, would you say that, is there something that, so for you, what has prevented you from feeling like you're productive enough, if that's the case? I might be leading that question a little bit but, or is that completely rubbish?

BS: So, there are a lot of like little things that probably draw my attention away from, like, the less urgent things like answering email, helping out with support, chasing and fixing bugs and things, like a common thing that will happen in my work day is I sit down and I, you know, I go and check our support email inbox and there are like some things marked for me that are bugs, things that I need to know about or that need some kind of input from me and often, you know, like there are some big tasks that I need to get done today, but first I need, like, first task of the day is to check this inbox, then I'll kind of get distracted by all these other little bugs and be like going and chasing around this thing or that other thing.

It's useful to fix those bugs in the big picture, but they draw away from time to work on these larger, you know, like larger projects or things, so being able to, one of the things about my maniac week is I, you know, said, I'm not going to do any support email this week, you know, it's on you, deal with it and my co-founder and our support just took care of it for the whole week so I didn't, like, I didn't even open email pretty much. That was really nice because I was able to then keep my focus on these, like, larger picture items that sometimes get, you know, get frittered away day by day because it feels like I'm going to need, you know, four hours to work on this and now I only have three left in a day.

PM: Yeah, I understand that, so what do you think, so have you taken any lessons or any kind of concepts that you would say help you to understand what the probable future scenario of the quantified self at work might be like? It's pretty much my last question, I've sort of tried to go through the whole what I wanted to ask in my head.

BS: I'm not, I don't know how I can speak to that. To whatever extent, you know, there's a lot more, yeah, like you were saying before, you know, there is kind of this change in the way that the hierarchy and officers and people leaving college are less likely maybe to go to us, into like a lower level entry position, like work their way up or they're doing start-ups and you know, finding places where they have more, I don't know, more control and more input into, like, the shape of the business. I guess that's the interesting thing about the start-up role. So, in these less structured environments, to the extent that that's becoming more common in the workplace.

PM: Oh, it's useful, yeah. It's kind of, yeah, it's a response to that changing world of work and so do you think there's a sort of a positive aspect to it or...?

BS: I know that I was far more interested in this more self-driven start up kind of, like, work environment when I was interviewing for jobs after grad school and after like a half a year I took this leap of faith, to work on Beeminder, so I know that that appeals to me.

PM: And during that week, did you feel, so what did your track, your emotions at all to track or...?

BS: I didn't track my emotions at all. That's one that is interesting to me, I know about Moodscope which I think is maybe a pretty good one for tracking mood. It's still subjective, I always, I'm suspicious of my own ability to like reflect and have any idea about my emotional state, [laughs], like, I don't know how to be self-consistent with that kind of subjective tracking, so...

Interview with Robin Barooah

PM: I think I am interested in wearables and self-tracking technologies (WSTT) because they aren't really something I'd picture myself using: I don't know whether they suit my personality. I guess the stereotype is that people are... well, obsessive? Detail oriented? Not like me... well....

RB: There are people who are obsessed with WSTT as if the data were more objective! Thinking, 'ah, these are objective statements about me'. That thread is strong in the QS [Qualified Self] community and in reporting about QS but it's kind of annoying to me because there is less and less presence of this... there are so many alternative perspectives of QS and I'm one of the representatives of that non-common view. It's fascinating, the number, that reflect some aspect or yourself, they are not objective at all, we ... they are produced by mechanistic processes and we know something about these, and we know something about the origin of the numbers, but... who is doing the interpreting?! That is to me why they are interesting! And one's relationship with a given number changes over item, it's not like this thing that produces a truth... I know that people who have used my app, I showed that page, essentially showing using the same information, they go through a process, start off trying to be a perfect meditator, and feeling bad if they fail, and I know people that have got into nearly the 1,000s of consecutive days and there are people how will come to me at meet-ups and show me the app and the screenshots, and say, will it fail if I get to 999... will the app be able to handle bigger numbers? But then someone will fail... everyone fails in the end... and then the relationship with the number changes. One guy that was consistently showing me these higher numbers and then one day he missed one, and he says, I'm done now, I am still going to meditate every day, it's taught me something about permanence, attachment to perfection, he was always showing me that number, I was thinking, feeling like the Jedi master, he will realise he's really attached to this number... I think that, you know, the numbers are one thing and ourselves and interpretation in another and that's far from objective.

PM: When did you start using WSTT? How did you find out about them?

RB: That is a tricky question, so I found out, I had a long history of interest in technology, like very long, like I wrote my first computer programming using punch cards in the 1970s so ever since then I had my head connected to these things, I had one of the first pocket computers that existed, and I have had some kind of personal device since I was 12, my father was a scientist and he managed to smuggle a personal computer out of his lab and so by the time I was 14 I was aware or knew you could carry a computer around with you and I thought about making wearable in that time frame, a thing called Cord Keyboard. Conceptually you have five, six keys, and you make letters out of pressing combination of these, you could have basically a switch attached to each finger, you could type into the air, without a keyboard, I remember hearing about these, you know, you could have one in a glove, you could have a display like a Google glass and you could, it would be like a really cool thing...

Microwriter was made in London, actually... I got one of these but I never had the wearable... but I would sit on the underground with my hand in my pocket, writing reports.

My awareness of wearables goes back to my teenage years.

I don't think of that as a wearable, it's a PDA, funnily enough I may have never used a wearable, though I have continuously owned a pocket computer since I was 12 I don't think I've had anything like a specific watch, or a heart rate monitor, nothing like what we think of as a wearable.

PM: Why is there a trend around 'wearables'?

RB: Firstly there was a transition point when the IPhone came out, which was critically, we had personal computers before but they weren't really personal. For one thing they were somewhat shared and they never went along with you, you had to go to the computer rather than it going along with you, IPhone was first computer that would go into your pocket and create a general personal interface that most people could use. Obviously, there were machines before that that could do everything that the I-Phone could do but they were the first to make the pocket computers, and at that point, there was a shift to REALLY personal computers, and that's what made me think finally I can do this meditation app, I had wanted to do this for ages not because I couldn't technically do it, but who has a desktop computer with them when they are meditating? Finally, you can do things whereby you can bring computers into spaces where it would have been intrusive before, it can enter into space where it wouldn't have been acceptable before. I think wearables are an extension of that trend. Not as radical in some ways, they are now we really have personal computers, people don't share phones, it's your personal device, and now that people have their domain of computation, at least in principle (not distributed worldwide of course) but in principle we have this concept, there is this extension that well, why not have the computer know more about us, we have already learned/shared personal information with and through these devices so there is this understanding also that we are willing to allow technology into personal domains, that is basically why I think wearables are being used now, 20 years ago we had heart monitors, step counters, we could have developed them if we'd wanted to but seen as an obscure thing, it's not geeky to do this.

PM: Mainstream perception is that wearables started in the domain of health...

RB: The health demand was always there, but it isn't that we have suddenly realised we want to be more healthy, we have the techno-social readiness to use the tools for that purpose.

PM: What kind do you use? (including analogue such as diary writing)

RB: Personally I use, well, it's interesting, I use a few things, I basically I mean I use hardware wise, I use my phone and I use pen and paper. Like, some things I track using spreadshseets depending on what I happen to be near at the time.

PM: What activities would/ do you track?

RB: Meditation is one of them there are a bunch of things I have tracked to solve a particular problem I tracked my sleep but using my phone in a manual way, no sensor as such, it was special app that I made for myself. I discovered I was sleeping a lot less than I thought, which was a surprise to me, I was feeling exhausted all the time and everything seemed more stressful and I thought I was sleeping 6.5 hours and I was sleeping 3 hours, I was sleeping beside someone who was snoring, I thought I would wake up briefly but I would wake up and stay away for hours, that's one, sleep. I tracked very carefully I have this gluten intolerance, I knew that, I came to England for a year 2013, all products are obviously different than here and some I was having a reaction to, I didn't know what it was. I had a reaction to different kinds of breads, and tried to do this analysis to deduce the common ingredient and I did actually manage to single out an ingredient... but there are very few reports on this having talked to other people who have done food tracking, you can easily find that things with the same ingredients have contamination. I got to a single ingredient and I found a bread brand that I could eat though I didn't know. It was an obscure additive.

PM: Was there a trigger that inspired you to start using WSTT?

RB: So um I had been generally into self-experimentation when I was younger but I hadn't continued with that after my 20s and then I had a very stressful period and I thought I had to re-engineer my life and self-tracking to solve specific problems, I hate tracking technologies really, except that it is really useful, I don't want to be doing it unless I really have to.

PM: Did you find that you stopped using them at some point? Why? For how long?

RB: Often that is the case, I still feel my app for meditation I still like to have that feedback and I am happy to have... my phone has a step counter on it, most new ones do, I do look at it occasionally, my dog has a collar with a step counter, that is actually useful as well, it's not about me but it did change my behaviour in that it makes me take his walks more seriously.

PM: What does it feel like to use WSTT?

RB: Yeah, I mean so that's really interesting so for several of these things like the sleep thing and the food tracking thing and there was another thing I did about my weight a long time ago they feel like a lot of effort, I can't do many at a time, there is a project each stress of its own, for those kinds of things it feels like an effort, quitting my coffee, the tracking part takes a discipline associated with it. It doesn't feel like an effort to use step counter or the meditation app, obviously cause I guess they are taken care of, mostly by the technology.

PM: Has it helped your state of mind? How do you define/explain your feeling when you use/when you stop/when you start using again?

RB: Basically, my state of mind when started using again, something like, oh fuck this is a serious problem that I haven't considered/realised... well it hasn't been going away on its own and I am going to have to take it more seriously and think about it, and it's kind of a bit of empowerment, the fact that I am realising that something that I thought would go away, take control, recognising there is a set back and not as easy as I thought, so both empowerment and mild frustration.

PM: Have you ever used WSTT in relation to work/productivity?

RB: Yes I was tracking my productivity essentially using something like the Pomodoro method, you know of it, where I was using 25 minute blocks, 15, some unit of time I think it was 15, might have been 25 it is recorded somewhere, google it if you want to see... I was not strictly following the Pomodoro method but I like the idea of time boxing so I was using that practice and making a record of how successful I was at that, only recording successful time boxes, not recording that if I didn't make it through, later I realised having that kind of operational definition i.e. what a successful... applying it rigorously then I had a measure for insight of how productive I was.

Reason for using it? Well... not long after I had quit my regular job, was now trying to work on the meditation timer as a project and I had discovered that my concentration was shot after all this stress and I was struggling and not in a good cognitive state so I wanted to do something to get control of that. To build the muscle of concentration, I knew that I needed to put some effort into this.

PM: Would you have used it with the more traditional employment environment?

RB: There was a point where I made a transition from being a manager into being an individual contributor, and I during that time was tracking my time because there were loads of demands on me to remain parts of my previous job and there were also some weird blanks hours where I had no idea of what I was doing and so I definitely used in my regular job, and in my previously job I had done a lot of tracking of people I justified making their working hours more humane we had a staggered shift pattern, I made a case for a good work day, why are people staying until 9 pm?

PM: Do you tend to use WSTT for rest? For health? Productivity? What percentage of each?

RB: In practice this is more like the solar system, some tiny periods of time where I've been paying attention to these things, so it's pretty hard, and also I realise that one of the big things that I did some self-tracking around has not been included in that conversation and one that has been most consistent. I started a shared project, we were trying to re-cord emotional states, we initially were using words, emotional, anx-iety at random points at different points and we made Google entries in this shared calendar, and we looked at each other's scores, we had heard from John Cousins who had a company called Mood Scope and found that sharing his Mood Score helped elevate his mood, and he had bipolar and found that just sharing his mood helped him.

It turned into, over time, not so much a numeric process but more like diary-ing because it was hard to capture anything meaningful in a few numbers so that could be seen as turning away from quantified self into the qualitative realm, and in some ways it was, but then later, years later, we started in 2009 and carried on until 2013, and people would say you can do sentiment analysis and see if there are common patterns in four words, we didn't do anything first of all with the subjective data, I am quite a private person, but what I did do is I tried tracking frequency of making entries over time, and there were some fascinating results. The frequency of entry correlated almost identically with meditation. If you took a weighting of moving average of my mood entries, then you got a mirror image, graphs were fluctuated in the same way, had the same gaps, and that was like, and what does that signal mean, obviously ex-ternal events might stop... or both change behaviour and sentiment.

Level of depression or level of general activity or make me do both of those things, more likely to meditate and to make these mood en-tries, so it was pretty fascinating you can see in the graphs all these major events, like when my father died there's this radical change in the graph, or going to different countries, bunch of different events that changed the graph. One thing that I haven't done is to analyse the other person's data.

PM: Did you select number representations for each emotion?

RB: We started out by trying to have entries that were somehow numeric but we didn't succeed with this for very long, broke down, this is... I had separately tired tracking tools that tried to do that, they didn't break down, those broke down too, because I felt like I gave similar number though I was feeling different, in the moment when I am asked to you try to figure it out, I was feeling down a few minutes ago but I don't feel down now, so it's very hard to give a score. I actually asked this question I asked this at one of the QS conferences, how can you rate, how well you've been feeling over the past month, how about last day, how about right now? Put their hand up when they had a number, the longer the time period, the easier it is to rate your mood.

Interview with 'Ian'

PM: What wearable and self-tracking technologies (WSTT) do you use?

IAN: I use Python, that's a computer programming language to input data into Excel, hook up Python to Excel via a module called Excel Wings, and run algorithms to analyse data and spit out metrics.

I intend to create an app that will allow me to gather the same data but more easily maybe in 6 months. This is unchartered territory.

PM: When did you start using WSTT?

IAN: 2012, when I was living in Taiwan during my gap year, basically, after I had watched some QS videos that people are using technology to learn more about themselves, started to think about this concept and to use excel spreadsheets to do so. Well, more like, in the spring, 2013 I did this. I 'life tracked' every five minutes.

But I stopped because when I looked at the data I felt that too many important details was aggregated out e.g. if I was at my desk working and texted someone then it was lost by that five minute block. It wasn't as detailed as I wanted it to be because when I looked back at the data I knew that it wasn't representative of who I was. I knew that wasn't who I was. When I finished fourth year of University I wasn't doing any official tracking but experimenting with ways of tagging things, I just got too busy.

PM: How long did you self-track for at that time?

IAN: 3 months. No, more than that, a bit longer than that.

PM: About 3.5 months?

IAN: Yes, probably, I don't have the information with me now.

PM: Did you spot any differences between how you felt when you were life tracking and when you weren't?

IAN: In the first iteration, of the 5 minute one, I was able to go back and get a rough estimate of what I was doing but when I wasn't doing it I found myself being really curious, wanting to know, made me feel antsy, not having it made me want it again. I just wanted to have the ability to know how much time I spent on whatever yesterday, I like having the ability to know that, look at the data, I find it empowering to be able to know that.

PM: Why did you start using?

IAN: I am very very curious about what this kind of data can tell me about me. I have a hypothesis that at this moment in time that you and me and everyone here is defined by all previous experiences in my life, makes sense intuitively, really, as a way of figuring out what that is. If there is a way of knowing what I have done then I can gain insight into who I am.

Actually, I am hoping to change to using different software, the process is arduous, tedious, onerous, mind numbingly boring.

PM: Why do you keep doing it if it is boring?

IAN: That hypothesis is enough to overcome my boredom. The data represents/is a record of decision making throughout the day. E.g. right now coming to speak to you today is more important than anything else I made decisions about

PM: In looking at the data can you discern whether you apply a hierarchy of decision making?

IAN: Not really, more like a collection of a series of decisions that have been made, i.e. I decided to go on the tube today, I decided to do C++ for four hours today, so what the data represents is a series of decisions, aggregated to the larger scale begins to define who I am. Collections of results from decisions that I have made.

I hadn't thought about it that way (prioritising decisions), more that the data at a basic level represents decisions that I have made, so what that represents, a decision made against other possible decisions, it potentially tells me a lot about what is behind the decisions that I have made, looking at the data will begin to tell me about the processes that have gone on in order to make those decisions.

PM: What does it feel like to use self-tracking technologies?

IAN: If technology is a means to an end in the general definition. I am fascinated to look back at any point later about my present, I can tell you what I was doing on that day and for how long. That is incredibly empowering, to be able to look back in time, someone can't tell you that they spent 21 minutes watching TV. I find it fascinating.

PM: What is the feeling?

IAN: Let me express myself a bit more clearly, I feel very empowered because I have the ability to know more things about myself than the next person. For example, you may not know how much time you spent on your laptop yesterday, but I will know that. I make no judgment on the observation, for me this is purely observational, not judgment, if you use judgments then you would potentially not be the message/information, insight that you could gain from it. e.g for me, at an extreme: if you aren't interested in life tracking, you aren't interested in finding out who you are. But I am accepting of the uncertainty of the situation. I don't use qualitative terms because I want to stick to data integrity and eliminate any time variant bias. Trying to be as scientific and thorough as possible, geared around pure observations that don't change over time. In the previous incarnation of this software I was using e.g. 'p' for procrastination but that was my interpretation of the activities at the time, but when I look back on this I can see that this was an explorative activity. This is a way of recording data that doesn't change as I change. The representation of the data will not change as my opinions change e.g. instead of saying procrastination, I am saying, 'laptop', 'internet' now.

I'm not interested in looking at 'outcomes', that would go against my reasons for doing it, it's an exercise in curiosity, I don't know where this will take me.

I think of inputs as data I put into the spreadhsheets and outputs are actionable intelligence obtained through data analysis.

In my current state, productivity is purely being measured in minutes, so that's not really an outcome, it's a description of the data set, it's a query on the data set, so I get the tags and say 'does this count as productive work or not' and then I put these under a search tag of 'productivity' because I see that as productivity

PM: What do you mean by productivity in this project?

IAN: Productivity is a label to a set of tags. I have a range of things under the tag of productivity.

PM: Why do you keep using WSTT?

IAN: I keep using this because of sheer curiosity. I have the idea that at some point I will be able to glean really important insights about myself. This is super interesting, not just that I feel productive; the power of the data is that it is all encompassing. Much QS is localized, only about one aspect of your day, this is that I am viewing everything in aggregation, everything in isolation aren't going to tell you much about yourself, it's when you view your life as a system that you see the patterns of how they react around each other and you have a fuller data set.

PM: Do you know other people who are also using it?

IAN: Yes, someone contacted me to say that he was interested in doing a similar type of self tracking projects, dude who spoke before me at the meeting. He emailed me today. He thinks it's a really cool ideal.

PM: When do you mostly use it/why?

IAN: This is what I meant before, 'there is a certain time of day' the premise of my system is that this is all encompassing at an aggregate level. Maybe people are doing this already, I haven't encouraged it yet, not encountered anyone doing this to the same intensity or detail that I am doing it.

Buckminster Fuller was using for three years what he was doing every 15 minutes. But their resolution was 15 minutes, mine is every one minute.

PM: Have you had a negative feedback about this?

IAN: I haven't had negative impact though a friend raised the question, do you have people's consent when I put 'who I was talking to' in my data, which is a valid question, but no I don't feel that I need their permission to remember them if I were sharing my data set then ok, that would be a problem. Like, just by meeting me means you are giving me consent to remember you, whether I write it down or not.

PM: Why did you stop when you did?

IAN: I just felt that it wasn't seeing the kind of detail that I wanted to see, so I had a regroup and thought about it for a while, things got busy and I didn't get round to setting up, takes time to get it set up and to run it properly. Then when I had free time to spare I set it up again. So around then the decision to do university work outranked. The hierarchy is an interesting point, idea, because at that moment in time I perceived studying hard in fourth year more valuable than exploring this conceptual folly. Hadn't thought of it that way.

PM: In what ways has the use of WSTT affected your behavior?

IAN: It's hard to say, I don't have any definitive 'yesses' to that question because I've only been going at the most sophisticated version of my life track I don't have enough data to say yes definitely because that was an 'output' i.e. actively changing my behavior as an output, my data analysis tools aren't sophisticated enough to do that, but an interesting thing to see, when I was running linear regressions at certain activities/time, I got some interesting results, interesting statistically sign negative correlation between TV watching and number of productive minutes (summation of all activities under productivity tag, i.e. codes with descriptions, about 15 productive).

At the moment this hasn't changed my behavior, but it might change me in a way I'm not aware of, but surely that would be represented in this data in some way, but because I wasn't connected to the data before I was doing it, I won't be able to look at the structure of the data in any way. Other people have asked me, because if you know you are doing it, does that change your behavior? Does the process itself? I have been asked this question a few times but I don't know as I don't have evidence to back it up, it's kind of the whole reason to do this.

The 'point of doing this' is to gain information about myself that I can then learn from, irrefutable data that can't change, that stands the test of time.

I might make a decision to change my behavior after looking at the data e.g. resulting form negative correlation i.e. too many episodes of one series, but when I do that now I am more conscious of the fact that this can run away from me, and I'll get nothing else done during the day. It's a process of learning, although I should preface this by saying that I am a statistician almost by trade, but this is a relationship, whether causal, correlation is not causality, is it causal? I can't prove that yet but I am aware the relationships exist, but I wouldn't say there is a causal relationship because my tools aren't sophisticated enough.

PM: Has this impacted your motivation?

IAN: [doesn't really know how to answer...] motivation TO... what?... makes me want to do it more. I am a data junkie and I enjoy having the information in front me of, motivation to keep doing it.

PM: Has it helped you with making goals (short, medium, long)?

IAN: I have an idea say, learn to do yoga, then you do it a little bit, and then it carries on for a bit and you don't do it, and now I almost know that you have do something for a period of time, a concurrent time, maybe it has made me less inclined to frivolously take on new things, hadn't thought about it much. I'm concerned whether things are productive or not/ appreciate for time allocation to 'get into something' make it a part of my life.

PM: Is there a scarcity of time?

IAN: Yes, definitely, it is the only thing in life that you can't have more of, it's the fourth dimension, you can't stop it or changes it, you have to take it when it's there. This is why I'm curious about it, it is the most precious commodity we have, if we haven't been spending it well, my data is a representation of this precious commodity, you aren't spending it in the right way then you aren't getting the most out of your time that resonates as a fact.

PM: Does that mean it's ALL about setting goals for you?

IAN: I don't know really, potentially yes, by doing this I can really perceive how long i.e. learning a new skill takes, like if I want to learn a new skill then I have to work that into a fraction of my life, that is the balance of my life, allocating my time in the best way, to be most fulfilled in life, you have to get it just right, and what I am doing is helping me learn about that, informing me about how I can do it in a more optimal way, in essence.

PM: Is the right way different for anyone?

IAN: What would make you happy wouldn't be necessarily what makes me happy, but that would be representable in that system.

PM: The ultimate reason for life tracking is to achieve happiness?

IAN: Don't use happiness because you are still working with the assumption that you are working toward as a goal that there is an answer to this question, it's a heuristic process, my ideal level will change as well, as I get older, 'what I want now is not the same as what I wanted two years ago, what I will want when I'm older'

Working towards just one thing in life would be naïve because every day you are changing. If all I wanted to do was to be productive then

I would spend all day working but that wouldn't make me happy, happiness is derived through fulfilment, and that is different for everyone, it's getting the right balance. That is the target but the target is constantly changing based on daily activities. You can't achieve perfect fulfilment in that sense, but you can work towards it, but working towards it might be the fulfilment, it's too philosophical for me, I am a data scientist

PM: Has it changed your values?

IAN: (thinking) it's made me appreciate the need for getting the balance just right, the need for wanting to spend times I actually enjoy doing. So a good example, when I was applying for jobs etc. I was almost going to be an accountant, and I got to the final interviews and stuff, but it was the time spent during those interviews that I had to actively spend time learning about the profession and reading accountancy magazines, like becoming an accountant turned me off, I don't want to be doing this. So, that's almost me trying to fit a bit of accountancy into my life and me rejecting it, trial and error.

When I read into computer science, I was so interested in it then I actively pursued it, to learn more and more about it, almost like my preference for it determined my next time steps, minutes, willingness to do more of that thing. So like with accountancy, five minutes doing it where I hate it, the next five minutes wouldn't really do it.

Hasn't changed my values to put family and friends above everything else, values in the sense that I want to value what I do, want to be interested in what I do. So not my core values.

PM: Has it changed your well-being, emotions?

IAN: Not obviously, I couldn't conclusively say yes or no. In a similar way to what we were talking about before, whether or not it has/hasn't changed me, maybe subconsciously, I am not aware of it, but it would be evident from the data, but my future self is dependent on my present self. To know about the subconscious two sets of data I'd need two sets of data, previous and past.

6   Robot Army of Redressers?

Growing interest in software that measures corporeal experiences and traditional management interest in its purpose for assessing productivity is one reason we need to reopen debates around our own understandings therein, to reposition the discussion away from the neoliberal assumption that efficiency, speed, and growth of productivity are the only goals available to humankind. Exploitation and appropriation are being facilitated by specific advances in technology which presuppose dualism and advocate the health of the body as intimately linked to the health of the mind, whilst also reducing any corporeal agency. This recognition enables the current promotion of self-tracking, self-archiving devices that potentially serve productivity requirements of management. For these reasons, it is vital to revisit how the implications of ontology can inform possibilities for revolutionary change and to identify the techniques of control contained in technological advances; recognising the imminent threat emerging from networked labour in the cognitive industries and attempts to appropriate these via state surveillance and businesses' use of individual profiling.

The new materialist point is that matter is not dead, and even influences how things happen. This is demonstrated in the use of self-archiving technologies and the rise in a new 'employable self', or one who can manage herself through reducing all work to the quantifiable, tangible, and identifiable. The corporeal and affective turns in the humanities and social sciences try to uncover the depths of this assumed ontological Cartesianism and have developed the concepts of abstract machine, machine assemblages and cyborgs. Here, I have taken a close look at the biometric dimensions of self-tracking and the quantified self; looking at the recent evidence of the growing recognition of the monism of bodies and minds and the importance of the labour process theory arguments in assessing this current phase of Taylorisation of the workplace (again). The conclusion will summarise the book's chapters and conclude that the ambivalence of a quantified workplace movement must be critically analysed with regard to the emerging possibilities for control at work through control of both the mind and the body; the implications for workers' motivation, as well as the potential for an emergence of history whereby workers in the Fordist factory became some of the most organised in labour history or where we see a digital Army of Redressers. To identify how I view the imminent next stages in this emerging research field, I provide the description for the first of the three Debates in New Materialisms.

Worker tracking technologies tell us which working conditions or interactions appear to cause which emotions or social performances, but do not tell us how or why. They claim to show us what a body can do, but in fact they only show us what bodies have been seen doing, in a particular, determinate social formation which they co-constitute. This is characteristic of a shift from 'truth' to empty functionalism, from deductive science to a raw, inductive 'it-works' orientation. Coding 'individual' material then opens the distinct possibilities for other controls, such as selling and misusing data produced by wearable tracking technologies.

Contemporary neuroscience confirms the Deleuzian–Bergsonian contention that sense organs have a double capacity, part of which is oriented to participatory knowledge. The qualitative level 'allows us to apprehend the world as a field of forces that affect us and make themselves present in our bodies in the form of sensations' (Rolnik, 2011: 25). The denial of flow and becoming, of all the singularities of life, is crucial: it does not matter to capital if we laugh, cry, fear or go mad, it 'counts for nothing' – it is 'noise' in the information-theory sense (Guattari, 1996: 137). The epistemic underpinning of the quantified working self perpetuates the image that the mind controls the body, and thus, from a Spinozian perspective, serves to *contain* the body's power within a *mental* frame largely constituted by neoliberal ideology and subjectivity. Wearable computers were perhaps originally intended as tools, but have become a wearer's second brain, a technological companion, an extension of the self or a second skin (Mann and Niedzviecki, 2001). Potentially repressing and denying the qualitative aspects of bodily experience, tracking the self at work is an affective phenomenon in its own right; constructing certain kinds of bodily possibilities where it is hoped that a device and machine are become symbiotic (Viseu and Suchman, 2010: 162). Will machines soon know our bodies better than ourselves? In our interview in Chapter 5, Dancy predicts that soon, machines will tell humans how to be human. Given workers' experiences that are outlined in this book, this role for the machine in employment relationships is one we may soon see more explicitly than ever before.

From the new materialist perspective, what may be missing in emerging discussions about quantifying the self at work is any awareness of the dimension of life *as such*, or the field of the temporal, of becoming and differentiation, of the unique experience of life, in Marxian terms, of labour-power prior to its equivalential capture by capital. If quantifying the precarious self is *not* providing a unique expression of 'life itself', it is a deepened, extended and uniquely repressive form of discipline and repression of life/labour. The very existence of life itself, as something unrepresented within the system, is rejected; life is exiled from social life, assigned the abyssal status of 'bare life' (Agamben, 1998) or assigned a position of absolute incommunicability. At the point that the autonomous self is measured as related to work and production, it becomes striated and made abstract. Metrics thus become the sole remaining identifier. Yet, the repressed force of the qualitative returns in the form of psychological symptoms and problems borne by precarious workers. Future research should identify an emerging social movement like those seen in other emergent practices of social movements: people who are responding to the 'problem arising out of modern [post]industrial conditions ... aimed and safeguarding of some public interest against dangers inherent' (Polanyi, 1944/2001: 153) where the 'greater visibility of bodily information implies an associated responsibility to act' (Viseu and Suchman, 2010: 163). What kind of action will be inspired by data tracking? As I have argued in Chapter 3, affective solidarities are supressed by tracking, even in the communities that arise out of them. The confessional, competitive, self endorser tends to emerge in these arenas rather than the collective.

New uses of technologies in the quantified workplace are part of an emerging form of neo-Taylorism which risks subordinating workers' bodies to neoliberal, corporeal capitalism. In the short term, quantification helps corporations and self-employed precarians to keep up with cutthroat competition. In the long term, this approach undermines life to capital to an unsustainable degree, destroying the qualitative outside, which both provides the basis for capitalism (as use-value, labour-power, consumer desire) and the basis for resistance. At a minimum, we can speak of declining welfare for workers and the associated regime of total mobilisation and surveillance which corrodes workers' health and safety, creating anxiety, burnout and overwork. Neoliberalism continues to portray such problems as failures to adapt, personal psychological shortcomings or educational deficits. They seem, rather, to be systematic effects of a particular labour process. Labour movements will need to combat such corrosion.

If left unchecked, the spread of wearables in the workplace may be seen as an extension of a control society (Deleuze, 1992); based on a strengthened Cartesian dualism, and a subordination of precarious workers' qualitative being to capitalism in the form of a Taylorism which reaches into the body. Vaneigem (1967/2003) argued that '[l]ife quantified becomes a measured route-march towards death (35) ... rigorously quantified, first by money and then by what you might call sociometric units of power, exchange pollutes all our relationships, all our feelings, all our thoughts' (29). But 'there remain things unmeasured by the current, changing modes of capital accumulation' (Colman, 2014: 3).

Against a new regime of quantification, social movements can be expected to seek new forms of refusal and exodus, which must increasingly take the form of a refusal of data – a refusal to track the body, a refusal to subordinate the qualitative to the quantitative, a refusal of surveillance and a refusal to share data with corporations and the state. Scholars have celebrated the potential of smartphones and social media for social protest (Castells, 2012) and autonomous identity formation. But the use of big data which is now being generated by self- and other-tracking technologies in workplaces indicates a significant shift to logics that potentially work to circumvent protest. There is now an entire industry devoted to big data and finding correlations that work in an instrumental sense; informed consent is increasingly difficult to obtain. Refusing to share data is becoming a political act.

While terms like agility and flexibility evoke images of pleasure and freedom, I argue that our current phase in work design experimentation—the agile management system—is not one of reduced work or empowerment and exhilaration, but permits hyper-exploitation. In Chapter 2, I discussed the history of work design experimentation from industrial betterment to agility, noting the ways that the body and the machine are portrayed and adapted in each period. I concluded that bodies and machines are in a state of perpetual apprehension, testing the possibilities for limiting and facilitating agency. This analysis took me to the next chapter, where I theorise precarity in a material sense. Precarity is not exclusive to technologised workplaces, but it is exacerbated in the unequal employment relationship that emerges. Knowledge and material production emerge from incredibly exhausted, vulnerable producers who may or may not know who or what is meant to manage them. Concepts of self-management pervade 'management guru' literature and were part of the knowledge economy dream of the late 1990s and early 2000s. In this book, I have disputed the imaginative utopia of the entrepreneur by looking at the working conditions of the self-managed individual who carries the supposedly weightlessness of a cloud-based world. The entrepreneur, rather than being released from the drudgeries of everyday work, is perhaps the most controlled and, at least digitally, tracked worker that has ever existed. Problematically, the dream of the entrepreneur is usually only successful when s/he already has social capital from family relations or inherited asset-based wealth. The rise of the gig economy is the manifestation of the failed promise of the knowledge economy. The 'free' in freelance is not liberation but leads to work that is done for free, such as online reputational management which is outlined in Chapter 4. But in Chapter 3, I emphasise the undignified status of precarious workers and look to the philosophical treatises of new materialism, feminism and Marxism to make sense of this unresolved terrain. I concluded Chapter 3 by looking at avenues for resistance, particularly in the terrain of the affective.

In Chapter 4, I outlined the prominent digitalised working environments and their conditions, including platform and gig work and electronically monitored office and warehouse workers. In 2017 I was interviewed by Jane Wild for the *Financial Times* for an Employment Practices report. I argued that rather than being improved (as they are marketed), working conditions are debilitated by machines. Here is text from the *Financial Times* article (Wild, 2017):

> Transparency is crucial in forming that strategy, says Phoebe Moore, an academic who works with multinational companies and unions to devise codes of conduct about their data gathering practices. She adds that often workers do not realise the extent to which they are being observed, from their emails being read to voice and motion technology being used to analyse how great a contribution they make in meetings. Ms Moore recommends that employees are involved in the process of formulating a data policy and that the guidelines are very clear in stating why data are captured and what they are used for. "Communication [with staff] is very important," she says. "Who owns the data? Who stores it? Can it be sold?"

The quotes Wild uses emerge from work I have done with companies and unions to identify what processes should, at the very least, be in place before any decisions are made to track workers. The worst offense is when companies do not set up a contract with workers that at least creates a set of principles that are shared with employees and which management agrees to follow.

Kylie Jarrett projects a figure of the digital housewife 'whose cognitive and affective efforts in building and sustaining interpersonal relationships online, in communicating and coordinating activity with others, in producing and sharing content, is at the heart of the collective intelligence of digital media's commercial properties'. This housewife provides content to products and helps development of these (without pay) but also 'adds to that affective stickiness' (Ahmed, 2004a, b, cited in Jarrett, 2016: 9). A huge proportion of work in digitalised spheres is not paid and is under recognised; this usually unseen labour is appropriated and facilitates the reproduction of the unequal relations that I have outlined in this text. Are we all digital housewives now? Reputation generation has always been important for employability, but in the era of hireability, digital technologies provide a range of methods to improve and maintain reputations. As I have pointed out in Chapter 4, Uber drivers and Upwork freelancers must work constantly and carry out unpaid labour to remain competitive against other gig workers, to gain enough work (in the case of Upwork) and to avoid being fired (in the case of Uber). Likewise, people in knowledge professions like academics must keep reputations fresh by continuously updating Twitter feeds, using such platforms as Linkedin and Academia, while not putting too much private information on social media at the risk of being surveilled and accused of wrongdoing. Much unpaid labour is now used for predictive people analytics, where decisions are made about recruitment and collaboration. It may soon begin to feel like, if you do not have an online presence, or perhaps, if your labour is not digitally quantified, you may not exist at all.

In Chapter 4 I have looked at empirical cases of the quantification of labour as a method to control unseen affective and emotional labour; where this labour is about suppressing anxiety and dissent and where the algorithmic boss actively allows the measure of affect and emotion and all-of-life, through digitalised devices. I have revealed several cases where workers have been tracked and monitored, including the Quantified Workplace project where one company provided devices and interfaces for employees to improve both wellbeing and well-billing. My findings from the yearlong project show that workers are not ambivalent to self-tracking, but instead demonstrated a high rate of resistance.

Chapter 5 catalogues four interviews with specific individuals who are very well versed in self-tracking. Their stories and insights give exceptional weight to the book's arguments, not least because they have practitioner experience in a number of related fields. Interviewees were part of the initial stages of the quantified self movement. One man has been called the most self-tracked person on the planet. Another has used a pencil and paper to track every second of his life in a quest to understand himself objectively. One has used various methods of diarising and self-accounting to deal with emotional and stressful times as well as to overcome habits. People are aware of the possibilities for self-development in quantifying the autonomic self. Numeration is not something entirely divorced from lived experiences. While I outline the dangers and the exploitative aspects of too much technology and tracking in labour processes and the employment relationship, these four interviews provide both confirmation of the tragic possibilities and dark side, as well as some delightful counter positions to this book's darker arguments.

To conclude, I outline an agenda for research in the quantified self at work into the next decades. The issues I have outlined throughout this book will not disappear but are likely to intensify and expand internationally. Here I set out a series of provocations based on recent research on the quantified worker (most of which was not available when I started writing this book) and empirical examples of the rise of machinic management to inform the next steps in research in what is an emerging field of research on the quantified worker.

Wisdom of the Algorithmic Boss?

Striphas comments that 'algorithm is a less obvious keyword by means of which to make sense of culture today' compared to keyword possibilities such as "information and crowd"' (2015: 403). The wisdom emerging from algorithmic happenstance may be an elite outpouring that encapsulates the 'best of what has been thought and said' (Arnold, 1869/1993: 190, cited in Striphas, 2015: 406) which is what defines culture in the Arnoldian sense. Algorithmic trends can surprise, like the case of #AmazonFail in 2009. In this embarrassing case, one romance author could not find sales ratings for gay romances on Amazon and thought it was peculiar. Through contacting the help line, the author discovered Amazon's electronic filters recognised these types of books as 'adult material'. Thousands of Twitter users made comments that day about the discriminatory filtering system, a rampage that was seen to unseat the Prince of Peace that Easter (Striphas, 2015). Another example is seen through the quirky surprises that the progress in artificial intelligence developments have offered. A 'teen girl' chat robot was released by Microsoft in March 2016 and was permitted to chat with the public. Very quickly, uncensored chats began to inform her own words because, of course, computers can only restate what has been stated to them. The bot went from moody teen to offensive Hitler-endorsing incest promoter. In that case, the 'wisdom' of the public was one of dark cynicism as well as humour; Microsoft's corporate public relations stint was a soft hackers' paradise.

Given these recent anecdotes, it is provocative to ask whether an algorithm really should be trusted to replace a traditional manager. Crowdsourcing and shared working platforms like peer to peer were once thought of as a democratic space where all could play a role in producing the workplace and owning the means and mode of production. Against the hopes of early collaborators in newly digitalised economies, these spaces have been privatised and co-opted. Algorithms are the outcomes of surges, such as the ranking of workers who take more contracts in Mechanical Turk or the shuffle of a subscription or service request like in the case of Uber. The hierarchy that is well known in the regular employment relationship is symbolically altered to a technologically, seemingly chance driven system and the determinant for employability becomes reduced to a technological synapse. Inequality is obscured by these abstract moments in selection systems and allows backend actors to reap a huge majority of profits from its business model and leave those performing the service to, in the case of Uber, sleep in their cars. In February 2017 Uber CEO Kalinick yelled at an Uber driver in one of his cars, when the driver (who was secretly filming the encounter) asked why the company was raising standards and dropping prices. Kalinick insultingly told the driver that 'some people don't like to take responsibility'. Or in the case of the Amazon megalith, clients' takings rise as they race to the bottom to find the cheapest and fastest service provider; providers whose lives are increasingly made precarious (not to mention increasing the market share of Amazon itself). As stated by Karatzogianni and Matthews (2016), we are seeing the 'use of digital commons for ideological purposes'.

Robot Army of Redressers and the Privacy Strip Show

Strava, RunKeeper, Sports Tracker, Polar Beat, Endomondo, and Ghostracer are all fitness apps that track and store data about cyclists and runners. Users are encouraged to share their data with other runners and cyclists on active feeds that resemble the feed in Eggers' novel *The Circle*. In this novel, the Circle is a firm in the not-so-distant future (which resembles Google), where employees are not only encouraged but expected to take part in the company's social media engine (which are not very well disguised versions of Facebook and Twitter). Mae, the book's protagonist, fails to join in the 'socials' within the first few weeks and is called in to speak to Gina, the CircleSocial manager who is investigating why she did not join. When Mae explains that she has been busy settling in to the job and has not had time for extracurricular activities, Gina does not seem impressed. Gina points out that 'communication and community come from the same root word, *communis*, Latin for commons, public, shared by all or many' (95). Gina asks, how can communication be extracurricular? As the tale develops, Mae is drawn into a world where the Circle requires constant and complete exposure from those in the inner (the workers in the firm) and outer (everyone else) 'circles'. She begins to follow as many feeds, post as many comments, friend as many others as possible and watches the numbers of smiles and 'zings', visits to her site and the like with pleasure. She watches the recording of her blood pressure on her wrist and is 'thrilled' when it increases alongside the increase in numbers. Of course, Mae also watches her steps and other health data. The job that Mae does is customer service, and she is explicitly judged on customers' rankings of her service. Communication technologies in the world of corporate feedback loops consider communication to be quantifiable with an 'unhindered instrumental power' (Haraway, 1991: 164), so in call centre service work such as the type in this fictional account, communication's units are considered indisputable factors for analysis.

In the Circle, there is an acceleration of techniques to penetrate all of workers' lives; where 'privacy is theft'. This becomes a meme that playfully disrupts the anarchist Proudhon's comment that property is theft; people are asked to set up cameras inside their homes and to record and broadcast their daily lives in a manner resembling the reality television programme Big Brother in its most macabre sense. Those who refuse to be a part of this ever-invasive society are soon chased down by drones, which is live streamed and intended to be amusing and a bit of fun, an assumption which is not held by those being chased. In fact, this drone activity directly leads to the suicide of one of the characters. Of course the book is fiction, but the extremes of quantified life as it dominates the qualified in the story are disturbingly convincing. The Circle dystopia is where all of work and experiences of life are immaterial. It is a world that Karatzogianni and Matthews (2016) liken to Harman's zombie capitalism, where we see profit declining (like in the case of Uber) based on over-accumulation of things we can no longer even touch.

In a new dystopia like the Circle described above, people in (and even outside) any kind of collective are at risk of becoming the new informers without the intention to do so. Historically, revolutionaries were appealed to; to become moles or informers, as described by E. P. Thompson. Thompson writes about what he called the 'army of redressers' in the late 1700s and early 1800s who met clandestinely during the night across Yorkshire, Birmingham, Bristol and London to 'expose fraud and every species of Hereditary Government' and to discuss how to 'lessen the oppression of Taxes, to propose plans for the education of helpless infancy, and the comfortable support of the aged and destressed… to extirpate the horrid practice of war' (Thompson, 1963/2013). Attendees of these underground meetings were asked to say yes to the following three questions: (1) Do you desire a total change of system? (2) Are you willing to risk yourself in a contest to leave your posterity free? (3) Are you willing to do all in your power to create the Spirit of Love, Brotherhood and Affection among the friends of freedom and omit no opportunity of getting all the political information you can? (Thompson, 1963/2013: 418–19) to ensure they really were revolutionaries. The Home Office began to seek out its own sources for information, including from previously active reformers who were in need of money or the 'casual mercenary volunteers attempting to sell information by the "piece"' (Thompson, 1963/2013: 534). In those days, spying and surveillance was a very different matter than what we see today (which I have also discussed in Chapter 4). The state set out to identify who was a threat and targeted them through various tactics, including trying to divide and destroy by paying for revolutionary information. Now, just by being online, someone may inadvertently give away information about another person or event that could be used by a blame-seeking state. Data can now be used to criminalise in ways that would make Foucault turn over in his grave. While online, we give data about ourselves to the state, for free; usually without any intention to reveal clandestine information.

Now the wisdom of the online crowd becomes a new army of redressers, where technological accident becomes the determinant of redress. Having mentioned above other revolutionary movements from two centuries ago, it is appropriate here to introduce the Luddite movement. The Luddites were framework-knitters who saw the invention of the weaving machine as a direct threat to their work. Many jobs were precarious during this historical period, and these working class groups resorted to violence, destroying machines in a manner Hobsbawm (1952) called 'collective bargaining by riot'. The weavers claimed that management were using machines not to immediately replace their work (though that was feared as an eventuality), but to defend bad management practices. Though the time period is different and the machinery antiquated by today's standards, the Luddites' fears were similar to those we hold today: that technology is being (or could be) used for bad management practices and that machines could replace jobs. Chapter 4 detailed where this is happening. Now research must continue these investigations, identifying where technology is being used to make unqualified work related decisions and identify how workers could be protected.

Ontology of Quantification

In Chapter 2, I make an appeal to the scholarly community for a return to discussions of ontology. While the affective and corporeal turns have done so, quantification is not sufficiently discussed. I tie this claim to a similar caution I make to the discipline I have been associated with, international political economy (IPE). I have claimed that IPE tends to sit within a gully of Cartesianism, separating the body from the mind in theorization. New materialism of the feminist, poststructuralist traditions is a philosophical challenge to Cartesianism. Haraway imparts that 'labour is the humanising activity that makes man; labour is an ontological category permitting the knowledge of a subject', and reveals full 'knowledge of subjugation and alienation' (1991: 158). Haraway notes that socialist feminists have taken the 'basic analytic strategies of Marxism' by entering reproductive labour to debates in the wage relation. This is a start, but Haraway comments that this intervention is still epistemological, as it requires a social relation, asking women to build 'unity' rather than launching a call for 'naturalisation' (158). I claim that quantified self authors should make a choice in their philosophical commitments. My arguments begin in the article I published with Andrew Robinson (2016), postulating that quantification of work results in exacerbated distinctions between the mind and the body despite a naturalising of these where qualification can occur. The Quantified Self movement encourages people to live by numbers and to self-optimise (Ruckenstein, 2014: 70). Ruckenstein states that self-trackers have 'internalised the desire to know and to optimise, but also voluntarily act on it by sharing information about their tracking experiments and experiences with friends and followers, who are invited to monitor their bodily habits and mental states in similar ways' (Ruckenstein, 2014: 70). Bodies and minds are not generally unified in quantified self discourses but are placed in competition with each other, where the mind is assumed to have the upper hand (pun intended).

Ruckenstein indicates that 'personal analytics is thus firmly rooted in the externalisation of "nature" as something that people are able to transform: when bodies and lives are made more transparent, they can be better acknowledged and acted upon' (2014: 9). Self-tracking allows people to see new things about themselves, or what I talk about as the autonomic self, which leads to the creation of a data double. This concept emerges from surveillance literature where the idea of the body is equated to 'flows or streams' which are then reassembled into 'data doubles to be analysed and targeted for intervention' (2014: 9). It is interesting that a concept originating in surveillance literature has been translated as a liberating process, where people 'find value' in their doubles.

Debates in New Materialisms

In Chapter 3, I laid the groundwork for the next stages of research that will infuse and be infused by an emerging research area in the 'quantified self'. From 2015–2017, I ran a seminar series on new materialisms at the Universities of Westminster, Kingston and Middlesex, inviting the authors in new materialism from the Marxist, feminist and poststructuralist arenas to discuss the contemporary issues of austerity, repeating economic crises, poverty, inequality and the risks of digitalisation. My explicit intention was to begin to build a bridge between seemingly unresolvable theoretical and philosophical frameworks. I ran the first event with David Chandler and others (listed below) at Westminster University. The second was led by Helen Palmer at Kingston University who held it at the beautiful location of St Martin's. At both events, I spoke about the commitment to nature in Marx's work on species being and the breadth of politics and economics in feminist new materialisms. At the second event, I performed a monologue I had prepared and presented at FutureFest in London. In my monologue, I took on the personas of various quantified workers including a construction, office receptionist, and call centre worker.

In the final part of the present book's conclusion I include part of the description I wrote and posted on my blog after the first *Debates in New Materialisms* which I held at Westminster University 04 March 2016. The reason I have included this description is that researching and writing about new materialism for this event was an extremely affective experience. I became acutely aware of this in the preparation for the event and at the event itself. The description reveals the ways that all aspects of materiality affected my experience of the event. Others likewise expressed to me that they had felt significant tensions in the room, particularly around discussions of materialism and its significance.

What Is New in New Materialism?: Marxisms, New Materialisms and the Nature/Culture Divide

[The first part of the description outlines how I came to the conclusion that I would run the debates in new materialisms, building on what I had observed happening in the areas of orthodox Marxism and post-structural feminism.]

Thinking through these issues, I started to consider running an event where I could bring in researchers who are dedicated to both understanding what 'new materialism' is and want to contribute in new ways to this emerging area of work. I run the Conference for Socialist Economists (CSE) South Group and so hold funding to hold events based out of the CSE journal, Capital & Class. I began to speak to possible speakers for the event I began to envisage. I spoke to David Chandler, who runs the Materialisms Reading Group at the Westminster Forum who agreed to co-run an event with me, where we would bring interested speakers to try to identify what is new about new materialisms? Although she could not finally attend, I invited Daniela Tepe Belfrage who has recently written a paper critiquing the subset of Marxists who have written about 'new materialism' whose submission I coordinated to the journal Capital & Class.

I invited Felicity Colman, who runs a large European network on New Materialism and is writing about digital feminicities and Nick Kiersey who is writing about the anthropocene in a way that resonates with the new materialist interests in moving away from anthropecentric versions of current life. We invited Helen Palmer whose work on transversality and the subject as well as insights into the pedagogical and methodological aspects of new materialism would provide an excellent intervention. David suggested inviting Michiel van Ingen who is identifying how critical realism may or may not overlap with new materialism and Paul Rekret who is not convinced by the concept of the 'posthuman'. We invited Christian Fuchs to act as discussant. We agreed to seek out gender equivalence. The first panel was labelled as 'plenary' because we intended to outline 'what is new materialism?'. The second panel was intended as a platform to indicate what is 'newest', or perhaps better, 'cutting edge' in the debates we were to introduce in the preliminary panel. There was no intended hierarchy across panels nor set definition for 'newness' but we did set out to invite an equal number of early and seasoned career researchers.

The workshop was extremely popular, we discovered quickly. Registrations on eventbrite quickly added up. So on the day of the event it was not a surprise we were a little bit crowded in the room but there was a feeling of enthusiasm and anticipation. I began the first panel by going over some of the tenets I see coming out of new materialisms from their variety of interpretations. I reminded colleagues that when we talk about matter we need to be very clear what we mean by this. The key differences in the way Marxisms and new materialisms coming out of the postmodern debates view matter is that the latter do not see it as static and unchanging. Quite the contrary, matter is agential and transformational in the feminist and postmodern understanding. Domination over nature may sound empowering but it detracts from possibilities, from impacts that people have on one another that go beyond the cognitive and even the sensory. So I started the day by discussing atomism as envisaged by ancient philosophers Epicurus and Lucretius. Epicurus opined that we are unhappy because we have disassociated ourselves with nature. That is the origin of all despair and human tragedy. Lucretius however did not reject tragedy to the extent Epicurus did and accepted grief as part of the depth and richness of human existence.

The lectern I stood before was indeed an object, however atoms compose the lectern. I can't see the atoms but I know they are there. What I don't know however is how they came to be there nor what directions and paths they followed in order to get there, that is out of my control. I do know that the paths were in no way linear nor predictable. I accept the objectivity of the table nonetheless, also recognizing it has a subject, it has matter and it can at any moment, change, crumble, the earth may even swallow both me and the objects around me at any moment if there is an earthquake or a tsunami. I am not in control of the matter around me nor of the earth I stand on, nor, at least not completely, of my body.

At some point in my talk I felt very ill and had to tell colleagues that if I looked pained, it is because I was (I felt lightheaded). The room was full of bodies and chances are there was some kind of impact on me. The window was open to allow oxygen to enter, but the screams of the city were incessant, a pneumatic drill, a siren, signs of work and emergency. Haven't we all said at some point: 'my body is telling me something?' In the coffee break I told a colleague that I often do not know when I am 'stressed', but my body certainly tells me. The Spinozan point that 'the mind is the idea of the body' is highly convincing when we think in these terms. But materiality is often taken for granted or overlooked; taken as a secondary consideration, or something that is dirty. Matter is associated with pain. The way to emancipation was in pre-modernity thought, via abandoning the body. Materiality was seen as oppositional to spirituality, indeed many of those against Marx accused him of focusing on the way society is organized around commodities and materiality and distract from what could provide salvation. These understandings are limited and limiting. Coole and Frost postulated that the 'whole edifice of modern ontology regarding notions of change, causality, agency, time and space needs rethinking' (2010: 9). Indeed, materiality is more than mere matter, it is an excess force, vitality, relationality, emerges from difference that renders matter active, self-creative, productive, unpredictable. While new materialists tend to move away from the binarisms seen in Cartesian dualism, coupling is not identical to logical dualism. Life is complex. Forced compartmentalisations and divisions are the fodder of oppression but difference is not automatically antagonistic.

In 1976 Ollman said that the 'nub of our difficulty in understanding Marxism, whose subject matter is not simply society, but society conceived of relationally' (14–15). Capital, labour, value, commodities, etc. are all relations, containing within themselves the integral elements of what they are. We tend to see these things as externally tied. But Marx was not unaware of the corporeal nor of nature. This does not mean he would be a 'new materialist' today. It does mean that there could be space for dialogue across an age old 'divide' between Marxists and postmodern researchers (or so I hope). There are hints of an ontology that does not overlook the corporeal nor interrelatedness of life beyond the social. Objects are not separate from but were part of our nature as human beings, they were needed to 'complete... existence and to realise essence' (Marx, 1975d: 267, cited in Fox, 2015: 132). Marx's use of 'essence' looks like it follows a tradition of argument first developed by Spinoza. Fox argues that like Spinoza and Hegel, Marx rejected thinking about a being's nature in terms of substance. Marx also knew that all beings, including human beings, are interdependent. This makes the relationship between humanity and objects an 'inner relation' (Fox, 2015: 132, 3).

After I made some of these points, Felicity Colman spoke, asking us: 'what is newness?'. Felicity spoke of how work with the feminist new

materialist thinkers (such as Barad, Haraway, Van der Tuin, on the shoul-
ders of Braidotti, Grosz, Deleuze, Bergson), have recognised that there
is a need to develop an understanding of a 'quantum literacy', offering a
significant turn for critical discourses of relevance not only for feminist
metaphysics, but for all of those who are interested in thinking more ade-
quate terms for expressing knowledge production and the ethical terms of
life itself. Nick Kiersey then talked about New Materialism as an eman-
cipatory theoretical horizon for talking about nomad politics such that it
might be capable of scaling to address a global form of sovereign striation.
David Chandler then wrapped up the discussions by asking us to think
about the nature/culture divide and asked whether Marxists are ready for
full automation? After a half hour break, Helen Palmer, Michiel van Ingen
and Paul Rekret spoke. Helen spoke of a strategy of defamiliarisation com-
ing from Braidotti's work. Helen demonstrated the contemporary political
potency of this term through both a reading of its origins within Russian
formalism and a defence of its materialist concerns which counters the
traditional Marxist critique of formalism from the 1930s. Michiel talked
about what he sees as new about the new materialisms, an attempt to re-
vive what had until quite recently been considered an entirely discredited
approach to science and philosophy: vitalism. The new materialisms as
he reads them have sought to collapse or 'transcend' the nature/culture
divide. Critical realist philosophy on the other hand has sought to 'sublate'
the dialectic which has historically grounded their opposition. Paul Rekret
then challenged the concept of emerging hybrid entities, from medically
enhanced humans to full blown cyborgs and globally circulating human
tissues, announce the actualisation of the ontological assertation that the
human never was an integral, autonomous being exercising control over
itself nor mastery of its surroundings through the capacity for individual
agency and choice to begin with.

What stood out to me in the discussions that followed the two panels
were the ways that specific readings of the same authors seemed to in-
spire very different responses and interpretations. Symptomatic of long
standing theoretical and philosophical influences, there were points when
assertions and conceptualisations were seemingly quite different, if even
oppositional. The understanding of nature, the material and agency in par-
ticular differ in traditional historical materialist readings to feminist new
materialism, but that is not in itself a surprise. It was clear however that
much of the latter has not yet been fully circulated in established Marxist
circles (yet?). Like the points I make above, Marx must be re-read before
the proverbial gates are closed.

Nevertheless, as Orzeck (2007) wisely points out:

> *...insofar as the refusal to face up to the heterogeneous Marxist writ-*
> *ings on the natural body is a symptomatic of an anxious desire to seal*
> *the gap between Marxism and poststructuralism it is antithetical to*

these sorts of issues and crucially, to the discovery of incompatible as-sumptions. Compatible assumptions and findings give us a map of the land, but it is only incompatible assumptions that, at the risk of taking the metaphor too far, can reveal the impassable lakes and streams, forcing us to decide exactly where we want to stand.

The workshop lasted for five hours. We did not come to dramatic con-clusions but we did explore the possibilities for a discussion that has, as I have pointed out, been brought about with the urgency to re-discover the corporeal. We live in our bodies, on this planet. How we understand and relate to this does not have to be identical but if we share an ontological and epistemological purpose around change and emancipation there may still be capacity for transformation through continued experiences like this New Materialisms workshop in London, which we hope will be the first of many discussions. (Moore, 2016)

Last Words

A new dialogue between new materialism and international political econ-omy (the discipline where I began my research as a PhD student), is neces-sary to continue the debates that this first event promoted. As stated, two further events were inspired after I held this one; the final one on 7th April 2017, where researchers in the area of international political economy convened to discuss strides in the research in that area since its original conception. These debates have produced the space for a positive dialog for discussion as the worker becomes increasingly involved with machines. In this book, I have mostly warned about worst case scenarios and the dark sides of algorithmic rule which may happen if we assume the neutrality of technology and forget the qualitative aspects of life. The self becomes removed from qualitative relations with others when relations are mediated by measurements. While the employment relationship is structurally une-qual, numeration leads to reduced remuneration as work is not recognised for its qualification. The invisibilisation of labour in the domestic realm highlighted by Federici in the 1970s in the text *Wages against Housework* continues. Unfortunately, the labour of the digital housewife (Jarrett, 2016) continues. In a perpetual state of alienation in digitalised work, the body and mind must be divided, and the mind is expected to control the body by improving it, whether it wants to or not. The agency of the body is denied and affective conditions supressed. Improvements to, and controls over, the body are now considered a necessary workplace performance, not as a paid part of work, and ultimately are at risk of becoming the most invasive and intimate managerial methods to mask the anxiety and oppression of pre-carity, as well as deny affectivity in the context of neoliberalism. Research-ers must look closely at the ways in which workers have begun to explicitly resist the quantification of our work.

Bibliography

Agamben, G. (1998) *Homo Sacer: Sovereign Power and Bare Life* (Stanford, CA: Stanford University Press).

Castells, M. (2012) *Networks of Outrage and Hope – Social Movements in the Internet Age* (Chichester, UK: Wiley).

Colman, F. (2014) 'Digital Feminicity: Predication and Measurement, Materialist Informatics and Images' *Artnodes* 14: 1–17.

Coole, D. and Frost, S. (eds) (2010) *New Materialisms: Ontology, Agency, and Politics* (Durham, NC: Duke University Press).

Deleuze G (1992) 'Postscript on the Societies of Control' *October* 59: 3–7.

Eggers, D. (2013) *The Circle* (London: Penguin Books).

Fox, J. G. (2015) *Marx, the Body and Human Nature* (London and New York: Palgrave Macmillan).

Guattari, F. (1996) 'Institutional Practice and Politics', in Genosko, G. (ed.) *The Guattari Reader* (Oxford: Blackwell): 121–138.

Haraway, D. (1991) 'A Cyborg Manifesto: Science, Technology, and Socialist-Feminism in the Late Twentieth Century', in Haraway, D. (ed.) *Simians, Cyborgs and Women: The Reinvention of Nature* (New York: Routledge): 127–148.

Hobsbawm, E. (1952) 'The Machine Breakers', *Past and Present* 1(1), 57–70.

Jarrett, K. (2016) *Feminism, Labour and Digital Media: The Digital Housewife* (New York and London: Routledge).

Karatzogianni, A and Matthews, J. (2016) 'Evil Intermediation Platforms', prepared for the *Journal of Cultural Anthropology*. Available at: https://works.bepress.com/athina_karatzogianni/26/ (accessed 14/02/17).

Mann, S. and Niedzviecki, H. (2001) *Cyborg: Digital Destiny and Human Possibility in the Age of the Wearable Computer* (Canada: Doubleday of Canada).

Moore, P. (2016) 'New Materialisms Workshop', *Global Judgements and Ideas* blog post (by Phoebe Moore). Available at: https://phoebevmoore.wordpress.com/2016/03/14/new-materialisms-workshop/ (accessed 03/06/17).

Moore, P. and Piwek, L. (2015) 'Unintended Consequences and the Dark Side of the Quantified Self', Sustainable Societies Network commissioned paper. https://phoebevmoore.wordpress.com/2015/06/15/unintended-consequences-the-dark-sides-of-quantifying-selves/ (accessed 14/02/17).

Moore, P. and Robinson, A. (2016) 'The Quantified Self: What Counts in the Neoliberal Workplace' *New Media & Society* 18(1): 2774–2792.

Orzeck, R. (2007), 'What Does Not Kill You: Historical Materialism and the Body' *Environment and Planning D: Society and Space* 25: 496–514.

Polanyi, K. (1944/2001) *The Great Transformation: The Political and Economic Origins of Our Time* (Boston, MA: Beacon Press).

Rolnik, S. (trans. Holmes, B.) (2011) 'The Geopolitics of Pimping', in Raunig, G., Ray, G. and Wuggenig, U. (eds) *Critique of Creativity: Precarity, Subjectivity and Resistance in the 'Creative Industries'* (London: MayFly): 23–40.

Ruckenstein, M. (2014) 'Visualized and Interacted Life: Personal Analytics and Engagements with Data Doubles' *Societies* 4(1): 68–84.

Striphas, T. (2015) 'Algorithmic Culture' *European Journal of Cultural Studies* 18(4–5): 395–412.

Tepe-Belfrage, D. and Steans, J. (2016) 'The New Materialism: Re-claiming a Debate from a Feminist Perspective' *Capital & Class* 40(2): 305–326.

Thompson, E. (1963/2013) *The Making of the English Working Class* (London: Penguin).

Vaneigem, R. (trans. Nicholson-Smith, D.) (1967/2003) *Revolution of Everyday Life* (London: Rebel Press).

Viseu, A. and Suchman, L. (2010) 'Wearable Augmentations: Imaginaries of the Informed Body' in Edwards, J., Harvey, P. and Wade, P. (eds) *Technologized Images, Technologized Bodies* (New York and Oxford: Berghan Books): 161–184.

Wild, J. (2017) 'Wearables in the workplace and the dangers of staff surveillance' *Financial Times* 20/02/17. www.ft.com/content/089c0d00-d739-11e6-944b-e7eb37a6aa8e (accessed 14/02/17).

Index

For Product Safety Concerns and Information please contact our EU
representative GPSR@taylorandfrancis.com
Taylor & Francis Verlag GmbH, Kaufingerstraße 24, 80331 München, Germany

* 9 780367 872908 *